Thank you, Donna –
for your gift of
sharing smiles & memories
with little people.
God bless,
Debbie Gray

Colossians 3:17

THESE TRICKS ARE FOR KIDS!

T<small>RICKS</small> of T<small>HE</small> T<small>RADE</small>

for T<small>EACHERS</small> of Elementary Music!

A few ideas that might make your work a little easier and definitely,
a lot more fun!

Debbie Gray

Debbie welcomes comments about her work at
micahandjess@aol.com

www.debbieonthewebbie.com

authorHOUSE™

1663 LIBERTY DRIVE, SUITE 200
BLOOMINGTON, INDIANA 47403
(800) 839-8640
WWW.AUTHORHOUSE.COM

First published by AuthorHouse 11/03/04

ISBN: 1-4184-8124-6 (sc)

Library of Congress Control Number: 2004095481

Printed in the United States of America
Bloomington, Indiana

This book is printed on acid-free paper.

READER REFLECTIONS

These Tricks Are For Kids is far more than a book for beginning music teachers. You don't have to be a Veterinarian to enjoy "All Things Bright and Beautiful" and you don't have to be a teacher to find many wise and useful tricks collected and revealed in Debbie Grays entertaining book. Like her performances, the manuscript has energy, polish, and fun. Parents, camp leaders, *anyone* who works with children *or* adults will find fascinating stories, thoughtful quotations, and fun techniques. Be warned: there are a few experiences recounted that may change you.

~ *Randy Peterson, parent*

These Tricks Are For Kids is not only an excellent resource for a music educator but for all classroom teachers. Debbie Gray's "TRICKS" are not merely suggestions or ideas, but tried and true methods that she uses daily in her own classroom. Her sassy, smart, honest and inspiring "TRICKS" are very much a reflection of her teaching. She is a true master of music education and her words are noteworthy to anyone perfecting their skill.

~ *Katie Britt, educator*

Debbie Gray is a person who has inspired, taught, and helped me through some of the hardest times of my life. She has not only inspired *me*, but hundreds of other students who have passed through her music room over the years. She gives it to you like it is and is respected for just that. She is the "World's Teacher," leading many young people into the future with something to look forward to each day. And, if at age 21 and over a decade after having Mrs.Gray as *my* music teacher, I *still* visit her on my days off from college, then something has inspired me for the long-haul; some*one* has inspired me – that some*one* is Debbie Gray!

~ *Bobby Kerr, former student & drummer for AXIOM*

*Tricks…*is great reading! Even though the main audience is music educators, the thoughts and ideas are universally applicable.....very fun, thought provoking, and her writing motivates reflection! It's a great piece of work!

~ *Mary Franco, educator*

I enjoyed reading Debbie Gray's book as much as I enjoy walking into her classroom. Sometimes I come back early from my plan period just to slip into the room and watch the children delight in the experiences they have in her music room. Tricks of the Trade may have been written for music teachers, but the ideas for classroom management could be successfully used in any classroom that has a caring, enthusiastic, loving teacher. This would be a great gift book for any new teacher and has so many ideas that even some experienced teachers could find a wealth of techniques to explore to make teaching and learning fun.

~ *Melanie Caywood, teacher*

Table of Contents

INTRODUCTION

This whole project blossomed about seven years ago. I started jotting down random ideas during class that I wanted to remember to share with my student teachers and music education students doing their field observation with me. I made sure each had a copy of my list and continued writing things down as they came to mind. Several of these former student teachers, now successful music teachers, inspired me to turn my suggestions into a book. As I began assembling the additions, I realized my ideas were melding into clearly defined categories pertaining to extracurricular duties, discipline, motivation, lesson planning and presentation, classroom appearance, performances, and random TRICKS of the trade. Now, here I am nearly a decade later, offering a handbook so you can apply some of these ideas. Hopefully, you'll also be entertained along the way.

We teachers spend a staggering amount of time dissecting our motives, our methods, and our madness. Sharing ideas with our professional peers is a *great* way to evaluate our programs, our progress, and *especially* ourselves. For those of you who are new to the profession, this book is a great way to get off on the right foot and will prove to be a good, reliable resource *throughout* your career. For those of you who have been teaching awhile, you already appreciate the importance of trying different things that have worked for someone else, the value of sharing information, and the growth that comes in making changes. For those of you who, like me, have been teaching *forever and a day*, please write a book *I can read!*

Someone once said,

"We typically don't change until the cost of staying the same exceeds the cost of change."

This book is full of suggestions for change: change in your classroom appearance, change in your attitude toward music education, kids, and teaching, change in the way you discipline, and maybe even change in the way you present lessons. Change can feel weird. Sometimes change *IS* weird. And even the suggestion of change can cause fluctuations in our spirit and disposition because change isn't necessarily easy. Nevertheless, change is worth considering.

If you can be patient as you peruse these pages, wade through the warped wit, rummage for some randomness you haven't realized yet, and keep an open mind so you're not too timid to try some new TRICKS, there are bound to be two, ten, twelve, or twenty *worthwhile* tidbits to tune up your teaching techniques! (I know…I know…but alliteration is *totally too tempting to omit*.) ☺

I have no doubt that some of you, while reading this book that's abundant with assorted approaches, are going to think, "Sheesh…this Debbie Gray character is just totally WEIRD!" Others of you are going to think, "Wow…what a *COOL IDEA!*" or "I never thought of *that*!" Whatever your perception, I want you to know, I'm not attempting to sculpt you into my likeness. I realize there are many factors that could potentially create a chasm between my TRICKS and your trade. We may differ in our thoughts, methodology, feelings, beliefs, and abilities on at least some of the issues at least some of the time. But, when you salvage one miniscule shred of inspiration, get a glimpse of some silly new *fun* that you and your kids can have in class, adopt any new approaches, use a performance idea or two, personalize a goal, write a few more letters, have some good verbiage for recommendation letters, avoid a crisis, or sponge the smallest element of classroom management encouragement from it, *These Tricks Are For Kids* will be a *worthwhile* investment for you, in both time and money.

SO…WHAT'S *WORTHWHILE* ?

werth-hwil\ adj: sufficiently valuable to justify the investment

of time or interest.

~ Rhymezone

werth-hwil\ adj: being worth the time or effort spent.

~ Merriam-Webster

In order to be good at what we do, we must determine what is worthwhile - that is, how and where we invest our time, money, and energy. Teachers have so many different audiences to reach – all with *incredibly different* needs, learning styles, abilities, concerns, worries, backgrounds, demands, cultures, socio-economic roots, expectations, attitudes, limitations, and opinions. You are bound to feel bombarded and overwhelmed by it all. I *still* do, even after all these years. But you will, with time as your friend, gradually discover your limitations, your strengths, your needs, what is worthwhile, and what is a waste. As you travel through these pages, you might think you know which of these TRICKS will work for you. You may deem others worthy only of occupying pages better put to use as doodle art by filling in letters that have vacant centers. (The Sunday morning church bulletin has been a reliable color-in-the-letters fidget-fixer for me for as far back as I can remember!) But I urge you to step out of your comfort zone and give something different a try. You can always abandon it, but if you don't try, you'll never know.

"In life you are given two ends, one to think with and the other to sit on. Your success in life depends on which end you use the most. Heads you win, tails you lose."

~ Conrad Burns

Ultimately, I think our number one goal should be to develop our lessons into lessons that *put the kids, not the content, first.* Then, make sure our lessons can be *enjoyed by every single student,* urban, rural, happy, sad, talented, not-so-talented, old, young, bright or otherwise. These tricks should help you do just that! I sincerely believe, with every ounce of my being, that if kids *enjoy* coming to my music class – I can teach them almost *anything* once they're there. When they're happy and having a good time, their mood is better, their attitude is more balanced, their emotions fluctuate less, they can leave their concerns at the door (sometimes), and the defensiveness that sometimes blocks learning is diminished, sometimes even erased!

In reference to accepting my tricks, I've discovered that although it's a good thing for all of us to consider advice, ideas, and opinions of others, we all *have* to be authentic and true to *ourselves!*

"Be yourself. Who else is better qualified?"

~Frank Giblin

"Always be a first-rate version of yourself instead of a second-rate version of someone else."

~ Judy Garland.

"WHAT KEY ARE WE IN?"

An old song, *I BELIEVE IN MUSIC,* by Mac Davis, has some profound and very appropriate lyrics for every one of us: *"Music is a universal language and love is the key."* If we, as music teachers, embrace this basic thought as the foundation of our decision making, we are bound to inspire, make a difference, and make a success of ourselves, our program, and most importantly, our students.

The *"love"* I'm talking about, is multi-faceted and not the traditional kind of love that is associated with Valentines Day, engagements, and weddings. The love for our kids in class is the kind of love that is used in terms of empathy, accountability and appreciation, a liking for, a special feeling of interest and compassion, a penchant for helping, a connection, a relationship, and a positive emotion of respect and devotion.

I'm not so sappy or cliché to think what I'm suggesting is easy. On the contrary! I'm not even sure it is possible in some cases! We all have students who are flat out obnoxious and hard to like, much less *love*! All I'm saying is that finding a way to love our students should be one of our "umbrella" goals! On the opposite end of the spectrum, some kids are so adorable we could scoop them up and take them home with us for a lifetime. If you don't already know one of these kids who requires a conscious effort to find anything *at all salvageable* in their attitudes, their personality, or their lifestyle, you will soon. Every teacher has at least one...eventually. They are so unlovable; yet, it's up to us, their teacher, to make sure those who are disenfranchised have a franchise in *our* hearts. That kind of **love is the key** we're in.

Music is a more potent instrument than any other for education.
~*Plato*

In some ways, I think we music people have the capacity to love the unlovely easier than the classroom teachers, only because they have to deal with them all day long! They get on their nerves, frustrate, and irritate them *hour after hour.* We, on the other hand, only see them for the short duration of music time, maybe forty-five or fifty minutes! We can add something to their lives, if nothing more than a few minutes of good music, good times, and a good dose of patience and kindness.

"Kindness is a language
which the deaf can hear and the blind can see."
~ *Mark Twain*

Even if we have to be great thespians and fake it so they *think* we feel like they are loved, it can benefit them and it requires very little of us. It is easy to love the loveable – it's our responsibility to love the unlovable. As farfetched and maybe even impossible as all this may seem, there must be some value in making it a goal, and some promise in it since the Bible speaks of this same topic in Luke 6:32 where the Gentile medical doctor, Luke, wrote,

"If you love those who love you, what credit is that to you?
Even sinners love those who love them."

~NIV

Students with special needs like: English as their second language, learning disabilities, emotional disorders, speech impediments, behavior disorders, physical handicaps, students with difficult families or no family at all, as well as kids who appear to have the world by the tail, can all find some common ground through music. But music is just the *connecting language*. *Loving* students is the connecting step too often omitted by professionals. Loving them – even the unlovable – **is the key** to touching their lives and making a difference. I suggest that even if you can't love them with your heart, use your head and **act** like you love them - in a believable way. You know they say, actions speak louder than words.

Just as **love is the key to touching their *hearts*, fun is the key to touching their intellect**. It's important to be happy with what you've done, but we probably shouldn't always be satisfied with it. Keep changing, revamping, re-teaching, evaluating yourself, and practicing until you feel confident that it just couldn't be any better and it is obvious your students are having fun while learning volumes! Did you notice that I put "having fun" before "while learning volumes"? That's exactly what I mean, too...priority one in every elementary fine arts class, should be FUN. If it is fun for the kids and they LOVE it, they will stick with it. If it is fun, they will *want* to learn more about it! If it is fun, assessment and accountability, discipline and dialogue will be easier. If it is fun, they will have great memories of their elementary fine arts time and teacher. If it is fun, they may even choose to pursue a career in music or at least make it an important element of their adult lives!

On the other hand, if music class is NOT fun, multiple degrees, years of experience, the finest curriculum, the best equipment, the most incredible examples, the most splendid titles, and being the most accomplished musician *will not* make you inspire the majority of little kids. Let's face it...eleven year olds aren't dazzled by the fact that we have sung in operas and ten year olds don't care if we've performed in Carnegie Hall. Nine-year-olds couldn't care less that we studied with a world-renowned concert artist and it doesn't matter to eight-year-olds that we graduated summa cum laude from Julliard. Seven-year-olds aren't impressed with our three degrees, six-year-olds don't think that writing and publishing a book is anything particularly special, and it just isn't important to five-year-olds that we hold National Teacher Certification. Catch my point? All they care about is that music is fun, their teacher is nice (funny helps, too), and that the "stuff" they get to do is "cool!" Cindy Lauper almost had it right when she released the single, "GIRLS JUST WANNA HAVE FUN" That's right, baby...*but so do boys!*

I'm always amazed with the music teachers I hear singing the blues because another exploratory course "steals students" from their music classes. *HELLO!!!* It's just a simple statement of fact – KIDS FOLLOW FUN, they want excitement, they like energy, they love surprises, they are energized by suspense, and they LIKE "NICE." If we want to teach them, we *have to have them* in our classes. And if we want them in our classes, we have to determine what will get them there and keep them there (other than state requirements). If we put all of this together, it doesn't take a rocket scientist to see that music class *has* to be fun...and not just fun, but *REALLY* fun! There's a lot of competition out there – particularly in the middle school and junior high where other electives can be chosen over music. Massive amounts of movement, lots of activity, gobs of giggles, mounds of multi-media sights and sounds to bombard their senses, an overabundance of teacher-smiles, choreography, variety, "cool stuff."and kid-appropriate concepts are just a few of the components that will initiate conversation outside of class and lure the masses to you. (Just a side note. Kids DO talk – don't fool yourself into thinking that what happens in your room never leaves your room. They talk and they tell...they congregate and they converse...the crowd quickly decides if it's cool to be in music or if it's dorky to be in music. It is a contagious conclusion, too. It's up to us, no one else has the power to alter those out-of-class conversations.)

Some of my suggestions in this book are going to seem fundamental and absurdly obvious to you, but I've included them anyway, I guess because many of them didn't seem to become absurdly obvious to me until just recently. (Sometimes that proverbial light bulb comes on a lot later in life than anticipated!) I'm afraid that doesn't say much about how quickly I catch on...but, it *does* mean that even after multiple decades in the classroom with more than thirteen thousand kids, five different principals, and lots of parents, *I'm still learning* and *changing* the way I do things – every single day! I've heard that life-long learning is a very good thing, so you can congratulate me, I suppose!

My Principal sent us this quite apropos quote with our Monday Memo:

"He who dares to teach must never cease to learn."
~ Richard Henry Dann

However, I think Country Singer, Loretta Lynn, said it even better,

**"You've got to continue to grow
or you're just like last night's cornbread – stale and dry."**

In addition to the "duh-that's-obvious" information, I'm counting on there being a few things that will turn on your light and brighten your world! I think this thoroughly-opinionated (but yours to read, adopt, and enjoy… read, delete, and ignore…or…not read at all) manual has the potential to help your teaching experience be more satisfying and less stressifying.

REMEMBER…

- **Any and all advice, ideas, or strategies I suggest are always subject to avoidance!**

- **They probably won't work with all students, all your classes, or in every situation, but they are sure worth a try when you have tried everything else and everything else you've tried has made you seriously consider trying *anything* else to earn a living!**

- ***Nothing* always works all the time! Something always works some of the time. Anything always works when nothing and something haven't worked!**

- **Know that your job as a teacher of children is *very important!* If you give value to the Bible, you'll find it says in James 3:1 "Not many of you should presume to be teachers, my brothers, because you know that we who teach will be judged more strictly."**

- **"If you always do what you've always done, You will always get what you always got."**
~ Barry Elms

One of the most important things for every teacher to remember is that, no matter how many TRICKS you adopt, how many books you read, how many teachers you observe, how much advice you solicit, or how many methods classes you endure, you are still going to have to incorporate your own style, your own personality, and your own ideas once you're in your own classroom in front of your own crowd of kids. It doesn't take too long to find out what works for you, your students, and your area of expertise, and what makes you wish you had opted for a career as a Royal Gorge tour guide, riding a burro in blistering heat, leading a Chihuahua and 47 tourists who are afraid of heights, don't understand a word of English, and all have digital cameras and acid reflux. Yea…it takes very little time to learn that you must keep changing, revamping, re-teaching, trying new things, using your imagination, creating, taking risks, and practicing your presentations, assignments, and lessons so **you *and* your students** feel comfortable, confident, and your time together is *worthwhile* as you journey together through the fun and love of music! Take some chances – it'll feel liberating!

I've had some extraordinary student teachers during my tenure in elementary music education! I have watched both men and women enter and leave their field service with an enviable amount of energy and enthusiasm for the job on their horizon…only to become dismayed with music education itself and burn out far too soon after the torch was lit. They get discouraged with all the extra, non-music responsibilities, having little or no budget to keep equipment, instruments, music, and supplies updated, classroom discipline, fundraisers, and exhaustion. But mostly, living with the pressures of performing a multitude of programs with very little preparation time and the eternal onslaught of requirements established by people outside the field of music who are unequivocally clueless as to what it takes in time, energy, talent, and materials to make little kids performance ready, that they just choose to leave the field. It's sad! The kinds of teachers *we need* give so much that they can't see themselves doing it for the rest of their lives, so they bail before they get so financially entrenched in the profession that they can't afford to leave. I visited with several of these extraordinary music teachers who are now working in the business world or have turned in their resignations, who had proven to be awesome educators but then decided to resign before ever completing their fifth year of service. In every case, once we funneled all their comments, complaints, and concerns into a congruent cause – it seems they all bailed because they were frustrated. So…please continue to meander through these wads of wisdom, opinions, quotes, and quips so that you may experience success and *"thrive, not just survive!"*

"Success lies not in being the best, but in doing your best."
~ Anonymous

"If you love what you are doing, you will be successful."
~ Albert Schweitzer

"The only time success comes before work is in the dictionary."
~ Vidal Sasoon

"I don't know the key to success, but the key to failure is trying to please everybody."
~ Bill Cosby Ed.D.

"MUSIC, AN AVENUE TO THE HEART"

I agree with Dr. Cosby and I am relatively certain that my opinions on the following topic will definitely <u>not</u> please everyone…but that's ok, too – as long as they inspire you to consider the opinion, think about your stance, and uphold your reasons for supporting or disagreeing with me. (Deep breath...here it goes!)

First, we *definitely* must design lessons that meet our boss's expectations and the states' standardized testing criteria. Equally, if not *more* importantly, we have to be specifically focused on *our own personal principles and standards* for our students! As we gather those criterion and standards that we believe will make the kids and ourselves reach our highest potential, allow me to comment on a few fundamental aspects of teaching that may surprise you.

Consider first, that for most kids, music is going to be an *enriching element* to their lives, *not a career!* Granted, students being able to identify form, read complex rhythm patterns, play a melody line, understand and effectively use music vocabulary, know how to write chords in different inversions, sing pure vowel sounds, recognize musical symbols, identify operas, composers, and instruments is *very impressive* and clearly makes them look brilliant and us like "master teachers." But **I believe we <u>have</u> to put *our* love for music in *their* perspective.** Mastery of the state fine arts standards, while well and good, is simply *not* enough. It is *not* going to make a difference in a kids life when he is facing the inconceivable pressures our kid's face today! Music terminology and concept mastery just won't matter when they are abandoned, introduced to gangs, tempted by drugs, faced with teen pregnancy, have dropped out of high school, or collapsed beneath peer pressure.

Before anyone gets defensive and goes into attack-Debbie mode, you have to know that I *totally* understand how these educational elements of music teach complex thinking, responsibility, cross-curricular inferencing, and have unlimited additional benefits. But sometimes, we music teachers get so caught up in performances, perfection, schedules and standards, that we place more emphasis on *music* than on *kids!* That is backwards. It *has* to be the other way around for both student and teacher to be successful!

More than likely, we've all experienced the life-changing power of music or we wouldn't be in this particular profession! From either experience or observation, we know music is one of the major thoroughfares available toward building self-discipline, self-confidence, self-control, and self-improvement! Our career affords us such an amazing opportunity to be role models, fashion character, and teach LIFE LESSONS *through* music! So…**let's use *music* as our *invitation* into their lives** so that we might help them mature their integrity and character along with their understanding and appreciation of music. Let's get passionate about preparing them for their future and use music as our inlet. *Together, let's commit to making a difference – in their lives – in their character - and when they learn great music along the way – that's the bonus!!!*

Before we delve into the nitty-gritty. Let me share a story with you about a student I had about fifteen years ago. As horrible as the circumstances were, in retrospect, no other single event has affected me, my philosophy, the way I teach, and why I am writing this book to you, more than:

MY DECEMBER WITH AARON

It was early in my teaching career – back when I thought I knew all there was to know about teaching, music, and children! Fifth-grade Aaron wanted to play the part of Santa in our musical and I must say, had potential to be a smashing success! That child could sing, dance, and deliver lines like a Pro! He was bright, happy, reliable, a remarkable student, and as cute as a button, too!

As the performance date crept closer and all the students *polished* their lines and practiced their solos, our old buddy Aaron, had fallen apart. Our "Superstar" could not get through a single sentence without dropping lines and missing entrances! He mumbled, shuffled his feet, talked to the floor when he did finally say something, and spoke so softly that he couldn't be heard from two feet away. Each day I grew increasingly more impatient with him! I *knew* Aaron was capable, but for some reason, he was not learning his lines and *he had the lead!* Even after days and days of being extraordinarily nice and patient, working with him during lunch, before and after school, trying to help him memorize his speaking part and solos, he would not sit still or stay focused long enough to get anything accomplished! It was so frustrating.

I tried the old consequences and guilt-trip routine that was so popular back then: *"Aaron, if you don't learn those lines, I'm going to have to give someone else your part!" "I thought you wanted to be the lead character! Everyone is depending on you!"* In spite of nagging him, he only got worse and it was too late to find a replacement! *What on earth was I going to do?* This talented ten-year-old little boy had me over a barrel! He was going to ruin the show for the rest of us, make me look completely inept, and I couldn't do a thing about it other than keep harping at him and making him miss out on other things in order to work with me on memorization!

A few days after Aaron struggled through the musical, dropped nearly every line, stammered through sentences like he'd never seen them before, seemed to be clueless on blocking, and couldn't sing his solos to save his soul, I learned what was wrong. Aaron's daddy was hurting him. His mommy knew it was happening, too, and had done *nothing*. While I was *pushing* Aaron to learn the happy-go-lucky, charming lines of dear old St. Nicholas and sing about what a jolly fellow he was, that precious little guy had a jagged, broken pencil shoved up inside his rectum. He had steam-iron burns on his buns and if *that* wasn't enough, he was carrying the secret of knowing his two little twin sisters were being sexually abused, he being forced to watch, but could tell no one without fear of further danger to all of them.

After over twenty years in the profession, **Aaron's story** is still the single most life-changing, most heart-wrenching story I have ever experienced. To think, I thought a <u>musical</u> was important. I was worrying about what people were going to think of *me*! *Oh my gosh!* The lasting impression of Aaron's life changed my entire perspective on teaching *and* kids! **Aaron's story** is also probably why things that put other teachers and moms in orbit, don't rattle me too much. It definitely has a way of keeping *everything* in perspective.

Ever since that December, it is my goal to teach **children <u>first</u>** *then* I worry about content. I know now that every child who comes into my music room has the potential of being another Aaron. That thought tempers every word that comes from my mouth. It shapes every goal I set. It helps to keep anger distant and empathy close. It makes me more sensitive to changes in behavior and appearance. And, it makes me want to be the one who makes sure that all my students have a friend - someone they can trust, and someone who does everything possible to help them find some sense of happiness, security, and comfort in their little lives.

> **"Developing relationships as well as intellect with our kids, sometimes has a 'sleeper effect.' The effects of our intervention and influence may not show up for years but we need to *know* that we have offered *our* very best to *every* child."**
>
> ~ *Anonymous*

Now…let's move on to some less-emotional information.

DEBBIE'S DOSSIER

or…

A BONA FIDE BUT BASICALLY BORING BIOGRAPHY

I realize "About the Author" typically appears at the *back* of a book. However, after much deliberation and seeking advice from others, I decided to introduce myself to you at the *beginning* of mine. By the end of this section, assuming you decide not to skip over it *like I probably would*, you will know more about me than you ever cared to know. Sharing my personality and the foundational "me" from which I'm drawing the contents, hopefully will establish some credibility. Knowing that, it might be easier for you to consider the TRICKS I trade. Once those little metails (that's details about me) have been covered, we can proceed with this very opinionated collection of suggestions, thoughts, and advice I've compiled *just for you*.

I have a bachelor's degree in Music Education (BME) from the Conservatory of Music - University of Missouri at Kansas City, with K-12 Kansas and Missouri vocal and instrumental lifetime certification. While working on my BME, I performed in the Accordion Orchestra and the Accordionaires, under the direction of world-renowned performer, adjudicator, conductor, clinician, educator, and composer, Mrs. Joan Cochran Sommers. I also had the honor of singing for four years in the UMKC Chorale / Heritage Singers under the masterful and inspiring direction of the legendary Dr. Eph Ehly! While at UMKC, I was a member of the Percussion Ensemble, conducted by the late Charmaine Asher Wiley, and took private marimba lessons from a graduate student, Dr. Dennis Rogers, who is now professor and percussion department director at Missouri Western University and mastermind behind STICKS OF THUNDER – a delightful, audience-active percussion extravaganza that premiered in Kansas City. Although I have been blessed with many, many fine teachers, these music educators in particular, inspired, motivated, and had such impact on my life that if you know them and me, you'll recognize their profoundly positive influence on my career and my life!

I received my Masters of Arts in Teaching, with emphasis in educational computer technology, from Webster University and am now narrowing my selection of schools for my Ed.D, hoping to begin as soon as I complete the details of this TRICKS project, assuming I can find a statistics-free doctoral program.

My classroom experiences stem from teaching general music, since 1980, in the Blue Springs RIV school district. All but one of those years I have had the honor of teaching at Daniel Young Elementary, Kindergarten through fifth or sixth grade, depending on the year. Daniel Young students, under my direction, have supplied the kid-vocals in many radio and television commercials! We've done the *nationally* televised vocal spots for Kansas City's famed Country Club Plaza Christmas commercial - titled SHINE ON, Toastmaster's Kiddle Griddle store loop and ad, plus Missouri Tourism's WAKE UP TO MISSOURI. We also had the honor of being selected to sing the vocals for a *nationwide*, animated cartoon advertisement for **Blockbuster Video** that aired on Nickelodeon as well as all major networks! My students have sung the National Anthem for the openings of Kansas City Chiefs games, Special Olympics, and the Shrine Circus! Daniel Young singers can also be heard on the *Sniggles, Squirrels, and Chickenpox* CD by Miss Jackie Weismann. (You can order SNIGGLES at: www.jackiesilberg.com. Incidentally, this is a tremendous collection of fun, original songs written, accompanied, and performed with every imaginable voicing and instrumentation – appropriate for all ages from pre-school to fifth grade. *Sniggles...* also incorporates nearly every musical style you might like to include in your curriculum! It is rich with marches, blues, jazz, a sprinkle of gospel, and a spiritual or two tossed in for good measure. I selected the singers, taught the music, and then directed all the kid-vocals of Volume II in the recording studio! It is truly a masterpiece collection, is expertly recorded, and professionally performed! I would love to see it listed as a prerequisite purchase for the completion of an elementary music degree – it's just *that* good!)

In addition to teaching school, directing the commercials, and helping to produce the recordings, one of my career *highlights* was having the distinguished honor of being a clinician/presenter for Dr. Eph Ehly's **INTERNATIONAL** CHORAL SYMPOSIUM! Imagine how I felt when offered the opportunity to speak to educators, many with Ph.D's, from *thirty-three different nations of the world*! That occasion represents some *very special* memories and emotions for me – not only for what I was entrusted to do, but because of the honor, appreciation, devotion, and respect I hold for Dr. Ehly.

At the collegiate level, I am a supervising teacher (and love it!) and have the privilege of serving on the University of Missouri's Teacher Education Advisory Council (TEAC) which keeps me abreast of the latest educational trends, demands, and assessments for all education majors.

I have been honored by fellow educators and community as the JAYCEE'S OUTSTANDING YOUNG EDUCATOR, (you can tell by the adjective - *young* - that *that* was a while ago!) As BLUE SPRINGS TEACHER OF THE YEAR building representative I stepped through that selection process four different times, and former students have nominated me to WHO'S WHO AMONG AMERICA'S TEACHERS in 1996 and 2000. I was honored to have been nominated for the DISNEY'S AMERICAN TEACHER AWARD in 1999, 2000, and 2002.

I am a member of PTA, the Superintendent's Advisory Counsel for the Blue Springs School District, and I am a member of three professional organizations: Music Educators National Conference (MENC), Missouri Music Educators Association (MMEA), and I serve as a district delegate for Missouri State Teacher's Association (MSTA). My community involvement and memberships include church, the Community Services League, Sports Car Club of America (SCCA), and the metropolitan area's Critical Incident Stress Management team (CISM) – a community response team that is activated should a catastrophic event occur. I was a collegiate member of Sigma Alpha Iota - a professional music fraternity - and am now an active member of Delta Kappa Gamma - an international honor society for women educators promoting professional development, personal growth, and excellence in education.

One last thought: God has and continues to influence the very fabric of who I am. *Hey, that could be my next book!* (Now *that's* an idea! – Shhh…. *just don't tell my husband!*) ☺ Because of God's constant authority on my life, you'll find what I believe to be spiritual truths appropriately, but sparingly, interspersed with my TRICKS. Please don't let them offend you if you're not inclined to believe the way I do – just *ya da ya da ya da right over them* and proceed to the input you *do* value. Remember, though, those sparse scriptural and faith-based comments don't devalue the TRICKS that can be helpful. On the other hand, if you are someone who finds my Believer-based interjections beneficial, thought-provoking, or inspirational, then I am thankful I didn't resolve to exclude them!

I have no doubt that people would describe me as a bold, verbose, abstract communicator who is preoccupied with morale, motivation, feelings, and character.

> **"Personality is what a person does when people are watching;**
> **Character is what a person does when no one is watching."**
> *~ William May*

I always seem to follow my heart - probably because my head isn't very discerning and tends to listen to *everything!* ☺ I trust my heart-over-head intuition and judgment, and have found it to be a blessing when working with kids. However, I've learned that trusting my instincts, often to a fault, and allowing my *feelings to dictate my logic* has created some complications for me in the past four and a half decades. That's probably just because I take an inordinate amount of pride in being authentic and strive to develop that same quality in my students. To quote Popeye, **"I yam what I yam and that's all that I yam."**

There is an ample collection of drawbacks to my personality type that are only fair for me to admit, I lose interest in people and projects if they become routine. I get impatient with superiors and tend to side with the underdog. I don't tolerate whining, brown-nosing, tattling, and especially, lying. I do a *great* job instigating ideas and projects, but struggle with seeing them through fruition. (That's why I consider this book such an amazing achievement!) I have issues with anyone who fails to carry their end of the rope, and I like to dodge anyone who wants to squelch my freedom to exercise my creativity and right-hemispheric preferences. I find that my work is often more difficult and time consuming than necessary because I am such a forgetful scatterbrain. I have to work like a Banshee to be even remotely organized. (Thanks to Cingular Wireless, I can reflect my personality with a ring tone download from Wizard of Oz – *IF I ONLY HAD A BRAIN!*) Ironically, I can get down-right disrespectful with someone who is not being respectful – I know…I know…and the older I get, the less patient I am with adults and more patient I've become with children…go figure.

I love to read, but even more, I <u>love to write</u>! My husband can't figure out how I can have such a penchant for writing but can't seem to write ATM transactions and check amounts down in our check registry. I can't explain that – like many of the things in my life – but I'm working on it! I absolutely love watching our youngest daughter, Jess, manage an academic scholarship that requires a 3.7 GPA while playing collegiate basketball *and* softball at MidAmerica Nazarene University. She also is a highly skilled driver in the Solo II *auto racing circuit.* In fact, she won the National Championship in 2004! She is the lighthearted side of my life and always makes me smile! Also, I bask in the excitement of sharing in the journey of our oldest daughter, Micah, as she struts toward Med School on full scholarship at UMKC. Micah was a brilliantly talented catcher and was offered multiple softball scholarships, but declined in order to focus on her personal goals. She is an amazing young lady, to say the least, and I couldn't be more proud of both girls! Last but certainly not least, I'm unbelievably proud of and in love with my husband, Mike! He owns his own business designing and developing race car motors, races a formula car with SCCA, is the best daddy and hubby in the world – and loves me – in spite of my weird idiosyncrasies and quirkiness! His hobby, his career, and especially, his commitment to "his girls" have been an integral part of our lives and have actually been a very cohesive element for our family! I am so blessed.

My *most favorite quiet-time thing to do* is to **collect quotes**! I am a quoteaholic! I have so many you could read through the Old Testament, complete with begats, before you could finish reading through all the cool quotations I've collected over the years. Many are anonymous, unfortunately, only because I read them on the Internet, but they're still awesomely thought provoking! *Oh how I wish I could credit the thinkers of the thoughts!* You will find a smattering of them sporadically dispersed throughout *These Tricks Are For Kids*. I hope you enjoy them as much as I do!

"Listen to advice and accept instruction and in the end you will be wise."

Proverbs 19:20

"Successful people are those who have failed many times and have chosen not to give up."

~Anonymous

"People seldom become famous for what they say until after they are famous for what they've done."

~Cullen Hightower

"You should not confuse your career with your life."

~Dave Barry

Chapter 1

Ahhh Yes...those DELIGHTFUL EXTRACURRICULAR DUTIES

or...

YOU DO IT BECAUSE YOU HAVE TO

There are so many time-consuming responsibilities teachers have to do that may be indirectly beneficial, but just do not seem to directly apply to your students' education. I am discussing them right off the bat because I've been told, more than a few times, that these "extra things" were the beginning of the end for many of the music teachers who bailed out of this career. Recently, I've realized that those responsibilities have rapidly reproduced like rats and rabbits. When I first started teaching in 1980, my responsibilities were to show up on time, write lesson plans, teach songs, assess student mastery, provide two short programs each year, attend three PTA meetings a year and one faculty meeting a month. That was pretty much it. Since then, in addition to that short list...PTA meeting attendance is now required every month, we have *at least* two faculty meetings and one departmental meeting a month, nearly every grade level performs a show with a *minimum elapsed time* of 30 minutes (required, not suggested), we are required to create mission statements, compose philosophies, write annual goals (and rewrite them), update curriculum, serve on multiple building and district committees, design sub folders, archive almost everything written or spoken, contact every parent, and write recommendation letters for students, cohorts, and administrators. I've been asked to submit a written justification supporting why music should be kept in the public schools as well as writing responses as random as defending why the Physical Education teacher and I combine classes for our dance unit. You will, no doubt, throughout your career, have the same and exponentially more "**opportunities**" for EXTRACURRICULAR DUTIES! So....I've included my responses to some of my "opportunities" within the confines of the next few pages. You have my permission to use them, lose them, edit them, ignore them, springboard from them, adopt them, or you may opt just to disregard this whole section altogether and skip to another chapter. I'm fine with that, too! It's one less extra duty for you to manage. (But I'll lay odds that sooner or later you'll be asked to whip out some serious paperwork within one of those "by-noon" deadlines, and then you'll love my first chapter…and me! OK…maybe not *ME!*)

MY MISSION STATEMENT
or…
I'M ON A MISSION
or…
WHAT CAN I DO TO MAKE ALL OF MY STUDENTS SUCCESSFUL?
(At this time, please securely fasten your rose-colored glasses.)

My mission is to do whatever is necessary to ensure that *all* my students, without exception, know that I believe in them, that I will not give up on them, that I like them or *something* about them, that I am their *friend first – teacher second*, that they will look forward to music because they know there will be something for all of them, that they are loved, they will have fun, they are important to me, and they are safe - not only from physical harm, but from bullying, hurtful sarcasm, or *anything* else that has the potential to make miserable music memories.

When God gives us responsibility, He wants us to work diligently. I think He expects us to make the best from what has been entrusted to us. At the close of each day, at the close of my career, and at the close of my life, it is my desire to hear,

"Well done, good and faithful servant: thou hast been faithful over a few things, I will set thee over many things; *enter thou into the joy of thy Lord.*"

~Matthew 26:21

Oh yes…just so you know…I DO own my very own personal pair (of glasses) – in light fuchsia.

"God will do everything you can't do…if you do everything you can!"
~ Dr. Paul Bazalgette

"What is best in music is not to be found in the notes."
~Gustav Mahler

2

"To give anything less than 100% is to sacrifice the gift!"

~ Steve Prefontaine

OK...SO WHAT IS PHILOSOPHY
AND WHY DO I NEED ONE?
I'M IN *MUSIC* EDUCATION!

(fi los' *o* **fē)** *n.* The logical study of the nature and source of human knowledge or human values; the set of values, opinions, and ideas of a group of people or individuals.

- Webster

I think, whether you are just beginning your career, you've done it for a few shy of a bazillion years, like me, or you are somewhere in between the extremes, it's important to give regular, serious evaluation to your objectives and teaching philosophy. Begin by:

➢ Describing your personal feelings and beliefs about *teaching in general* – not just music.

➢ Include your own ideas of what makes you (or you hope will make you) an outstanding and loved-by-the-students and respected-by-your-peers teacher. (That's right, you can be a respected educator *and* loved by the students! The teachers in our building are living proof of that!)

➢ Consider what makes your students outstanding and admired-by-the-*community* and how you can help them achieve that citizenship success.

➢ Know what values you embrace and to what extent can you model them in class.

➢ Evaluate how your beliefs about teaching are demonstrated in your personal teaching style, the way you make your students feel, and in the way your classroom looks.

3

➢ Decide on the single most important thing you wish to leave with your students.

I've answered and revised my thoughts on this topic at least two dozen times over the years and it is interesting and amazing how drastically my expectations and priorities have changed and how dramatically my values have strengthened over the past two and a half decades. The fact is, if I knew back then what I know now, I would probably have to write letters of apology to all of those students who endured those first few years with me. The objectives and behaviors that were important to me fresh out of college, though still significant, are way down the priority list now that I'm old and uh…*old.*

> **"The age of a woman doesn't mean a thing.**
> **The best tunes are played on the oldest fiddles."**
> **~ Sigmund Z. Engel**

I realize I place myself "on the line" by revealing what is probably a controversial philosophical strategy, nevertheless, here is the number one part of Debbie, the teacher:

MY PHILOSOPHY – PART ONE

The foundational formula of my philosophy is taught in the New Testament book of Matthew 7:12 "So in everything, do to others what you would have them do to you…" (NIV). In other words, I like to be liked – *so I like my students.* I like to have fun – *so I make class fun.* I like my time to be valued – *so I make music time worthwhile.* I like to be respected – *so I respect others.* I like to be complimented – *so I compliment.* I like to be my best – *so I help my students be their best.* I like to learn – *so I teach them how to learn.* I like to be entertained – *so I entertain.* I like variety – *so I ensure variety.* I like surprises – *so I include surprises.* I like novelty – *so I create novelty.* I like to try new things – *I offer new things to try.* I like to hear stories – *I tell lots of stories.* I like people who are friendly and smile – *so I make an effort to be friendly and smile.* I like enthusiasm – *so I am enthusiastic.*

I don't like to be bored – *so I try not to bore.* I don't like busy work – *so I don't assign busy work*! I don't like being told where to sit – *so I don't tell kids where to sit!* I don't like confusion – *so I plan extensively to avoid confusion.* I don't like to sit still very long and be quiet – *so I get my kids moving and talking at regular intervals.* I don't like people who drop the ball – *so I <u>anticipate need</u> and help others.* Can you catch the point I'm making? When planning your life with students, faculty, family, and friends, consider how you *would* like and *have liked* to be treated, and then treat them in an identical way. The only way I can see you going wrong is if you're someone who hates to be around happy, positive people, you love to be isolated, you don't like challenges, you've been treated badly and now it's your chance to be vindictive, you're content to do the very minimum of what is required, and/or you don't like people. If *any* element of that last sentence in any way is a description of you – please put this book down, go to Monster.com or the Help Wanted section of your newspaper and find yourself a different career!

"Choose a job you love, and you will never have to work a day in your life."

~ Confucius

MY PHILOSOPHY – PART TWO
or...
MY THREE R'S! (WITH AN F)

RELATIONSHIPS, RESPECT, and RELAX! (with a FRIEND)

Being a teacher is a lot like being a salesperson. We have to be the **best** salespeople in the country to be master teachers and, in order to do that, we *have to know our product and our customers!* We have to make sure our "customers" believe that what we are "selling" is valuable and worth the investment of their time, energy, hard work, and attention. However, even more importantly, our "customers" have to be able to trust us, feel safe with us, and know that we care about them more than they could ever believe possible!

If given the opportunity, most of us would probably prefer to purchase a car from a *friend* as opposed to a person we don't know. There are probably several reasons for this. First, we figure, a *friend* is going to care enough about us to give us a good deal, not let us down, and not let us get mixed up in a bad experience. Secondly, we expect a *friend* to be truthful and helpful so we know that what we get is the best there is for our investment. Next, a *friend* could be trusted to tell us if there is anything that needs work to improve our investment and will probably help us close the deal. Yet perhaps the most important benefit of having a *friend* on our side is the simple fact that the ***relationship*** and the ***respect*** between us removes much of the risk, the fear, and the insecurity that we might otherwise feel.

The balanced combination of **_respect_** for one another and the **_relationship_** between each other is what makes us a confident customer.

Analogously, if given the opportunity, most students would probably prefer to take a class from a *friend* as opposed to anyone else. There are probably several reasons for this, too. First, they figure, a *friend* is going to care enough about them to give them the best learning-experience deal there is on the market and not let them get mixed up in a bad experience. Secondly, they expect a *friend* to be truthful and helpful so they know that what they get is the best there is for their investment. Third, the **_relationship_** with a *friend* is **_relaxed_** and based on trust. A *friend* can be trusted to tell them if there is anything that needs work in order to improve their investment. A *friend* will probably help them close the deal! Again, perhaps the most important benefit is the simple fact that the **_relaxed, respectful relationship_** between the two, removes much of the risk, the fear, and the insecurity a student might otherwise feel. These **_three R's_** make him or her a confident customer or in our case, student and friend.

The mark of an excellent salesperson and quality product is a return customer. The mark of an excellent teacher is having students who feel successful, important, loved, and **_respected_**, who believe they've learned useful information, and who have a personal connection with their teacher.

Storytelling is one of my favorite **3-R's-with-an-F**-building tools. I *love* it and use it often! Stories evoke many emotions, create mental pictures while at the same time, deliver very potent, unforgettable messages. More importantly, telling stories helps kids relax, helps build a student – teacher connection and bridge the inevitable gaps. Storytelling helps my students learn about me, my family, my history, my sense of humor, my hopes, as well as my expectations. Storytelling also makes *me* vulnerable. That vulnerability often elicits empathy, which in turn, can fashion friendships. Disclosing personal things about myself helps me create a **relaxed**, open **relationship** with my students. They learn about my mistakes and my successes, my compassion and my indifference, what makes me cranky and what makes me hysterical, about my fears and worries, and about the conclusions I draw from different situations. Students recognize those things, they relate to those feelings, and consequently, they relax and are more receptive to my guidance. Because I am their *friend* and they *want* to come to my place, we get a lot of learning accomplished and we have fun doing it!

"Folks don't care how much you know until they know how much you care...."
~ *Glenn Fray*

"When love and skill work together, expect a *masterpiece*."
~ *John Ruskin*

"Be kind, for everyone you meet is fighting a hard battle."
~ *John Watson*

STORIES? WHAT KIND OF *STORIES*?

I TELL STORIES ON A BOX,
I TELL STORIES WITHOUT SOCKS!
I TELL STORIES ALL THE TIME
I TELL STORIES THAT EVEN RHYME
~ *Debbie Seuss Gray*

When I first started teaching, I found a quality quartet of books by Doug Nichols. The collection, entitled <u>A Nichols Worth</u>, has many great little songs, but one of my favorites is called <u>Misery To A Kid</u>. I typically teach it to fifth grade and extend the lesson by having students write their own lyrics. I sing the song for them, encourage them to sing along on the simple chorus, and then *subito,* stop right in the middle – as if this story just occurred to me! Milking as much attention from my audience as possible, and being an actress extraordinaire, I slowly stroll around to the front of the piano, exaggerating my facial expressions to continue baiting my crowd, and begin telling about a miserable experience of mine:

"Ya know how sometimes you just start craving something for no apparent reason? Well, I don't EVEN like milk that much, but for some bizarre reason, one steamy, hot Missouri mid-morning, while I was down in the backyard mowing the horrible hill my husband calls the WIDOW MAKER, I got this sudden, obnoxious urge for a tall, icy glass of milk! I stopped in my steps, released the handle-safety-trigger so the mower stopped whirring, and I headed up the steps – lunging over multiple stairs at a time. (Obviously, this was a few years AND a few pounds ago!) I grabbed a tall glass from the cabinet, poured it to the brim with milk, splashed a drip or two on the counter, stirred in a couple of heaping (and I mean HEAPING) teaspoons full of powdered chocolate, and started chugging! I didn't even stop to take a breath – I was so incredibly thirsty! It wasn't until I had pretty much gulped two-thirds of the eight ounces, that I...hit a clot – a clump – a mysterious, gross, gagging glurb about the size

7

of a large curd of cottage cheese! It was only then that I realized that my milk was not only soured and clumpy, it was in my stomach!!!"

I wait for clues that reveal evidence that they grasp the reality of what had happened. The momentarily delayed onslaught of gags, groans, and gasps verifies their revelation and sends me back to the keyboard for another round of the chorus: *"...that's misery I'm a-tellin' you – that's misery..."* We no more than complete those four phrases when my eyes light up, yet again, with still another story that has just dawned on me to add to my personal experiences of misery. I saunter back to the front of the piano, in full-thespian mode, and I see in my peripheral vision, the kids relax from their front-of-their-chairs-both-feet-on-the-floor-backs-straight posture to their Sunday-afternoon-in-the-recliner-watching-the-Chiefs-game posture. Smiles of anticipation are wrinkling their freckly faces and I proceed with yet another miserable story from my past:

"Let's see...Micah was born in '83 and this happened to me when she was four so you can do the math and figure out how long ago this grossness transpired. My mom and dad were babysitting the girls while Mike and I went to the movies. When we got to the theater, the show was sold out so we bought tickets to the late show. Now, this was before anybody had ever even heard of a cell phone much less owned one, so I had to use a ____ (and I allow them to fill in the blank. This is a great tactic for keeping your audience absorbed.) *I inserted the ____ in the slot, dialed the ____, and got a busy signal. What do I do now?"* (It's actually amazing how long it takes someone to come up with: you reach in the coin return for your change...but someone eventually catches on to my pantomime and comes up with the answer. Thank goodness!) *THAT'S RIGHT! So I open that little silver trap door thingy that is on the front of all pay phones, stick two fingers in to retrieve my quarters, and as I slide them out with the money beneath them – I realize my change is marinating in sticky, gooey, disgusting slime."* (Pause for emphasis) *"Yep – someone had spit in there and I'd drug it out with my fingers!* **<u>DISGUSTING!"</u>**

Accompanied by noisy responses, I hurry back to the keyboard side of the piano and a chorus of, *"That's misery I'm a'tellin' you! That's misery!"* At this point, I don't need to tell you how their little minds are cranking! They're thinking about how totally gross my stories were, how they were totally true, how the second one was even worse than the sour milk story, and all the while...somewhere in the recesses of their amygdaloid body, hippocampus, and cerebral cortex, they're conjuring up their own memories of miserable experiences! VOILA` This is exactly my objective! Sometimes – particularly with this age group – *shock and awe* is the best way to initiate thinking. ☺

I'm only a little apologetic if all this is too disgusting for you - hey, they're not fabricated stories…they really DID happen! The only part I left out was how I held my hand out the window, in sub-freezing temperatures, as far from the rest of my nose and body as possible, all the way to the gas station where I could finally wash my loogified fingers!

And then there was the time… when, *"…it was Meet The Teachers Night for PTA. Our former principal always had her staff sit in chairs at the front of the gym, facing the parents and students in the audience while she shared personal quips, thoughtful compliments, and honors held by each of her staff members. I sat there, listening to this overly-exaggerated and embellished introduction of myself, waiting for my name to be called. I have to admit, I was feeling pretty heady and proud of myself after hearing all of her phenomenal compliments about me and my accomplishments. As I stood up, eager to acknowledge the 300 plus people sitting right in front of me staring, smiling, and applauding, I realized that the entirety of my skirt failed to accompany me when I stood. My hem was beneath the toe of my shoe so my skirt stayed down when I didn't. There I stood, blatant bare belly exposed to the embarrassed masses, complete with panty hose, seam, and shirt hem visible for all to try not to have to see! I think the audience of parents, all doing their best to avoid gawking and gasping, were as shocked as I!"*

After sharing something as unforgettable as that, students totally find a place in their hearts for their sour-milk-chugging, phlegm-encrusted-phalanges, abdomen-displaying music teacher who is asking them to now think of something they could write about that was miserable to them!

I've also shared the story of how I turned on the attic fan in the middle of winter, with all the doors and windows closed, to help suck out the smoke that had engulfed my house because I'd neglected to open the flu prior to starting a fire with newspapers. The details of that story, which includes the parts about having to replace our brand new carpet and repainting the recently painted walls because the burning ashes of the newspaper kindling engulfed the room, sucked by the attic fan, and dropped fiery bits of burning paper all over everything, left quite a mental picture. As tragic as it sounds, every student who has heard the story can tell you: **1.** What a "flu" is (which is one of the words in our song and was the instigator of the story in the first place), **2.** What can happen if you ever forget to open the flu before starting a fire; and **3.** What will probably happen if you turn the attic fan on while there's a fire in the fireplace! Oh yes…they'll probably add a fourth conclusion as well: Mrs. Gray is a dork!

Stories not only build teacher-student rapport, they are tremendous developers of critical thinking, vocabulary, they are impacting lessons that, because of their ownership and sharability, are remembered far longer than simply stating facts and instigating reactions.

So...my philosophy for building **relaxed, respectful relationships** includes storytelling. Include a story every time you can – even if it has to be embellished a bit to make it entertaining, interesting, applicable, and generate a smile or two!

"If you smile at me I will understand, because...
that is something everyone everywhere does in the same language"
~ Crosby, Stills, & Nash

"Everyone is trying to accomplish something big, not realizing
that life is made up of little things."
~ Frank Clarke

A PHILOSOPHICAL FINALE

Like so many of the teachers I know, I have had the honor of having many happy, satisfied, "return customers." I believe that is testimony to the power of building strong **relationships** with students, treating them with *compassion, love,* and mostly, ***respect.*** It also comes from making sure they experience an atmosphere where they have a good time, feel safe, and important while they're "shopping" for all the things they want to remember, take home with them, and treasure for a lifetime! YOU are the one who ultimately can make the difference. YOU are the one creating the memories!

There is an overabundance of critics attacking education and educators – more now than ever before in my career. But remember...they are not there! They are not there to see what you are doing for those children and *they will not be there* when those children come back to you as an adult and say, *"Thank you for being so special in my life!"* Their state-wide objectives and standardized tests aren't what will bring them back or make a difference in their lives – YOU have that distinct honor!

"It is not the critic who counts, not the man who points out how the strong man stumbled, or where the doer of deeds could have done better. The credit belongs to the man who is actually in the arena; whose face is marred by the dust and sweat and blood; who strives valiantly; who errs and comes short again and again; who knows the great enthusiasms, the great devotions and spends himself in a

worthy course; who at best, knows in the end the triumph of high achievement, and who, at worst, if he fails, at least fails while daring greatly; so that his place shall never be with those cold and timid souls who know neither victory or defeat."

~ Theodore Roosevelt

GOALS

(gōl) *n.* A purpose; the terminal point of a race or journey.

"The indispensable first step to getting the things you want out of life is this:

<u>Decide what you want.</u>"

~ Ben Stein

"If you can't see where you're going, you may not like where you end up."

~ Anonymous

I've learned that the people who require us to write goals often have a preconceived notion of what those goals should be and how they should be written. So, after years of submitting goals that were deemed "not acceptable" even though they were what *I* considered my purpose and what *I* hoped to accomplish throughout the course of the year, *I am still learning* what are "acceptable" and what are "unacceptable" goals:

QUASI GOALS

(…of the "unacceptable" variety.)

- I will do what is necessary to help all of my students look forward to and enjoy coming to music class.
- Each child will mature his or her musical aptitude.
- I will write a note to as many students and parents as possible throughout the year.
- I will run my schedule efficiently and on time.
- I will accept all offers and opportunities to be a workshop clinician or presenter.
- I will begin the completion phase of the book I am writing.

After having **my** personal objectives and purpose for the nine-month long journey ahead of me deemed unworthy, I went back to the drawing board and contrived a new set of "acceptable" goals. If you are going to use any of these ideas or verbiage, these would probably be the ones you would want to use as your springboard – rather than those mentioned first, although *I would be pleased with the "Quasi Goals" if I were your administrator reading them.* (That, however, I will NEVER be!)

"GOOD" GOALS
(…of the "even more acceptable" variety)

I am dedicated to ensure that by the time the children I have had since Kindergarten graduate from this school, they will:

- Understand the basic concepts and elements of music (rhythm, melody, harmony, texture, form, dynamics, expression, style) and be able to communicate that knowledge effectively.

- Have experienced the opportunity to be in at least four performances.

- They will have a large repertoire of songs they can sing, the majority with actions or choreography.

- Third, fourth, and fifth graders will be able to sing in two-part harmony. First and second graders will be able to sing Partner Songs and simple Rounds.

- All grades will have an age-appropriate mastery of proper vocal technique, know the elements of movement, dance, improvisation, space and an introductory knowledge of theatre terminology (props, staging, costumes, scenery, sound effects, etc.).

or…

"GETTIN' THERE" GOALS
(now we're approaching "close")

- Concepts will be introduced and taught in a variety of ways so that all students can learn.

- Students will acquire the knowledge and skills to decode music.

- Students will acquire the knowledge and skills to communicate music vocabulary effectively.

- Students will acquire mastery of state and national fine arts assessment objectives and test.

Then there are Administrators who expect goals to be written like objectives: "80% of the students will master raising their hands before speaking." Although I believe that those percentages are fabricated estimations and are of little value when setting goals or objectives...if this is required, this must ye do. So 80% is always a good handy and seemingly acceptable number for proficiency, so just wedge it in there somewhere between your goal and who you want to meet the goal so you are in compliance with authority. Unless you're instructed to do so, though, it's probably not very important. Seriously, **why settle for only 80%? Hold them _all_ accountable! Help them _all_ learn! Teach until they _all_ get it.** Have fun writing...

(My goal was to keep this section short and sweet.)

(My goal was to keep this section short and sweet, to shut up about goals, and move on to our next topic.)

(My goal was to keep this section short and sweet, shut up about goals, and move on to our next topic so that at least 80% of my readers stayed interested enough to read to the end.)

Amen

"Some goals are so worthy, it's glorious even to fail."
~ George B. Shaw

"Never give up on a dream just because of the time it will take to accomplish it.
The time will pass anyway."
~ Napoleon Bonaparte

"Dreams determine what you want... actions determine what you get!"
~ Unknown

"Those who stand around thinking about goals are generally being passed by those reaching them!"
~ Unknown

"Never give up on what you really want to do. The person with big dreams is more powerful than one with all the facts."
~ Life's Little Instruction Calendar

"There is no such thing as just staying the same. You are either striving to make yourself better or allowing yourself to get worse."
~ Peter Williams

SUBSTITUTE FOLDERS

or...

SURVIVAL STUFF SO YOUR SUB DOESN'T STINK!

(I mean, SINK! *SINK!* That's it! **SINK!**)

This is one of those EXTRACURRICULAR DUTIES I have found to be an extremely beneficial requirement and not at all in the "busy work" category. It is my opinion that you should always have a SUB FOLDER for when you must be absent. Look at it this way, when you're sick or something comes up that keeps you away from school – the last thing in the world you want to do is worry about what your sub is going to do and how your students will be while you are absent! Consider it a personal **gift to yourself**...all wrapped up in one little three-ring notebook.

I usually always leave my Sub Folder on my desk in a very prominent place, but I have also been asked to leave it with the secretary so when my sub checks in, my sub folder is handed to him/her and there's no chance he or she can't find it in my classroom. I prefer, though, to keep it on my desk, because I find that I regularly update it and change things if it's right in front of me all the time. My awesome friend and right arm across the hall, knows that anytime I'm absent, I appreciate her checking in on my sub and making certain he or she finds everything needed to make the day run smoothly. She's the best and I, of course, return the help in any way I can!

I do not ever leave MY lesson for the sub to do. Quite often, a <u>music</u> person does not sub for music teachers so you'll do best if you leave some <u>generic plans</u> that the non-musical person can use successfully. Here are the things I've done to make my subfolder all-encompassing, concise,

14

easy-to-understand, very self-explanatory, and cover me from liability (I hope) for what goes on while I am absent.

In addition to detailed lesson plans, my folder includes:

- Location of all materials needed for lesson plans.

- Class lists and/or seating charts (**I *never* use seating charts**, but I'll expound on that topic later in the book).

- An asterisk beside the names of students who are dependable, trustworthy, responsible leaders who can help.

- Schedule

- Extra duty responsibilities and rules or guidelines (recess, lunchroom, hall duty, bathroom patrol, etc.).

- Directions for operating all your equipment, including CD and/or tape player, VCR, DVD, television, and…record player - if you're like me.

- Emergency procedures (fire, tornado, earthquake, intruder, loose tooth, etc.)

- District, school, and classroom rules.

- Written directive that **corporal punishment is not allowed or acceptable**. (You could even use *"forbidden"* if you wanted to emphasize this guideline.)

- Written directive that **no child should be released without express permission from the office or administrator.**

- Written directive that **no student(s) are to ever, for any reason, be left unattended.**

Here are some examples of different kinds of sub plans I leave. If you notice, I've written different styles for different preferences. Some subs WANT to use their musical skills, other's were on sabbatical when God was passing out musical talent and so would prefer something non-musical. Some prefer written work, some prefer dramatics, others like games, and most like the no-brainer plans. I think I was probably feeling for the person who has to come in and take over an unfamiliar class when I designed such a wide variety of options. (These are all in a three-ring binder with tabs marking each section.)

- **OPTION 1: Use the teacher's manuals and student books.** An objective is stated, page numbers, approximate length of time needed to cover the concept, recordings, and even a script/dialogue are typically available in most Teacher Editions. You may choose whatever lesson, song, review you, or the students wish. (Your choice.)

- **OPTION 2: An entire packet of hands-on experiences are available**: Scripts, (for the students to act out short skits); pictures with caption bubbles to create conversations, illustrate a song, or design your own music cartoons; worksheets with puzzles, word searches, and other games tucked inside the pockets of the folder. (I collected some of my packet materials from HELP! I'M A SUBSTITUTE MUSIC TEACHER – a Collection of Games and Activities for Survival in the Classroom by Cheryl Lavender! Nevertheless, I always keep my eyes open for good sub stuff to add to what I've already provided. Music and Educational conventions, the Internet, and classroom resources are your best bet for finding new ideas.)

- **OPTION 3:** Have students research famous composers, musical styles, or music eras, and give either a written or oral presentation at the end of class. (I typically request that none of these activities be held over for the next class time simply because I hope to return to the curriculum as soon as I return). They may work as individuals or in teams of two or three... sub's discretion. For whatever it's worth, I don't like this idea much at all...just because if I were a student in the class, I would *hate* having to do this assignment and would consider it busy work. Nevertheless, it is an option that is repeatedly suggested by music educators as a good choice for subs – so, I included it so as not to be too much of a maverick.

- **OPTION 4:** Musical SIMON. Great practice for working in small groups and improving tonal memory through competitive play. (I will include directions at the end of this chapter for making this a class game that involves everyone.)

- **OPTION 5**: Substitute may use his/her own MUSIC plans for the class. (Some subs will appreciate this option because it gives them the freedom to do it the way they prefer, so it is personal, comfortable, and familiar.)

- **OPTION 6**: (This is my personal favorite!) Show one of the five videos in the INSTRUMENTAL CLASSMATES video collection. This particular video series, in my opinion, should be on every elementary music shelf! The videos are superbly done in an entertaining, elementary age-appropriate, educational way! They are appropriate for ages one through five or six and the information is extraordinary. The format and action moves quickly enough that students don't get bored and restless so classroom management isn't a concern. There are enough videos in the collection that students never have to see the same video content more than once. I have a chart in my Sub Folder for the substitute to list which tape each class has seen to prevent repetition, although they are good enough that students don't mind watching them more than once. With the lengthy illness of my father, knee surgery on my daughter, and several bouts of pneumonia, I have had to enlist the use of a sub more than usual over the past couple of years. The result though, is that I have seen a remarkable improvement at every grade level with instrument identification and orchestral family facts!

- **OPTION 7:** Using saved music catalogues and magazines, allow students to work in groups making posters that include cut-out pictures of the instruments. Have them place them on their poster in the sections of the orchestra labeled: strings, woodwinds, brass and percussion. (Typically, this requires students to bring their art supplies that include glue and scissors, crayons, colored pencils, or markers to music class, unless you use some of your meager music budget, your own money to stock your room with these art supplies, or are lucky like me, and have a kind and generous art teacher who will lend some supplies.)

I like to display the posters that are correct and prove to be good study guides. Some students work in teams and make a different poster for each orchestral family while others put all four families on the same poster. The kids seem to enjoy this activity and in order to help them with their projects, I have made PowerPoint programs for each family of the orchestra for facts, review, and photos. I set them to loop, so they recycle themselves over and over.

If I ever need a sub around Halloween, I leave a collection of Piggy Back song lyrics otherwise known as "Pumpkin Carols" for my sub to teach. Most of the melodies are familiar and the words fit the tune easily. Another fun holiday sub activity is to have students write new lyrics or verses to 12 Days of Christmas for any holiday, like: Halloween: 12 ghouls a groan'in…. or for Thanksgiving: 12 turkeys gobbling…11 pilgrims hunting…10 Indians dancing… or Valentines Day: 12 couples kissing…11 girls a'giggling…10 guys a'groanin.' St. Patrick's Day you could have 11 leprechauns leaping and Groundhog's Day could include 7 clouds a'floating. You can even have students make up their own choreography to match their lyrics but **beware on the 12 couples kissing!!**

If I know ahead of time I am going to be absent, I record myself teaching the lesson to another class in each grade level so all the sub has to do is plop in the tape, monitor the kids while letting me teach.

I typically do a run-though of any activities I place in my sub folder, just so the kids aren't totally depending on the sub for instructions. I just make this a concept lesson early in the semester so I know it's been covered with every class.

SIMON SAYS, "HERE'S HOW YA PLAY IT."

or…

ON YOUR MARK, GET READY, GET SET….GO!
(I DIDN'T SAY, "SIMON SAYS!")

The SIMON game is in the cabinet above the sink. How to play: Upon pressing "start," SIMON will play one sound and simultaneously light up a color pad. The person on that color team presses his/ her lighted pad – echoing what SIMON played. SIMON will then add a second sound to the first – chaining a two-pitch, two-light sequence. The first player presses his/her pad first and the second bar is pressed to match or echo what SIMON has played. The player of that team color is to press his/her pad. I.e.: green team only presses the green pad, red team only the red pad, etc. but they must follow the sequential order. The sequence continues, adding an additional pitch with each play.

If using this option, please use the following guidelines:

1. Students will have been taught how to play, but you will need to remind them of the directions of play previously given.

2. Lights off.

3. Place the piano bench in the center of the room with one student chair placed on each of it's four sides.

4. Give game directions and guidelines <u>before dividing class into teams</u>.

5. Divide the class into four teams: red, yellow, blue, and green.

6. To keep score, write the four team names in columns on the chalk board.

7. Be sure SIMON is set on game 1, level 4.

8. The students on the "green team" are the "starters." This means that the *seated* green team member will press the start button at the beginning of each new round. (Please advise the student to wait until all players are settled before initiating the round.)

9. Play continues until an error is made, indicated by a buzzer. At this time, ALL FLOUR PLAYERS HAVE COMLETED THEIR TURN <u>even if their light never lit and they never touched SIMON during their round.</u>

10. When the error color flashes and buzzes, it indicates that THAT player is to go to the end of his or her line. The other three players proceed to the score board and tally a point for his/her team. ONLY THE PLAYERS OF EACH ROUND may write on the score board. (This prevents confusion caused by other players giving points.)

11. Please **announce before play begins**: The minute *anyone* talks, seated or standing, the other three teams are awarded an extra point! (Teacher must tally the extra points so no student is forced into the disciplinary/bonus position.)

Please enforce this rule consistently and immediately (even for whispering) and you will have very few discipline problems!

(This rule enables the players to think without distraction and it eliminates students from one team telling another to press their light pad when it isn't their turn, and consequently, causing THAT person to get "out" rather than the one talking.)

12. Play continues during time allotted. The team with the highest number of points is the winner. That group may be the first to line up, share a treat if available, "go pop" (see the chapter on Motivator Magic) or offer nothing for the winner – your choice.

WRITE? RIGHT!

or....

I RECOMMEND WRITING RECOMMENDATIONS

Hopefully, you will have opportunities to write letters of recommendation for your peers, your friends, your Administrators, your students, and families. Please jump on those chances!! Accept the request or offer if your help isn't solicited! (They can always lose it on purpose if they don't want to use it.) A recommendation letter is your opportunity to honor, compliment, and lift up another person in your life. What a wonderful opportunity! It will make them feel great, successful, and honored that someone has noticed their hard work and talent. It will make a new friend out of an acquaintance or make a good friend a great friend!

It is not without some personal benefit to you, too! It forces you to analyze and put into words what qualities are the trademarks of a master teacher, administrator, friend, person, or family! Writing a recommendation letter is a bonus-brimmed task that everyone, including your students, should be able to do.

It is very important when writing one of these letters, to follow the instructions very precisely, but there are also a few general rules of thumb to guide you through the process.

- Letters that have the most influence on selection decisions usually describe how long and in what context or capacity you know the person.

- The letter you write should provide information that is not likely to be available from other sources.

- The letters can address the applicant's special interests, motivations, personal qualities, or background as well as their strengths and talents.

- The letter could indicate how the applicant compares to others you have known or observed in a similar capacity.

- The letter should express your supported opinion as to why the person deserves to be the recipient of the honor, admission, position, etc.

- The letter should include specific examples of the applicant's expertise, talent, ingenuity, mastery, compassion or worthiness of the honor.

Isn't it easy to see why someone might relish receiving such words of kindness and perception!? Whether they are actually rewarded with whatever they are seeking by the recommendation letter or not, your words will be a treasure to them for a lifetime. **Maya Angelou** says it best,

> **"I've learned that people will forget what you said,**
> **people will forget what you did,**
> **but people will never forget how you made them feel."**

Most of the time, the guidelines for the letter include placing it in a sealed envelope then signing your name over the seal to protect it's integrity. I do that every time unless directed otherwise, but I also <u>always</u> make a copy and give it to the candidate so he or she knows exactly what was said.

You may be thinking, "…what if what I wrote wasn't something I want them to read?" Then I say…DON'T WRITE IT. If you are asked to write a RECOMMENDATION LETTER for someone you cannot recommend, then simply DON'T WRITE IT. This is a very important time **not** to fabricate truths or construct untruths in order to classify someone into a deserving role. If you are asked, express your regret - simply say, "*I'm sorry. I'd rather not. I could proof read your essay or is there some other way I can help you?*" Whatever it is, avoid expressing your personal opinion, just come up with something gentle, but concise to say, so he or she knows you will <u>not</u> be helping out on that particular aspect of their application. It's your reputation on the line as well as theirs. If you recommend someone who turns out to be a total failure or disappointment,

21

you do not need or want your good name associated with endorsing them for the position. It not only jeopardizes your integrity and causes others in authority to question your judgment, it also is bad for the students who will be directly affected by your candidate's position. It's just not worth it. I must admit though, this is not easy to do…particularly if you are friends with the applicant.

I had a young, second-year college student doing field observation in my classroom and was asked to write a recommendation letter for her, to accompany a job application to teach music in a day care situation. Something about the phrases, "*My daddy knows….*" and "*…just a formality…*" made me know she was going to get the job regardless what my comments were, but I still felt I had a *moral obligation* to the little ones in that school, to share my impressions with the human resources person. I don't remember exactly how I worded it, but I probably could have won a blue ribbon in a creative writing contest with my entry.

I informed them that she was punctual…*about 3% of the time over the course of one semester*; that she was clean, dressed appropriately and professionally…*on picture day*; and that she seemed to do a little better being patient with the children…*in the mornings than in the afternoons.* I went on to mention that her piano skills had improved…somewhat, *since she'd been able to add the V chord in the key of C to her repertoire*; that she did what I asked her to do…*once;* and that there had been one afternoon during her multiple-weeks worth of visits that… *she actually joined the kids and participated in the lessons being taught.* I explained that she spoke loud enough to hear her speak…*if you were sitting on her lap;* and her rapport with the students was acceptable…*as long as those associating with her were the cream of the crop.* (OK…I admit, I exaggerated on the speaking loud enough to hear her part – I promise…I never sat on her lap to verify that theory. I actually think I said, *whenever she was angry.*)

Regardless of the practice-what-you-preach methodology, I can honestly tell you, in this particular instance – common sense prevailed - I did not send my student a copy of the "recommendation" letter I mailed to her prospective employer. <u>She was hired.</u> She also returned to me for a second recommendation letter about two months later, because they had "some cut-backs." I told her I would be happy to send the same letter I'd sent to her most recent employer. ☺

I have no idea what you may be thinking about me right now – but it is fair to say that I may have exaggerated a tad regarding my "recommendation" letter, but I *do* have a clear conscience regarding the actual letter I submitted, because I did not lie. There was no way I could honestly say that this student deserved a position in education, and

I submitted it to protect the children! She was deficient in every aspect of the process and not only do the children and staff not need to have to deal with someone so remarkably unsuitable for the job, you and I don't need someone like that tainting our profession or spoiling our reputations as educators!

Please remember, if you're drawing conclusions about me...that in twenty-plus years of teaching and hosting college student teachers and observers, that was the only time I *ever* had to be covert and brutally honest about someone's deficiencies. My student teachers from the Conservatory have far exceeded outstanding and have been well-prepared for their teaching experience. This isolated example though, gives me reason to believe there are others out there. We owe it to our profession and even more, to our students, not to encourage the placement of such individuals. Don't let guilt, friendship, or peer pressure persuade you to write a recommendation that shouldn't be written.

Here are a few of many, many letters I've had the <u>honor</u> of composing in order to praise someone's expertise and help them attain their professional goals with a letter of recommendation:

A LETTER OF RECOMMENDATION FOR

A DISTINGUISHED EDUCATION FELLOWSHIP

To Whom It May Concern:

It is my *privilege* to write this letter of support for Mrs. Betty Beal, eighth grade science teacher at Moreland Ridge Middle School in Blue Springs, Missouri. She is an outstanding candidate for the Albert Einstein Distinguished Education Fellowship! From personal experience, I will share with you the variety of ways her extraordinary teaching, expertise, creativity, and insight has influenced my daughters.

As a parent of two children who have been in her class, I have observed, first hand, how she allows her students to utilize their personal talents and ability levels to enhance their motivation and move through the information at their own pace. Her multi-faceted methods of teaching and reinforcing concepts allow students to learn by designing models, acting in plays, writing scripts, poetry and songs, playing games, experimenting, making movies, taking hikes, creating PowerPoint projects, listening to guest speakers, and using familiar objects to delve into and compare things that are unknown. Every child, regardless of ability and *learning style*, has the opportunity to succeed under the tutelage of Mrs. Beal. She is

<u>always</u> supportive, respectful, and appreciative of her students' thinking, their effort and their work, and she stands as an ever-present resource.

My oldest daughter was in Mrs. Beal's class during the 1996-97 school year. She is a student in the gifted and talented program and up until eighth grade, had absolutely no clue which professional path interested her. Mrs. Beal sculpted her lessons and *daily* labs so that not only did her delayed and average learners enjoy success in her class, this gifted child was inspired and motivated to develop each discovery to a greater extent. By the second week of school, I found myself taking her to school an hour early just so she could "…spend time in Mrs. Beal's lab and do extra experiments." Mrs. Beal's innovative approaches to learning, her development, and implementation of new experiences created valuable, unprecedented opportunities.

Today, that same daughter, a junior in college, has a clear-cut focus on her career in the field of science. She intends to go to medical school, specializing in surgery and medical research. I firmly believe that Mrs. Betty Beal is the person who initiated and developed this interest and love for lab work, this enthusiasm for helping others, and the motivation to drive toward a career goal that will affect my daughter's entire life. Mrs. Beal has had an unbelievable impact on her life!

I have the privilege of speaking from another perspective with my bright, 4.0 GPA - but not "gifted" second child, who, unlike her sister, perceives school as a bit of a push. Again, this is a child who, upon entering eighth grade, showed no interest whatsoever in science of any kind. After having Mrs. Beal, I saw a whole new interest and determination blossoming from her. Each evening at dinner, she shared stories of what was done in science lab; we got questioned about science quips that she had learned, and we searched the papers daily for articles that pertained to science so she "could" read and report on them in class. Because of Betty Beal, another science-related field will be inheriting an avid, curious student, and career-oriented young lady!

If students' response to their teacher, their enthusiasm for learning, their involvement, and their self-confidence is directly proportionate to exceptional, effective teaching, then Betty Beal is the epitome of excellence! I strongly recommend Mrs. Betty Beal as an Einstein Fellow because she is self-confident, an extraordinary communicator, and a master of innovative approaches to learning. No one could be more deserving of recognition for total, unselfish contributions to the success of our future!

or…

You'll see some similarities. I am a firm believer in

VARIATIONS ON A THEME!

<u>A LETTER OF RECOMMENDATION FOR</u>
<u>TEACHER OF THE YEAR</u>

To Whom It May Concern:

It is my *privilege* to write this letter of recommendation and support for my fellow teacher, Jason Gross, fourth grade teacher at Daniel Young Elementary School in Blue Springs, Missouri. He would be a tremendously outstanding candidate for the Blue Springs School District's Teacher of the Year award! From personal experience, I will share with you the variety of ways his extraordinary teaching, expertise, creativity, and insight has influenced the children in our school.

I have observed, first hand, how he allows his students to utilize their personal talents and ability levels to enhance their motivation and move through the information at their own pace. His multi-faceted methods of teaching and reinforcing concepts allows students to learn by designing models, acting in plays, writing scripts, poetry and songs, playing games, experimenting, making movies, taking hikes, creating projects, listening to guest speakers, and using familiar objects to delve into and compare things that are unfamiliar. Every child, regardless of ability and *learning style*, has the opportunity to succeed under the direction of Jason Gross. He is <u>always</u> supportive, respectful, and appreciative of his students' thinking, their effort and their work, and he stands as an ever-present resource.

Mr. Gross sculpts his lessons and *daily* activities so that not only do his delayed and average learners enjoy success in his class, his gifted children are inspired and motivated to develop each discovery to a greater extent. Mr. Gross' innovative approaches to learning, his development, and implementation of new experiences create valuable, unprecedented opportunities for every child and every learning style.

I firmly believe that Mr. Gross is a person in each child's life who initiates and develops interest and love for learning. His enthusiasm for helping others and the motivation techniques he assembles to drive his students toward meeting their individual goals will affect young lives exponentially.

After having observed Jason's teaching and frequently discussing various aspects of education over the past few years, I have seen consistent new interest and determination blossom from both him and his students. He is a voracious reader, a continuous learner, an incredible role model, a patient gentleman, and a man energized by coming to work each day – facing new challenges and a classroom full of students to influence, teach, and love.

His classroom reflects his penchant for novelty and his uniquely fun personality. Jason has a giant sofa, lamps, and a throw rug for the kids to enjoy. He has a reading corner with huge paper tree limbs and leaves hanging down making an especially cozy spot for readers. He moved out the traditional reading, computer, and teacher's desk and replaced them with giant wooden, desk-high cable spools! He has a class tarantula who was named Harry - - until they had to change it to Harrietta. Jason's students are bombarded with creativity and out-of-the-box thinking. His students are taught *how* to learn, not just *what* to learn and for all of these things, I honor him as a master teacher!

If students' response to their teacher, their enthusiasm for learning, their involvement, and their self-confidence is directly proportionate to exceptional, effective teaching, then Jason Gross is the epitome of excellence! I strongly recommend him for Teacher of the Year because he is self-confident, an extraordinary communicator, and a master of innovative approaches to learning. No one could be more deserving of recognition for total, unselfish contributions to the success of our future!
Debra L. Gray (parent & educator)

Or…

ANOTHER LETTER OF RECOMMENDATION FOR TEACHER OF THE YEAR

To Whom It May Concern:

Penny Bowerman is an extraordinary Counselor – always helping the students, parents, and staff at Daniel Young Elementary. Her heart reaches out to so many people that it is impossible to recognize how deeply she has touched lives over the course of her career.

It would be easy to list the many activities and honors she has been associated with during her decades of dedicated service to the community. Along with being the Daniel Young Elementary Teacher of the Year – numerous times, and Jaycees Outstanding Young Educator, she was also the Phoebe Epperson Hearst building candidate and first runner-up at the NATIONAL level!

In addition to her counseling, she has served in multiple capacities, year after year, as a PTA Board member, PTA officer, as the PAFLE Coordinator, building Coordinator of the district-wide Adopt-A-School program, and of course, a member of the CHOICES Core and Intervention teams.

There are clearly many other accomplishments that I could list, but the important and wonderful part about Penny is her extraordinary gifts of showing unconditional love and compassion to EVERYONE, her positive attitude and creative personality, and especially, her wit and wisdom that make this co-worker, teacher, and counselor an irreplaceable friend and professional.

Respectfully Submitted,

Debbie Gray

or…

A LETTER OF RECOMMENDATION FOR

AN ADMINISTRATIVE POSITION

To Whom It May Concern:

It is my *privilege* to write this letter of recommendation and support for Kindergarten teacher, Mrs. Jeanne Peve. She is a tremendously outstanding Principal candidate. I have had the pleasant opportunity to work closely with Jeanne for the past nine years at Daniel Young Elementary in Blue Springs, Missouri. She is an amazingly talented teacher whose educational expertise has created an impressive number of young readers and writers in her Kindergarten classroom. Her ambition and support, however, reach far beyond her abundantly successful work with the five-year-olds. She has collaborated on many school-wide projects, filling a very definite leadership role. I am pleased to say that Jeanne is very professional, punctual, a kind and sincere individual, and an ideal coworker. She is a clear, concise, communicator and has an intuitive way of anticipating need.

Jeanne was my summer school Principal in 2002 and I thoroughly enjoyed working for her. She was in my classroom every single day, without fail, offering help, encouragement, and friendship to both the students and me. She always does more than her share of the work on the committees and projects in which she participates and I am quite impressed with her enthusiasm, how she often takes the initiative with new ideas, and picks up the slack when things need attention and experienced ingenuity. Her work as a teacher is thorough, comprehensive, and just as when she is teaching, she is conscientious and gregarious when serving in an administrative capacity.

I certainly believe Jeanne has what it takes to make a wonderful Principal. I strongly recommend her because she is self-confident, capable, an extraordinary facilitator, organized, and a master of innovative approaches to learning. She will definitely be an asset to any faculty concerned with the success of our future!

Sincerely,

Debbie Gray

Or...

A LETTER OF RECOMMENDATION FOR A STUDENT

To The Campus Ambassador Selection Committee:

I have the distinct honor of recommending Mr. Taylor Hill to the Ambassadors Program when he enters UMKC in the fall of 2004. Having known Taylor for years, both as an educator and his friend, and being somewhat familiar with the philosophy, mission, and expectations of the University Ambassadors, I believe, without a doubt, that Taylor would be an integral addition to your already quality program.

Taylor has communication skills and professional preciosity beyond his years! He is an eloquent speaker, an enthusiastic people-person, an extraordinary academian, and brings with him to UMKC a rich resume of involvement in DECA at the International level, student government, his entrepreneurship experience, and at least two years of business ownership and leadership!

Because of his understanding of and appreciation for *diversity*, the quality example his *life style* exudes, his extraordinary ability to *manage his time*, his *organizational aptitude*, his penchant for being extremely *responsible*, his talent for *getting along with and motivating others*, and his loyalty to getting things *accomplished*, Taylor is an exceptional candidate for Ambassador and clearly more qualified than any student I have ever taught! His work ethic is unlike any college-age student I know and his determination to succeed and impress is unprecedented.

Taylor's "away message" on his computer exemplifies his goal-oriented thinking. He writes: *"I believe there is little difference between obstacle and opportunity and that hard work, vision, and determination make it possible to turn both to their advantage."*

I urge you to consider Taylor Hill for a position on your staff. He will be an asset beyond anything you might ever anticipate!

Sincerely,

Debbie Gray - BME   MAT

UMKC Conservatory of Music Alumni (1979)

A LETTER OF RECOMMENDATION FOR A

STUDENT TEACHER

To Whom It May Concern:

It is my *privilege* to write this letter of recommendation for Mr. Dan Edwards. I believe him to be an outstanding candidate for the music opening you have available! My professional relationship with Dan began and extended through his observation classes and student teaching with me in the Blue Springs School District at Daniel Young Elementary. Though I have only observed his teaching in a general music classroom, the rapport he established with the students and staff, his preparedness, talent, enthusiasm, punctuality, professional demeanor, character and integrity are distinctive qualifications that would make him an ideal teacher for any position, primary or intermediate level.

I observed, first hand, how Dan allowed the students to utilize their personal talents and ability levels while progressing at their own pace. His multi-faceted, face-paced-but-thorough methods of teaching and reinforcing concepts allowed students to learn by singing a wide variety of songs, learning age-appropriate musical concepts, writing lyrics, playing musical games, playing instruments, incorporating artwork, and listening to guest speakers. Every student, regardless of ability and *learning style*, had the opportunity to succeed when Dan was teaching. He was <u>always</u> supportive, respectful, and appreciative of his students' thinking, their effort, and their work, and he was an ever-present resource for all.

Mr. Edwards planned his lessons and *daily* activities so that not only did his delayed and average learners experience success in his class, his gifted students were inspired and motivated to develop each discovery to a greater extent. His imaginative approaches to learning, his smooth curriculum development, and his ability to sculpt new experiences created valuable, unprecedented opportunities for every child.

After having observed Mr. Edwards teaching and frequently discussing various aspects of music education, I have seen consistent new interest, new ideas, goals, and determination blossom. He is a voracious reader, an accomplished musician and composer, a continuous learner, an incredible role model, a patient gentleman, and a man who seems to be energized by new opportunities.

If students' response to their teacher, their enthusiasm for learning, their involvement, and their self-confidence is directly proportionate to exceptional, effective teaching, then Dan Edwards is the teacher you want on staff! I *strongly recommend him* because he is self-confident, a fine communicator, and a congenial staff member. No one could be more deserving of a career in music education!

Respectfully submitted,

"Do unto others as you would have them do unto you!"

Luke 6:31

INVENTORY INFORMATION

The Blue Springs School District requires us to keep a running inventory of all the large, furniture items we have in our rooms. At one time, however, we had to write *everything* we had in our classrooms – from pencils to pianos. Because I was part of that generation, I kept my list and have added to it, keeping it updated each time I receive a shipment of supplies or equipment. I have that Inventory List saved on the hard drive of my computer, on a disk at my house, and I send the list as an attachment via email to my home so I have it saved in My Documents there, too.

It will take a long time to do this, but I urge you to, just so, in the event you lose equipment for some reason, you have a list of all your sheet music, instruments, CD's, Videos, tapes, furniture, everything you would want replaced if insurance requested a listing of losses. Rather than letting it overwhelm you, just work on one category at a time. Maybe ask someone to help you by standing at your file cabinet and reading aloud the titles, order numbers, publishers, and quantities of your sheet music while you sit at the computer and type what they dictate. You may want to do the same with your audio-visual supplies, then equipment. Move on to your text books, then furniture. Don't forget your piano(s) when you tackle the instrument category and when you've finally logged all of the big ticket items, then you can start listing the smaller things like your staff drawer, metronome, posters, bulletin board supplies, art supplies, construction paper, globe, maps, staplers, tape dispenser, electric pencil sharpener...anything like that. I also suggest placing an asterisk* by or listing in a **bold font,** all items that belong to you, personally. (I have lamps, silk Ficus trees, curtains, couch, chairs, mirrors, a rattan bird cage, and framed pictures on my asterisk list.)

Don't try to do this all at once. Maybe make it a five-year project or at the very least, give it what you consider to be a realistic timeline. Enlist the help of a friend or relative – my mom, Micah, and Jess have been lifesavers for my inventory list and me! Just don't try to do it alone...and remember, summertime, when the building is relatively quiet, is a *great* time to work on duties like inventory listing.

You could, instead, do a picture inventory by taking photos of everything in your cabinets, drawers, files, and room. This would definitely be quicker and just as accurate if you make sure to include necessary close-ups. If you use a digital camera, you can download the photos and still send and save them to various locations.

Good luck...and remember always to update it as soon as something new arrives for your room.

JUST JUSTIFY YOUR JUSTIFICATIONS

Remember me telling you that once I had to write a justification for combining PE and music classes for a dance unit? I guess what seems incredibly obvious to some is obscure and surreptitious to others. Nevertheless, I followed my directive and came up with the following support statements. Incidentally, I included it on the back of the program for all the parents to see the night of the first grade dance performance!

WHY COMBINE MUSIC AND PE FOR A DANCE UNIT?

Music & PE classes are combined for our dance unit because dancing develops the physical education of *endurance, coordination, teamwork, listening, and fitness* while incorporating the musical skills of *tempo, steady beat, expression, phrasing, and form.* The Missouri Assessment Program also identifies dance skills as pertinent to the total education of each student, so we cover terminology, techniques, and activities included in the Missouri expectations for music and physical education.

HOW DO YOU BEGIN?

We begin our dance unit by teaching "personal space" (a place where you can stand and someone can walk completely around you without touching anything else.) Then, we build on that concept by adding movements like shaking, making shapes, bending, twisting, stretching, twitching, and rocking inside their "personal space." The next step is to help them learn to move while taking their "personal space" with them. They gallop, skip, hop, spin, jump and leap, staying aware of the others working in their group and maintaining that bubble of space around them. We extend that lesson by adding multi-thought processing requiring students to mirror, imitate, improvise, move left and right, move directionally, and at different elevation levels such as high, medium, and low movement. Dancing doesn't only develop spatial awareness, concentration, and listening skills; it increases coordination and most definitely, endurance.

31

Debbie Gray

HOW IS DANCING DIFFERENT THAN MOVEMENT?

Dancing IS movement but dance is an awareness of movement and generally in an organized, predetermined order. To successfully perform a choreographed dance, students develop complex thinking skills like: chaining, patterning, memory, and of course, concentration. Students first have to learn the actions and work to develop the coordination to do them, then listen to the music to determine how and where those actions fit together, then finally, to remember the order in which those actions appear. Of course, we are aware that dance does not have to be pre-prescribed choreography. You will see some improvisational dancing combined with our choreographed dances.

HOW ELSE CAN DANCE BE BENEFICIAL TO MY STUDENT?

Making up their own simple moves, steps, or dances taps into their creative abilities and imagination. It is awesome and amazing how emotion, energy, and intensity often become evident when they are just allowed to express themselves in silent motion. Watch for their improvisational skills in Bean Bag Boogie.

Just like in many experiences in life, details are important in choreographed dance. For example, we emphasize to the students simple things like: palms up, knees stiff, looking up, faces toward audience, elbows bent and high, backs flat, bend from the waist instead of the knees or from the knees instead of the waist, stiff body, floppy arms, curled fingers, etc.

WHAT'S THE PURPOSE OF TONIGHT'S PROGRAM?

Our purpose in this evening's program is not precision and perfection, but a reflection of the kinds of things we do in our first grade dance unit and how much fun we have doing it. Perfection, and especially the repetition required for precision, can take the fun and energy out of performing... particularly for five and six year olds...so we hope you find our dances entertaining, light-hearted, and just plain fun!

"If you can talk, you can sing. If you can walk, you can dance!"
~ Zimbabwe Proverb

WHY KEEP GENERAL MUSIC IN OUR SCHOOLS?

Now more than ever before, music education programs are being threatened by budget cuts, time constraints, and lack of support. Although NO CHILD LEFT BEHIND legislation by President George W. Bush has uprooted some major problems, it is, as far as I am aware, the first piece of national legislation in history to not only identify music and art as *core subjects,* but to authorize funding for music education in schools! In light of this and in order for this significant promotion to experience all of the potential benefits it represents, it would behoove us to have a strong arsenal of spur-of-the-moment, tip-of-the-tongue facts to support keeping and funding music in our schools for our kids! I'm sure you've read many supportive documents, but to help us do our homework so that we might be better prepared for debate, there are several websites I visit for *sound* information. The first we'll visit together is from the Ronald McDonald House Charities at http://www.rmhcbayarea.com/music1.html

According to some of their Fun Facts About Music and Education, they state:

➢ Music education builds brain power, helps "at risk" students succeed, and helps improve academic performance.

➢ College-bound students with music backgrounds scored 52 points higher on the verbal and 37 points higher in math on their SAT scores than their peers without arts instruction.

➢ Districts with music education show a 21% decrease in drop-out rates than those districts without that opportunity afforded to their students.

➢ A Texas Commission on Drug and Alcohol Abuse reported that students involved in band or orchestra have the lowest current and lifetime use of any substances.
Other resources for supportive data and great thoughts are:
http://www.amc-music.com/musicmaking/thebrain.htm
http://www.education-world.com/a_curr/curr123.shtml

This topic could be a book in itself, with all the research that is being collected regarding the benefits and justifications of a music education – but I will leave that to one of you - some other author whose house doesn't need cleaning as much as ours.

CONCRETE CURRICULUM

Throughout my career, I have been asked, at least three times, to produce my objectives for grades K – five. Like ours, most districts have established an elementary music *curriculum*, but for some reason, you may be asked, as I was, to write your personal curriculum guide that encompasses the district curricular guidelines but reflects your personal objectives. I have included mine – for your reading pleasure. It is *very foundational* and I am positive you will want to expound on it in every way, but it's a springboard for your thoughts.

All objectives are designed to 1) develop confidence in individuals so they are able to make music alone and with others; 2) to develop a vast repertoire of songs to sing; 3) to build the understanding and use of a musical vocabulary; 4) to develop an understanding of musical notation; 5) to introduce a wide variety of music, musicals, and musical styles; and 6) to create a positive, happy learning environment where students are motivated, involved, respectful, have self control, and tools to resolve conflict.

Kindergarten Music Objectives and Activities

The Kindergarten student will:

1. Sing a variety of age-appropriate songs in unison

    a. Nursery rhyme songs

    b. Color songs

    c. Number songs

    d. Vocabulary-building songs

    e. Fingerplays

    f. Action songs

    g. Game songs

    h. Patriotic songs

    i. Holiday songs

2. Sing with confidence and enthusiasm

3. Experience movement or choreography with every song

4. Recognize voice differences (timbre)

   a. Man

   b. Woman

   c. Child

   d. Baby

   e. instrumental

5. Identify the difference in music and sounds:

   a. animal sounds

   b. sounds of nature

   c. sounds of transportation

   d. sounds from the home (doorbell, toaster, disposal, etc.)

   e. sounds in the office (phones, computers, printers, etc.)

6. Create (and sing) lyrics to familiar songs

7. Identify beginning elements of form

   a. introduction

   b. interlude

8. Move to the steady beat

9. Read simple rhythms

10. Move to musical style or mood

11. Move to:

    a. fast – slow

    b. loud – soft

    c. long – short

    d. high – low

12. Enjoy and look forward to coming to music class

13. Display self-control and appropriate music room behavior

14. Display methods of conflict management

    a. cool off, calm down

    b. listen to the other person

    c. talk it over

    d. try to see other's side

    e. decide on options

    f. choose the best solution

15. Display good sportsmanship and manners

    a. Selecting partners

    b. Lining up

    c. Forming a circle

    d. Hands and feet off limits

    e. Sharing equipment

    f. Respecting property

    g. Don't whine, hit, argue, or tattle

First Grade Music Objectives and Activities

In addition to the competencies given for the previous level, the first grade student will:

1. Sing a variety of age-appropriate songs in unison <u>with reasonable pitch accuracy</u> in a limited range.

2. Partner songs and rounds

3. Read and play simple rhythmic patterns on rhythm instruments

   a. quarter note

   b. quarter rest

   c. eighth note

   d. half note

4. Move to the melodic beat

5. Identify high and low pitch

   a. going up

   b. going down

   c. staying the same

6. Use and connect correct terminology

   a. Identify loud and soft sounds (dynamics)

   b. Identify fast and slow (tempo)

   c. Identify long and short sounds (duration)

7. Identify classroom instruments

37

8. Identify recognition of sections of songs

    a. A B form

    b. Phrase

    c. Verse

    d. Chorus

9. Learn performance manners, techniques, and procedures for readiness and rehearsal for grade level musical production.

10. Participate in a dance unit – team taught with music & PE teacher

    a. square dance

    b. line dances

    c. exercise dances

    d. 50's dances

    e. create-your-own dance

11. Display good sportsmanship and nice manners when:

    a. selecting partners

    b. solving problems

    c. finding and staying in personal spaces

    d. knowing the difference between tattling and informing

    e. respecting others' time, space, and focus of attention

    f. saying thank you and please

Second Grade Music Objectives and Activities

In addition to the competencies given for previous levels, the second grade student will:

1. Sing a basic repertoire of unison songs:

   a. Traditional folk songs

   b. Standard songs

   c. Camp songs

   d. Silly songs

   e. Action songs

   f. Multi-cultural songs

   g. Partner songs

   h. Rounds

   i. Piggyback songs

   j. Hand clap songs – requiring coordination, crossing center line, patterning, and memory

2. Increase vocal range and improve pitch matching

3. Sing with good

   a. diction

   b. breath support

   c. posture

4. Sing and/or move with sensitivity to mood or meaning of lyrics.

5. Create choreography

6. Prepare for annual grade level production

7. Identify space and line notes

8. Rhythm:

    a. Read and perform simple rhythmic notation patterns on percussion instruments.

    b. Create their own rhythmic patterns and perform

    c. Rhythm dictation on board

    d. Half rest

    e. Dotted half notes

9. Move

    a. to the steady beat or pulse of music

    b. melodic beat

    c. combination of steady and melodic

    d. double time

10. Listen to story songs to sharpen listening skills and be introduced to classic literature

11. Identify instruments of the orchestra

12. Recognize the relationship of size to pitch

13. Maintain self-control in all situations

14. Display and be rewarded for positive character traits

    a. helpful

    b. responsible

    c. anticipate need

    d. safe

    e. prepared

    f. considerate and respectful

15. Follow music class expectations, guidelines, and rules

Third Grade Music Objectives and Activities

In addition to the competencies given for previous levels, the third grade student will:

1. Sing songs

    a. by rote

    b. staff notation

    c. emphasis placed on pitch matching

    d. emphasis placed on tonal memory

    e. personally created lyrics

    f. with choreography created by teacher and students

2. Correctly use basic musical terminology

    a. tempo

    b. rhythm

    c. melody

    d. steady beat

    e. melodic beat

    f.   style

    g. dynamics

    h. form

3. Compose new lyrics to familiar songs

4. Be introduced to melodic direction

    a.   Step (up and down)

    b.   Leap (up and down)

    c.   Repeat

5. Identify and write notes on the staff

6. Perform and read more complex rhythmic patterns

    a. Add sixteenth notes

7. Prepare annual grade level production

8. Identify orchestral instruments

    a.   by name

    b.   categorize by family

    c.   by sound production or timbre

    d.   relationship of size and pitch

9. Can identify musical symbols and terms:

    a.   bridge

    b.   verse

    c.   chorus or refrain

    d.   bar line

    e.   measure

    f.   treble clef sign

    g.   time signature

    h.   double bar line

<u>Fourth Grade Music Objectives and Activities</u>

In addition to the competencies given for previous levels, the fourth grade student will:

1. Sing age appropriate songs in unison and harmony

    a.   solo

    b.   duet

    c.   trio

    d.   quartet

    e.   sextet

    f.   septet

    g.   octet

    h.   full chorus

    i.   from notation

    j.   correct vocal production

    k.   concise diction

2. Aurally identify major and minor keys

3. Compare and contrast musical styles

4. Compare and contrast musical styles with various art medium

5. Prepare for annual production

6. Rhythm

    a. dictation on the board

    b. dictation on paper

    c. abandoning "note nicknames" (ta, ti, ni) and read by number

7. Create or compose "Piggyback songs" by writing their own lyrics to familiar melodies.

8. Identify step, leap, and repeat

    a. movement

    b. written

    c. aurally

    d. perform on bells and keyboard from dictation

9. Know and use the expressive notation and symbols of dynamics

    a. pianissimo

    b. piano

    c. mezzo piano

    d. mezzo forte

    e. forte

    f. fortissimo

g. crescendo and decrescendo

10. Be able to play simple melody lines

a. diatonic bells

b. keyboard

10. Can identify musical symbols and terms:

a. Rehearsal numbers

b. bridge

c. verse

d. chorus or refrain

e. endings

f. bar line

g. measure

h. treble clef sign

i. time signature

j. double bar line

k. repeat sign

l. D.S. al fine

m. coda

Fifth Grade Music Objectives and Activities

In addition to the competencies given for previous levels, the fifth grade student will:

1. Understand and use music vocabulary and notation

2. Sing a wide repertoire of unison and two-part songs

3. Match Pitch

   a. singing

   b. aurally

   c. identify dissonance

   d. identify consonance

   e. in-tune harmony

4. Write musical notation

   a. notes on staff

   b. using dynamic symbols in music (*pp, p, mp, mf, f, ff,* < and >)

   c. using directional symbols in music (repeat signs, coda, D.S. al fine, rehearsal numbers)

   d. correct stem direction

   e. compose simple melodies

   f. notes on ledger lines

5. Rhythmic notation

   a. quarter notes and rests

   b. eighth notes and rests

   c.   half notes and rests

   d.   dotted half notes and rests

   e.   whole notes and rests

   f.   sixteenth notes and rests

   g.   dotted quarter notes and rests

   h.   syncopated rhythms

   i.   dictation (pitched and non-pitched, alone and within a melodic line)

6. Prepare for fifth grade performances:

   a.   Winter musical

   b.   Singfest

   c.   DARE graduation

   d.   Grade level graduation

   e.   Concert choir concert

Debbie Gray

Chapter 2

The First Day Of School Blues!

or...

Sheer Terror

After five full years of very comprehensive training at the Conservatory of Music at UMKC (University of Missouri at Kansas City) and my schedule pelted with classes in music methods, instrumental techniques, conducting, music theory, counterpoint, ensemble practices and performances, instrumental and vocal private lessons, music history, music appreciation, psychology, hours upon hours of practicum/observation, and then, of course, a whole semester of student teaching, it just never occurred to me that I would ever be experiencing SHEER TERROR on the first day of school!

Like you, I was so ready for that first job (and paycheck)! I faithfully took care of all the requirements for certification, I dutifully put applications in everywhere I could possibly apply, I went to countless mock and real interviews, I rehearsed responses, and had not a concern in the world, other than signing a teaching contract. I knew I was ready! I'd been told, taught, and showed! Now it was, *"JUST BRING IT! I'm ready to take on the world!"* It was going to be so much fun! Well, I was broadsided by one huge, gut-wrenching, nerve-shattering WAKE UP CALL!

If I remember correctly, it blasted into my frontal lobes about the middle of August after I'd signed <u>my</u> very own teaching contract, spent hours decorating <u>my</u> very own classroom, putting up <u>my</u> very own bulletin boards, writing in <u>my</u> very own grade book, and doing all the other incidentals required to get ready for <u>my</u> new school year. Then it hit! The realization that I was a teacher!! I was going to have to dress professionally rather than my comfortable, college slobbery. I was going to have to set the alarm hours earlier than I had since high school! I was going to be called MISS SMITHEE, instead of Debbie! I was facing seven hours in front of 25 different aged students each hour, and I felt SHEER TERROR!

Even with all those years of extraordinary preparation, some of the finest educators in the country, and every possible class to get me ready

49

for <u>my </u>very own life in the classroom....it dawned on me that I had no clue what to do on that very first day of school!! I knew how to teach…I thought I knew how to manage a classroom, I trusted that I was ready to do <u>my</u> very own thing and become Teacher of the Year as a rookie…but *oh my gosh!* I started imagining twenty-five perfect strangers wandering into my music room. Would they sit or stand? If they sat – would it be in chairs or on the floor? What do fifth graders like? What can Kindergartners do? What if they don't like me? What if they think the songs I'm teaching them are "baby?" I realized that first impressions could make or break me – especially as a teacher and particularly with older kids! I wanted them to like music, but honestly, even more…I wanted them to like ME!

The more I thought about it, the more <u>my</u> very own anxiety grew. I started having heart arrhythmia and palpitations. I had chronic sweaty palms. Sleeping at night became a totally non-existent event. I was nauseous pretty much twenty-four-seven and I was simply miserable. But the fact is, the time just kept ticking away and that first day of school kept marching right toward me, ready or not, in spite of my SHEER TERROR!

I can't possibly write lesson plans for every grade level for the duration of the year…and, you wouldn't even bother reading them if I did. I know I wouldn't! You've got your text books and teacher's editions for that kind of information, if you like using them. But, it is my strong opinion that if you make that first day **memorable and fun** - *not* all "talky and full of rules," – you'll have kids loving you, loving music, and talking about how "cool" it is! This establishes you and your class for success the following days - and then everybody is looking forward to coming to your class! If they WANT to be there, half your battle is won because you don't have to deal with nearly as many discipline problems, oppositional behavior, or bad attitudes when they like it and want to be there. So…here are a couple examples of things I do the first time I meet my students at the beginning of school:

FIRST DAY FUN!

I make an effort to have students enter the music room and stay standing in a personal space for some kind of movement activity or game. They've been sitting most of the time in their regular classrooms, I want them to associate movement and fun with music. So…they enter and stand in a circle. Familiar and appropriate Top 40-type contemporary music is filling the air.

We start class with a game. We play a rhythm game that I'm sure most of you are probably familiar with – it is sometimes called "Categories," but I just don't name it. ☺

I establish a tempo with "*one, two, ready, watch!*" and I slap my legs two times. I say it again and instead of "...*ready, <u>watch</u>*" I say "....*ready <u>go</u>*." They echo what I just did. Then, following the same procedure, I add the next two counts. (If you do the whole pattern first, you are sure to lose some kids – even fifth graders will get confused or overwhelmed and either start jacking around or just quit trying.) Counts three and four are claps. So now it's knees, knees, clap, clap. They repeat. The last two beats consist of a finger snap with one hand, then the other. So now the pattern is: knees, knees, clap, clap, snap, snap. Repeat enough times to build confidence and security. I always say in tempo, "*Do it again*" on finger-snapping beats of five and six if I want them to continue repeating the practice pattern and I say "*Ready stop*" on those same two beats when I'm ready for them to wind down and stop. The final step in the game is for students to keep the rhythm pattern of snaps and claps going while they say their first name on the first snap and their last name on the second snap. We go all around the room and it is an entertaining way for me to learn names and students to get to refresh their memories of classmate names.

This game can be used later in the year for a dynamics review by having you call out what dynamic level you would like them to say their name. For example, on the first two beats, you will say "FORTE" so they, in turn, have to say their first and last names on the snaps in a FORTE voice. It's fun, but don't expect them to do really well the first couple of times you ask them to try it, because they're struggling with coordination, remembering what to do and when to do it, what the term you're dictating actually means, and oddly enough - - - some are trying to remember their names!

Next, I move them from their stand-up circle to sitting down in chairs to introduce a totally fun and silly song. I teach a spoof on the **William Tell Overture** by Rossini. Much of the way you introduce anything that is silly depends not only on *what* you say but *how* you say it. I always take the very serious, formal introduction approach – sounding like a very serious (boring) topic is impending. I preface it by saying, "*Fifth grade is much different from other grades. By the time you get to be this age, it is time to stop being so silly and start realizing that music has a very serious, cultural side.*" I continue by speaking a bit about the composer and the style of the piece being classical, then establishing the fact that the lyrics are "*very serious.*" Once I have their total attention – they are already dreading the unexpected new approach to music and wondering if

Mrs. Gray has flipped out, then…based on a pregnant pause - I sing it for them:

I'm a ping, I'm a ping, I'm a ping pong head
I'm a ping, I'm a ping, I'm a ping pong head
I'm a ping, I'm a ping, I'm a ping pong head
I'm a ping.......I'm a ping pong head.

Chorus:
I'm a ping, I'm a ping, I'm a ping pong, ping pong, ping pong, ping pong, ping pong head
I'm a ping, I'm a ping, I'm a ping pong, Ping pong, ping pong head

Honestly, it is so much fun to see just how long it takes them to realize that this, in fact, is *not* a serious piece of music literature, that I haven't become some music ogre, that they're still going to get to be kids and have fun, and that I was just kidding during my introduction!! That's about all it takes and I have them caught up in music. They love being able to laugh and see me laugh with them. It's fun for them to try something totally new and crazy, and it's a pressure-free environment. Silliness builds relationships with young people!

"Laughter is the shortest bridge between two people."
~ Victor Borge

Once I have them secure with the words and the melody, I divide the seated class into three sections. ALL three sections *sing* the entire song, however, section one is to jump up (although I tend to use the words "pop up" which, for some reason, helps to keep their lack of self-control to a minimum) and right back down again every time they sing the word *PING*. The middle section pops up on the word *PONG*, and the third section pops up on the word *HEAD*.

Before attempting it for the first time, use your conducting skills, (and use that word because it's a good vocabulary builder) over-exaggerating your movements as you would if you were bringing in the different sections whenever they jump, and sing it for them. Then they try. I always accompany them…beginning slowly, of course, and each time I see them, we increase the tempo. I always sing it three times, alternating the sections so the middle group of singers are my "PINGS," the right side become the "PONGS," and the left side group get to be the "HEADS."

From that, you can extend it into a lesson on teaching **form** - this being an ABA piece. So...encapsulating the lesson and the extensions you see how you can use ***one song*** to teach:

DICTION

("ping" can sound like "pig" if they don't concentrate on enunciating!)

TEMPO

(I teach "*accelerando*" with this piece, too.)

CONDUCTING

FORM

MUSICAL STYLE

COMPOSER

FUN

EXERCISE

They were seated in chairs for PING PONG HEAD, so now, only for variety's sake, I move them to the carpet in a different corner of the room, facing a different wall and use that change as our transition to another fun and beneficial activity using flash cards. With various patterns of simple rhythms written in four four time, we read from rhythm flashcards. I use the nonsense syllables of ta, ti, ni, and two for my K - 2nd graders, but I introduce counting them as in one, two-and, three-ee-and-uh, four-and... *with numbers* with third graders and older. Incidentally, I call the ta's, ti's, ni's, etc., "nicknames" so when it's time for the transition to quarter, eighth, sixteenth, etc., they have the understanding that they are in fact, called quarter notes, whole notes, etc., but when we READ them, we use their "nicknames" or their numbers.

So...with that in mind and flash cards prepared, I establish the tempo (which spirals the learning from the handclap game and PING PONG HEAD) and have them read the rhythms. IF they haven't done it before, be sure to model what you want them to say...and model and repeat... or "loop" that model *at least three times* before expecting them to do it correctly. Once they've mastered being able to read the rhythms, keep it interesting in future classes by:

- Having them read it back to you in the same way you say, "*1, 2 ready read...*" and then you can say the preparatory beats in a high and low pitch, a loud and soft voice, a whisper, a growl, and as a mime would do it. (You can support core subject curriculum by adding "opposites" and "pattern" into the discussion.)

- It is a blast to do sound effects: say, "*1, 2, ready pop…*" (they pop their lips in rhythm) or "*1, 2, ready click…*" (click tongues)...ready blink, ready kiss, ready whistle, ready shhhhh; whatever you can come up with to add variety will keep it interesting, bring smiles, and make memories.

- Add movement: Have them stand and you say, "*…ready stomp,*" or "*…ready hop,*" or "*…ready tip toe,*" "*…ready march,*" "*…ready clap,*" "*…ready jump,*" and with this, you're adding movement (in rhythm) - which is essential, particularly if you've had them seated for more than four or five minutes. And yes, this is appropriate for upper elementary grades, too! In fact, they like it and do a better job at it than the younger ones.

- We always have fun changing the first syllable of the "nickname" words. For instance, "ta" becomes "wa" or "la" or "ja" or "ka" or "ba." (Just be careful not to use W's if you use the "ni" nickname for sixteenth notes unless you're prepared to deal with "wee wee wee wee's.")

- Another fun, more advanced way to review rhythms is to give them different sounds for each note value. For example, have them pop their lips for quarter notes, click their tongues on eighth notes, buzz (raspberry) their lips on half notes, etc. Not only do they begin to associate different sounds with rhythms, it's a super introduction or reinforcer for tone color, sound effects, and fun!

- We play Boomwhackers sometimes when we read rhythms. For short notes, we tap different things in different ways but for long notes – like half notes (or two's) we talk into the ends of them like a megaphone, and say, "*TWO.*" Or, we start with the tube at our shoulder and slide it down our arm for the duration of the half note.

Finally, they've been sitting on the floor, it's time for another change! Kids love change and it helps their attention span last so much longer! Rather than spending a great deal of time on rules, going over emergency drills, or apprising them of my personal expectations that the first day, my **ONLY goal is to establish a love for my class** - and believe me - those kinds of informational details <u>definitely don't</u> meet that objective! (Many teachers miss that small window of opportunity to bait and hook their kids to love music – just because they insist on all that other junk. Of course that other junk has to be taught – but hold off a class time or two – until after you've established that your place is a very good place to be! You may have to sprinkle in a rule or two if they talk while you're talking or start pounding on the piano – but don't stand in front of your little people and inundate them with that other junk!

Next, I teach them about "personal space." "Personal space" is something I teach to every grade level – though it takes less and less emphasis each year, so by the time they're in fifth grade, it's pretty much ingrained in them, second nature, and it's only the newbies who need a crash course in not crashing - but it is absolutely an essential lesson to teach and re-teach if you plan to have kids up and moving in your class! (And you will!)

Unfortunately...many music teachers have their students seated most of the time. (I'm letting my opinions slip in, aren't I? Oh wait...I already warned you that this book is chock full of my opinions, so it's OK!) I, on the opposite end of that spectrum, refuse to use chairs – *ever* - except with my fifth graders - but even then, only for about a quarter of the class time when we're reading sheet music or something - then I have them sitting in sections. If you have chairs that are the right size for little people, the big people have to wad themselves into a small ball to fit. If you have chairs for big people, the little people legs dangle and swing, kick, and constantly move. They probably fall asleep, too. In between sized chairs will work best if you insist on using chairs...just keep them stacked and collecting dust most of the time, please!

Anyway, it's no big deal really... I call it **PERSONAL SPACE.** Our PE teacher uses it, too - so our lessons compliment one another. It's just about making sure they know that they have to have a space around them, no matter where they move; a space that would allow someone to walk completely around them without touching another person or thing at any time during class! We practice it with pop music that they hear on the radio. I make sure it is age-appropriate so I can use it at all grade levels... just be sure you check out the lyrics so you don't play something that is "iffy." With the younger kids, I usually use the extraordinary music from SNIGGLES, SQUIRRELS AND CHICKENPOX or our series. The learning game is a little bit like musical chairs - without the chairs. They move around the room to the music, concentrating on steady beat and "looking cool." When the music stops, they are to show that they can stop in a personal space. Always be careful to use those same two words every time so your expectations are clear and their memory doesn't get scrambled.

Good luck - I hope these ideas will help to spare you some of the first day jitters that might plague you. Thanks to my former student teacher, Patty, who suggested I include some first-day lesson plan ideas.

CHAPTER 3

PERFORMANCE AND PROGRAM POINTERS

or...

THE SHOW MUST GO ON!

1. **_KEEP YOUR STUDENT'S BEST INTEREST YOUR TOP PRIORITY._** It is far too easy, with the pressures of minimal rehearsal time, scheduling conflicts, concert length requirements, and recent experiences at the collegiate level, to get so caught up in rehearsals and performance *perfection* that we lose sight of what is *best for the kids!* My advice: *Relax and have fun!* Swallow your pride…it doesn't *have* to be *perfect.* As you strive for quality, remember, they are only kids. Keep "the bigger picture" in perspective. In the larger scheme of things, **_the kids_** are our first priority, not the show, our reputation, or the attention we receive or don't receive for our work. When they're twenty-five, will they remember that performing was fun or that they hated it because it was miserable, awful or too stressful?

2. **_WORK HARDER THAN YOU EVER IMAGINED._** That's what it takes. Expect nothing in return other than the satisfaction of seeing your students prosper and succeed! (Honestly, I am still working on the "expect-nothing-in-return part of that advice. But I know that's the healthiest way to work.)

3. **_COMMIT WHATEVER TIME IT TAKES TO CREATE QUALITY PROGRAMS._** Don't expect any one grade level to be easier to prepare for a performance than another – each group shares their own little idiosyncrasies that add the word "challenge" to your project. Fifth graders may have more talent in part singing, learning more difficult pieces, and in matching pitch, but they are also more aware of their peers, more likely to succumb to "what's-hot-what's-not" attitude, and are very much self-conscious of the way they look, feel, sound, and smell, so their musical talents are sometimes hidden far beneath the façade of COOL. On the opposite end of the age spectrum, we

57

have our Kindergartners. Most are wonderfully boinky, bouncy, and boisterous, clueless about performing and have miniscule attention spans – and those are their *positive traits!* The music they learn is simple, the range is manageable, the accompaniments are playable, and the lyrics are age-appropriate. They're so cute you could do nearly anything with them and they'll be loved – but…the typical song for five year olds is ONLY about *thirty seconds long!* That's about two songs per minute. Next, multiply 60 seconds times 30 minutes of required programming, figure in the components of a 30-minute show, and you will quickly discover how many songs you have to teach! You will find out how many seconds you have to entertain and the most anxiety-inducing information of all is how little time you have to squoosh all those lyrics, melodies, rhythms, and actions into their wittle bwains! THEN, my friends, is when the panic strikes! There's nothing easy or insignificant about *that* challenge! All I'm suggesting is that you allow equal time for preparing programs with any elementary grade level – don't assume that one will be less complicated than another.

4. ***ALWAYS GIVE CREDIT AND SHOW APPRECIATION TO YOUR COHORTS.*** Being the director, we usually are the one in the spotlight, but *we know* there are many who have helped behind the scenes, to make the performance a success. Please always publicly *recognize the work, help, and support* of *all the contributors* to the performance. Saying nothing and ***failing to recognize,*** compliment, and thank *every*one who is deserving of your appreciation can be very ***hurtful and demeaning*** and actually, fall equivalent to publicly humiliating him or her.

Imagine how terrible you would feel if, after your many hours of work to make a beautiful performance, your Principal never introduced you? It initiates an *awful* feeling inside, so do whatever it takes to remember your helpers. Make yourself a list ahead of time and practice remembering them – or, I always write those names in my program so I have it right there in front of me, ready to announce at the end of the concert. If I miss saying it for some reason, they receive recognition and appreciation in ink.

5. ***DISSEMINATE INFORMATION.*** Keep everyone…teachers, secretary, custodians, and parents, well informed regarding your program plans! Keep them apprised of expectations, notified of changes, and appreciated for their help and support. Anytime I assign speaking parts, either the classroom teacher or I **contact parents**

personally, over the phone, to make sure they realize how special it is for their child to have been selected for the part and how important it is for that child to attend the performance. The younger the performer, the more imperative it is to make this call. It takes time but since I started doing this, the numbers of last-minute absences that leave you high and dry, have decreased considerably.

6. ***ESTABLISH PROCEDURE*** for students and parents in case school is cancelled. Our district has already addressed this issue but it is important you make sure everyone knows what to do or not to do. If school is cancelled, <u>all</u> after school and evening activities are cancelled in Blue Springs.

7. ***SEE PIANO. SEE PIANO BLOCK MOMMY, DADDY, GRANDMA, & GRANDPA'S VIEW.*** For years, I have rolled the big ol' Kawai in front of the risers, plunked my big ol'self down in front of the kids, and done my thing while they do theirs. Meanwhile, half the parents behind me couldn't even see their wee one because of the big ol' piano and big ol' me! I knew I wanted to change that…and now, twenty-some years later, I *finally* found a solution! With the help of Dan, a fantastic former student teacher, I located an *excellent* recording studio here in Kansas City called *ICEHOUSE PRODUCTIONS!* Jason, the owner and highly talented sound engineer, helped me produce a professional-quality recording at a reasonable price! So now, before each *little*-kid concert, using my own money, I spend an hour or so in the studio recording a piano accompaniment for our PTA shows! Then, come concert time, I sit on the floor, plunk in my trusty *ICEHOUSE PRODUCTIONS* recording, and direct the kids…with *ME* at the piano, only it's a *recorded* version of me instead of a *live,* block-the-view me! Everyone in the audience can now see their short little sweeties on the risers. As the kids get older and taller, quite a bit of our music already has nice SHOW TRAX accompaniments but when I *do* use the piano, third, fourth and fifth graders are ordinarily tall enough, mom and pop can see them in spite of my Kawai and me.

On this same topic, I always…*ALWAYS* record from a CD to a cassette tape, in spite of the fact that I lose sound quality! Here's why: if someone accidentally trips over your electrical cord and stops a CD, you've no easy way of relocating on that CD exactly where you were forced to stop the performance. On the other hand, if your accompaniment is on a tape and the power is interrupted, as soon as you turn it back on, your tape is exactly where it was at the time of the outage.

Also, don't forget to record entering-the-room-and-getting-on-the-risers music and getting-off-the-risers-and-exiting-the-room music. Sometimes, I stop at the end of each verse or chorus and play a chord for each step the kids need to take – as a cue for when they should step up. You'll want to plan ahead and get it thoroughly organized in your mind before going into the studio so you're not paying for your thinking time. ☺

8. *I WRITE THE PERFORMANCE DATE ON THE INSIDE COVER OF THE MUSICAL OR ON THE OUTSIDE OF THE FOLDER* anytime we perform a musical or octavo. This helps me remember from year to year how recently it was performed. Computers are a great way to save this information, just use whichever one works best for you, or do like I do and use both methods. When you're searching through your files, it is just good to have the information at a glance right in front of you rather than having to refer to your hard drive, disk, or CD.

9. *SAVE AND FILE ALL WRITTEN PROGRAMS.* If you do, you will always have your front cover artistry, program notes, dates, locations of performances, and names of choir members who participated - including soloists and speaking parts, if any. Ideally, this little strategy should help you avoid recycling the same show that was performed by an older sibling. (Believe me, you DO forget!) However, I must confess…one Christmas, I dug out Roger Emerson and John Jacobson's SANTA'S HOLIDAY HOEDOWN, knowing that it had been *at least* five years since we last performed it. I didn't check the names. Not good! Now there are at least six sets of parents, accompanied by their family and friends, who think that, because an older brother or sister had done the exact same show when he/she was in fifth grade, that SANTA'S HOLIDAY HOEDOWN is perhaps the only winter musical I know or can teach! Argh…what's the practice-what-you-preach advice?

Another advantage I've discovered by saving my programs are the pictures. The art teacher in our building was always excited about sketching a program cover! I have beautiful artwork, lettering, and fun caricatures! Computer-generated clip art and fonts are always fine – but I've found that I love to recycle the old-style, handmade masterpieces from a real honest-to-goodness artist! I just cut and paste them onto my new name lists. It works great! If you have time or if your art teacher or classroom teachers are game…you could ask the students to design the cover of their program. You can appoint someone to do it. You could turn it into a contest. You could just allow the students to vote which design they want to represent them. Or, there are a number of other ways this could be handled.

The day of performance, the teachers are usually thrilled to have the kids add some color to the programs with markers, crayons, or colored pencils, because they know it gives them a personal touch. If your PTA meetings are traditionally long, this is also a good project for the time they're in the classroom, waiting for the PTA meeting to conclude so they can perform. The drawback to this plan is that when time starts getting short, they hurry through their work and then we have some less-than-masterpiece-worthy programs. The classroom teachers or I appoint several students to pass them out before the beginning of the show as guests arrive. It's all about variety and fun. Do what works for you, but don't be afraid to try something new and different.

10. ***REHEARSAL BEFORE REHEARSAL:*** I love to begin my first, *on-the-risers rehearsal* on Monday – when the kids and I are fresh off of a weekend, relatively rested, and ready to face the new week. As crazy as this sounds, though, I have a rehearsal before that rehearsal on Friday. This "sneak peek" offers me the opportunity to see ahead of time where our best prepared parts of the program are, where we are deliriously deficient, where changes need to be made because of height or microphone access, and where I need to divide the *pockets of personalities who are potential problems.* I then have all weekend to think about it, make mental adjustments, make changes to the script, and anything else that needs to be conquered so Monday's rehearsal starts off positively.

> **"Mental preparation is the single most critical element in peak performance."**
> **~Jack Nicklaus**

I am hearing more and more that music teachers are not given the opportunity to have rehearsals in the performance area with the performance equipment, causing the first time students actually experience that feeling is at the performance. If this is you, you deserve a Purple Heart and a sympathy card! Seriously, I suggest you have a heart-to-heart with your administrator. Express your concerns, support your reasoning, establish where the glitch is, *beg if you have to*…and then pray he or she will help you solve the problem and get those kids on the risers or stages at least four times prior to the concert. This is so not fair to the kids or you, but if you've already been a squeaky wheel and still never got the grease, so to speak, then I would try to recreate the scene as closely as possible and spend time telling the students what to expect.

If you are one of the fortunate ones who are honored with access to the performance area, please don't take that for granted! Write thank you notes to *everyone* who makes it possible for you to combine classes, to use the performance area, and to squeeze in some good rehearsal time.

11. *ASK FOR HELP AND DELEGATE!* I do fine working alone and preparing *my choir* for a performance because I see them after school, all together, and over the <u>course</u> of an entire year. It is entirely different, however, when it comes to preparing for a 30-minute grade level PTA performance! I only see those little ones *once a week*. Their retention is sparse and my time with them all together is so limited that I *have* to enlist the help of the classroom teachers. I seldom have adequate time to meet the expectations required of me, but I work hard, stay focused on the goal, and *ask for help*.

- I make sure the classroom teachers know how few school days are left to prepare so they can share the same sense of urgency I carry. Realizing a deadline has a real way of motivating.

- I make sure they know I *intensely depend on their help* with speaking part practice, prop collection, dispersing information from me to the students and parents, etc.

- I make sure they know I deeply appreciate their support, flexibility, and willingness to do a little extra work in the classroom to help me prepare the kids for a successful show!

- I make certain they know our daily rehearsal time is extremely limited and that arriving on time is very important.

- I put all instructions and requests for help *in writing*.

- I make sure they know exactly what I need them to do.

- I make sure they know where and when to meet for rehearsals.

- I ask them to line up their students in order, ahead of time, *before every practice*. (Students get accustomed to who they stand between, who is behind and in front of them.)

- Ask each teacher to remain with students until another teacher relieves them. (Teachers have so many things to accomplish in their few minutes of break time that they are incredibly anxious about starting their break right on time! Realizing that set-up of risers, sound equipment, microphones, props, stages, accompaniment, music stands, etc. takes time and energy so asking them to manage their students until everything is ready to go is imperative. The good thing is, these practices don't last forever and usually only mean abbreviated break times for a week or so.)

- Practice all speaking parts in class and include a reminder that repetition is the best teacher.

- Prop open the doors that students will be using to enter the performance area.

- Keep parents apprised with regular reminders of performance dates, times, what to wear, time to arrive for the performance, and where to meet.

- Provide a single-column list with each student's autograph for the program. (I will explain why in a later chapter.)

- If a student is absent, write his or her name on the list so no one is left out.

- I beg them to remind me to notify the custodian if I change a rehearsal or performance schedule so he/she does not set up unnecessarily. (I usually do a good job remembering to inform our custodian, but just this year, I goofed and felt terrible about having him set everything up for me and I'd forgotten to notify him that we'd cancelled rehearsal.)

- I know I am *always* reluctant to have to ask for classroom teacher help – their plates are already so incredibly full, but because it's so urgent, necessary, and I've found no other way around it, I justify it by reminding myself that they typically get *extra break time* because rehearsals often go beyond the regular music class time. I also consider the fact that in *many* schools, the grade level teachers are responsible for PTA shows and they enlist the help of the music teacher. Since it's the other way around in my building, the little bit of time I ask of them is *exponentially smaller* than if they were having to write, rehearse, set up, strike, plan and produce the entire show themselves.

12. ***BETTER LATE THAN NEVER!*** There have been times in my years of performing, where a student arrived a few minutes late and stood in the back, heartbroken, that he'd missed his chance to perform with us. One experience with that and now I make sure my kids know that if they arrive late and the group has already begun performing, they are welcome to come right on up to their position on stage or on the risers and join in...sometimes late can't be helped. I am lenient....at least they made the effort! It's the kids more than the performance that are important.

13. ***CONGLOMERATION IS THE WORD!*** *Make your choir a melting pot. Get the popular kids, the academic leaders, and especially the athletes in your select performing groups* as well as the general populous of the school! They are leaders and you want them to lead the flock *into the music room.* Don't kid yourself, this WILL mean working around inflexible ball practices, games, track, dance lessons, horseback riding, music lessons, doctor's appointments, theater, dad's work schedule, mom's broken car, rush hour traffic, karate, bowling, archery, swimming lessons, weightlifting, dart tournaments, go-kart practice, BMX races, and, everything else imaginable. It also DEFINITELY means including some not-so-talented kids, but in the end, you'll come out the winner and so will the kids! There's not a better way to build a choir than to let it be one of the "coolest" things to do in the school – and most all of that hinges on two things: it's fun and who's in it.

14. ***A WORD ABOUT AUDITIONS FOR ELEMENTARY STUDENTS***
As much as I would *love* to have an elite performing group, a whole choir of kids who can sing on pitch, are perfectly behaved, can read music, and are cream-of-the-crop responsible, auditioning kids for membership is a tough journey. Think carefully before limiting your group to the best of the best. ***I would have never made that group!***

(Granted, we do have to figure out who will sing a solo part, but I'll include my methods for that in the next paragraph.) If you *do* choose to audition for an honors group, please write notes to every single one of the non-selected. Tell those kids how you admire their courage for trying. Let them know you respect them and honor their efforts even if they weren't selected. Evaluate and explain to them why you did not choose them – they deserve to know. Please find words of encouragement. Many of those kids probably didn't sleep much the night before and couldn't swallow breakfast that morning in anticipation of your auditions – wanting it so much, but afraid they might not make it. Many will never try again. Once is enough to go through that emotional trauma. Most will decide it wasn't worth it.

Don't be surprised when parents contact you regarding your decision to omit their child from your special group. Be prepared ahead of time to substantiate your selection and defend why you only want to work with the best students. Oh yea, let me just say…you probably won't hear a word from the parents of the kids who were chosen. You see…*it's easy to be the elite, it's devastating to be the discarded. Drop me an e-mail, I can tell you about that.*

15. ***LISTENING LEGACY:*** One of my first class times at the beginning of every year, I bring four students at a time to the piano, backs to the class, accompanied, and have them sing "Happy Birthday" to me. It's an easy song, everyone knows it, it has some very revealing intervals for me to hear, and I learn so much about each individual voice. I assure them I am not listening to give them a grade, I am only listening for their ability to match pitch and sing with good support, then I model five levels of sound, beginning with perfectly matching pitches and ending by letting them hear an example of monotone sounds. *I tell them (individually) what I write in my records only if they ask,* but they are each assigned one of five options: a **5** indicates to me that they match pitch well and have a full, rich, solo-worthy vocal quality; **4** means they match pitch well; **3** tells me they match most pitches but miss the octave jump; **2** indicates that they are struggling with pitch and support but can at least start on the right first note and end on the tonic; **1** tells me this child "sings" monotone.

This is confidential information seen only by me, sometimes but not usually, by the students. I then have a record of vocal improvement or decline throughout the course of their elementary years with me – which is a good way for me to assess my effectiveness as well as the students' progress. I want to interject that sometimes my **4**'s and even **5**'s have wavered into the **1**-zone. I really try to avoid allowing that to happen and I listen constantly and carefully so nobody slips through the cracks and I miss that transition happening, but the fact is, it does and it has. I'm not certain to what I can attribute that, but I think it may be self-consciousness based. As children journey through adolescence, they begin to develop reactions to peer pressure, their self-confidence often wanes, many outside-of-school factors effect them, and maturity often forces vocal change, especially in boys. If this happens, please don't assume it is your fault. Just nurture that singer, slowly but surely, back to his or her potential. One-on-one coaching is the best avenue for affecting this kind of repair.

16. ***SOLO YOU CAN'T HEAR?*** After awhile, some things seem inevitable. Wait until you have a beautiful program prepared and your lead gets strep throat with a 102 degree fever, laryngitis, your main soloist is admitted into the hospital for an unknown virus – of the mouth and throat, or the "du" part of your duet is still in the ER come show time because he fell down the steps on his way to the car for the performance. I could cite more examples from my twenty-something year collection of program panics, but I'll save you the nightmare of putting yourself in my shoes. Experience has taught me that it will alleviate lots of worry for you if you forget about auditions, **adjust the lyrics if necessary, and teach all solos to the entire choir.** There are not many things, performance-wise, that are worse than having soloists notify you right before the big concert that they're not going to be there and you have no understudy. (I tried having "understudies" with my children's musicals and I discovered you *have* to have at least two performances so both soloists get a chance to shine or you have some very unhappy kids with even unhappier parents because their soloist *"did all that work and never got to do anything with it!"* I don't blame them for feeling that way! After all, the understudy must rehearse just as much as the lead.) By teaching solos to the whole choir, you can have a choir back up in the event the soloist cannot perform or you can have your "understudy" right there in your choir – without him or her ever knowing they'd been pre-selected by you to be the sub in the event of an emergency. When teaching the choir the solo, just change the pronouns to agree with the story. For example, instead of "I will sing the wondrous story..." it is taught: "We will sing the wondrous story..." Use he/she in place of I, etc. It is simple...it builds confidence, and **it gives you an out when someone is out!**

This doesn't answer the dilemma that occurs when a primary speaking part is absent. That has only happened to me once and fortunately, I was teaching in two schools at the time and was doing the same musical with both fifth grade classes. I imported my Santa from the other school for the evening performance! I have no solutions for you or me if it happens without a second school doing the same show, with the same blocking, and the same teacher. Hmmm....a four-letter word comes to mind. ***PRAY***

17. ***SOLO SELECTION:*** I *love* having solos dotting my CONCERT CHOIR programs so I often *create* solo spots to feature my particularly talented singers. Rather than having formal, nerve-wracking auditions, I teach the solo to everyone, then choose a different volunteer to sing each rehearsal time. The students never really know who I will ask to do the solo(s) during practices or the concerts and they know if they don't want to do it that particular day, they just don't raise their hands. Often, the soloist(s) will be *different* if we do the same piece for multiple performances, spreading the opportunity to as many as possible. Everyone feels worthy, it keeps everyone at the top of their game, the number of "volunteers" constantly increases, it encourages rather than deflates kids, I always am assured an understudy, everyone who wants to gets the opportunity to sing on the microphone and be the *star du jour*, and parents are more content because their son or daughter hasn't been eliminated. I often find extraordinary talent by offering the microphone to someone if they know they won't have to sing in front of an audience. Some incredible voices unfortunately, aren't backed by incredible confidence – so this TRICK not only helps identify that singer, it also is a tremendous confidence builder! We all know what confidence, or lack of it, can do for a musician! I use the same TRICK when searching for kids to do speaking parts like introductions, narration, or show endings.

18. ***AUDITIONS FOR MUSICALS:*** I have had to resort to auditions when we do musicals because at the elementary level, it's not unusual for someone to be a *great* actor/actress and have the ability to memorize parts without effecting academics while being totally incapable of matching a pitch - even if their little lives depended on it! I have two TRICKS I use for this situation. First, although I know my kids abilities, I still refer to my "Happy Birthday" rating given at the beginning of the year (see above) so I don't mistakenly assign a major speaking/solo part to someone who can't match pitches very well.

Second, I write enough additional speaking parts so that *everyone who auditions* gets to at least be on stage in costume, most get a line or two to say, too! My only prerequisite is that whoever comes to before or after-school auditions must be able to come to before or after-school blocking practices. As much as I despise having to limit the lead parts to kids who have no transportation problems, it has become an unfortunate necessity. My daily schedule prohibits me from any time at all for working with students with blocking and speaking parts and class time is spent teaching the music. The only time I can possibly see students with speaking parts at the same time is before or after school. With our before-and-after-school daycare, I have to *relocate* all rehearsals, too. My music room is full of Kindergartners and First graders from 6:00 a.m. until school starts and from the end of school until 6:00 p.m. every single day, including holidays, snow days, in-service days, and all summer. (The same circumstances apply to the gymnasium, cafeteria, library, art room, and several of the classrooms – so we often rehearse in the front hall or, weather permitting, outside.) Weekend rehearsals are out of the question as well. A Karate class meets in there every Saturday morning and a church has services in my room on Sunday. The conflicts make performance preparation a true challenge, but I've had to learn to roll with the punches and make "flexibility" and patience two of my goals.

19. <u>AUDITION RULES AND FREQUENTLY ANSWERED QUESTIONS:</u>

Dear Fifth Graders & Parents,
    Several of us will be listening to all fifth graders who are interested in a speaking part for our December musical, SANTA'S STUCK IN THE 50'S.

1. Every student interested in trying out for SANTA, MRS. CLAUS, or an Elf part - please meet in the music room, ***<u>Monday, November 10th right after school – when walkers are dismissed</u>***. Be sure to have every elf line <u>memorized if you are trying out for an elf</u>. You will be asked to do all of them.

2. Every student interested in trying out for the NEWS ANCHOR, REPORTER, or CHILD part will meet in the music room, ***<u>WEDNESDAY, November 12th at 3:30 when walkers are dismissed.</u>*** Please have every child line <u>memorized if you're trying out for a child</u> because you will be asked to do all of them. If

you want to be Reporter or Anchor, memorize both parts because you may be asked to do both.

THERE IS A VERY GOOD CHANCE YOU MAY NOT BE ASSIGNED THE PART YOU TRY OUT FOR AND WANT. IF YOU DO NOT WANT ANY PART AT ALL IF YOU CAN'T HAVE THE PART YOU WANT, BE SURE TO TELL MRS. GRAY.
We anticipate being completely finished hearing everyone by 4:30, so please plan accordingly and have rides here promptly.

Parents will be responsible for providing costumes for their child, *however,* I do have a Santa costume.

Students must be able to stay after school two or three times between now and December 1 to block their places on stage and practice their lines with the others.

(Performers in several scenes will have to stay after school more often than students in only one scene. You will find a schedule of rehearsals on the back. It truly is a minimal amount of after-school rehearsal time, but it is essential due to the magnitude of the performance and the fact that rehearsal time with individual characters, during school hours is impossible.)

The date of the evening performance is Thursday, December 11ᵗʰ at 7:00.
Please keep this date open, especially if your child is planning to accept a speaking part.

A 2:30 all-school assembly is schedule on December 10ᵗʰ, for DYE students and guests. This is a great opportunity for those of you who are unable to attend the evening performance. Thank you for your support and interest!

~*Mrs. Gray*

I will be collecting this permission slip at the door so you can get in for auditions!

Keep it until then. *Please do not turn it in before your audition time.*

My child_____, in Mr./ Mrs. _____
room has my permission to attend auditions Monday, November 10ᵗʰ and/or Wednesday, November 12ᵗʰ. Please tell me how your child will be getting home at 4:30:

_____

Parent signature:_____

Frequently <u>Answered</u> Questions

1. *Students may audition for as many parts as they would like.*

2. *No one HAS to try out.*

3. *Parents are responsible for making, buying, or borrowing a costume for their child(ren). (I have a tired ol' Santa costume – that is all.)*

4. *The date of the show is 7:00, Thursday, December 11th. Students trying out <u>must</u> be available to perform in that evening performance.*

5. *Character parts MUST be memorized and spoken without their scripts for auditions.*

6. *Rides pick up time is 4:30 on the day of auditions and each rehearsal afternoon.*

7. *We will be listening for LOUD, expressive VOICES.*

8. *We will be watching for ACTING SKILLS, not just memorized lines, although preparation is very important since the show is so close.*

9. *Students with speaking parts must be able to stay after school several times for practices. Please see attached rehearsal schedule**

10. *Students must <u>keep their signed permission slips</u> and turn them in the day of tryouts as their admission-to-audition tickets. They are not to turn them in ahead of time to classroom teachers or me!*

11. *If someone is <u>sick and misses school</u> the day of tryouts, he/she will be allowed to perform lines during lunch recess, the first day he/she returns.*

12. *Due to limited space, auditions are closed to audience observation.*

13. *Parts not learned and memorized as scheduled for practices will be given to someone else.*

14. *There are only three weeks after try-outs to memorize the script. Students and parents should consider homework, after-school*

involvement, and memorization skills when choosing to accept this enormous responsibility.

15. Solos and other singing parts will be taught during class.

16. Anyone with a solo or large speaking part may (and should) bring me a blank cassette so I can make copies of the script and music to help them study. Please make sure a NAME and classroom teacher's name is written directly ON THE TAPE.

17. Dress rehearsal (students wearing their costumes) is Wednesday, December 10th.

18. There will be an all-school assembly at 2:30 on December 10th – everyone is invited!

Debbie Gray

20. *VIDEO TAPE EVERY PERFORMANCE*, especially the choreo-graphed ones. Why re-invent the wheel? And, don't count on your memory! Trust me, if I remember right, it vanishes. I also like to video tape during rehearsals and then show them, allowing the kids to analyze what they think they look like, what they actually see vs. what is expected. But now, time and new requirements prohibit that. Sometimes that analysis comes in the form of discussion but sometimes I have them *write* what they notice. Sometimes it's just better not to say anything and let the picture paint a thousand words.

21. *SCHEDULE A DRESS REHEARSAL THE DAY BEFORE THE BIG EVENING PERFORMANCE.* I always try to do this, plus I also beg someone to videotape the assembly so I can show it on the day of the performance! Unless we need it, we do not have a traditional rehearsal on that day…we rehearse by watching the tape, stopping, discussing, planning ahead, and proving the importance of speaking loudly, facing the audience, not upstaging others, being aware that people see them even when they are not speaking or singing, and various other infractions that can make a vivid impression when seen first hand! Thanks to our wonderfully flexible and helpful support staff, I combine all the classes: art, music, PE, library, and computers, and show the video. The special teachers enjoy having that few minutes of free time and it's a nice way for me to thank them for their input, help, and support.

22. *TAKE NOTES DURING REHEARSAL* while someone else manages the music, if possible. If I am using a recorded accompaniment, I have one of the other teachers start and stop the music so I can watch from a back-row perspective. From there I take notes about blocking, line delivery, choreography, upstaging, diction, dynamics, balance, etc. It is amazing what you can see if you are in the audience vs. in the director's chair. Be sure to take the time to go over the particulars with those involved in the necessary changes so the time you spent taking notes is productive and worthwhile.

23. *TAKE PICTURES DURING REHEARSALS!* Let me tell you something I tried that worked GREAT and you might want to give it a shot. It really was one of the coolest things I've ever tried – but it does take a lot of time! First, I used the digital camera and took tons of pictures of the performers during their first assembly when they were dressed in their fancy costumes and make-up. I got close ups, stupid shots, kids not paying attention, fingers in yucky places... all kinds of things...but mostly, just cute pictures. I tried to anticipate cute choreography in order to capture it on film. I also took notes during the second assembly performance and then combined the two to make a PowerPoint presentation with all my pictures and notes in it. I included directives like:

- "DON'T CLAP...EVER...THAT'S THE AUDIENCE'S JOB."

- PLEASE MAKE SURE YOU DO NOT MOVE YOUR MOUTH ALONG WITH THE DIALOGUE WHEN SOMEONE IS SPEAKING OR SINGING A SOLO.

- "ELVES, BE SURE NOT TO LEAVE THE RISERS UNTIL THE APPLAUSE HAS STOPPED,"

- "PAY CLOSE ATTENTION TO WHERE YOUR FINGERS AND HANDS ARE!"

- "BRAVO SANTA - YOU'RE SPEAKING NICE AND LOUD.... HAVE FUN TONIGHT!"

- "MRS. CLAUS - SLOW DOWN YOUR LINE WHEN YOU HAND SANTA THE COFFEE CUP"

- "BEE BOP, BE SURE TO FACE THE AUDIENCE WHEN YOU YELL."

- "CHOIR, YOU ARE AMAZING SINGERS! HAVE FUN AND SING YOUR HEARTS OUT!"

- "WAIT UNTIL THE AUDIENCE STOPS LAUGHING AT YOUR JOKE BEFORE YOU SAY YOUR NEXT LINE!"

- "MAKE SURE THE APPLAUSE HAS STOPPED BEFORE YOU START TALKING AGAIN."

- "IF I SPIN MY FINGERS AROUND IN A CIRCLE, THAT MEANS TO REPEAT YOUR LAST LINE."

- "IF SOMEONE IS ACTING INAPPROPRIATELY, LET MRS. GRAY HANDLE IT – PLEASE DON'T TELL ANOTHER STUDENT WHAT TO DO."

- "IF I IMITATE HOLDING A MICROPHONE, WATCH TO SEE IF I AM MOVING IT CLOSER TO MY MOUTH OR FURTHER AWAY FROM MY MOUTH. YOU SHOULD DO WHAT MY MOTION SUGGESTS."

- "IF YOU START FEELING SICK AND NEED TO LEAVE, DON'T WAIT FOR PERMISSION, JUST STEP DOWN AND GO TELL YOUR PARENT, TEACHER, OR GO STRAIGHT TO THE BATHROOM, IF NECESSARY."

- REMEMBER TO BE ABSOLUTELY QUIET OUTSIDE THE GYM – THE ADULTS ARE STILL IN THEIR MEETING.

- GO TO THE BATHROOM NOW RATHER THAN DURING THE SHOW.

(You *could* make your presentation more general to save time, making them reusable for other pre-performance learning and entertainment, but I've always created new ones that are personalized so kids look for their names and anticipate what I am going to say about/to them.)

Anyway, I filled about 40 slides with personal messages like that...instructions, comments, things I'd noticed that needed fixing or changing, and *especially compliments*! I then programmed it so it would "loop," meaning...just continually keep showing the show over and over. (I put each slide about 10 seconds apart.) Then, when the kids met in one room the evening of the performance, they wanted to read the TV information. They were so quiet and excited to see what the message was to them and if they had a picture of themselves to see. I tried to make sure everyone was in at least one photo or had something written to them. It was a new way to do last-minute comments - something I always have trouble with since they're so excited they have trouble being quiet and listening. Right before a performance, they are too excited to concentrate, some are taking inventory of who is missing, some are sad because someone special to them is missing from the audience, some are focused on how their hair or lip gloss looks, and some are just plain scared spitless! But that night, they WERE quiet...and, everyone was seated on the floor so everyone could see. When kids entered a little late, it was obvious what they were to do so I didn't have to keep interrupting with directions. Incidentally, if somebody talked, I just said, *"Please stand up, Cody"* and he/she immediately stood up and amazingly got quiet... just because most of the kids wanted to read and see. It took some time, but I must say...it was worth it!

On the flip side of that success, was total failure when I made a PowerPoint slide show as pre-Kindergarten program entertainment. There were no words for *them* to read, but I have two words: BIG MISTAKE! They were so wound up, all they did was laugh, point, and scream hysterically at seeing the photos of each other. It may have been a random, abnormal, once-in-a-lifetime reaction from five year olds, but I will never know because I will *never* try it again!

24. *I TAKE DIGITAL PHOTOS DURING PERFORMANCES* when I am not playing the piano and am using a recorded accompaniment. Then, at the end of each show, when thanking the audience for supporting their kids by making the effort to get them to and from practices and for coming to the program, I give my school email address and invite them to send a request via email, asking for program pictures, and I will send a PowerPoint collection back to them. I spend an hour or so after each concert creating a nice PowerPoint presentation that includes pictures, of course, but also the song titles and performers' names on it, the date, and title of the show. Parents

have liked receiving this little souvenir and it's definitely an easy way to win support for the kids and your programs. It is a dynamic way to build healthy relationships with your students, their families, and friends, too!

25. ***VIDEOTAPE AND SAVE, VIDEOTAPE AND SAVE!*** I ask my good friend and professional colleague, LeAnn, to videotape all of our performances. We just finished the Kindergarten program last week. Next year, the first grade program will be added to this new Kindergarten tape. Each year after that, we will record on the same tape, and film the PTA shows performed by the same class. Each grade will have one grade-level tape that is added to each year. By the time they get to fifth grade, they have a fun movie of every performance they've done since Kindergarten. They can see themselves as tiny little five-year-olds, see how they've grown, changed, and matured; they recognize new friends between one year and the next, and miss others they'd forgotten. It's also fun because they remember some long-since forgotten songs! It is such a fun package of music and kid history by the end of six years of collecting, everyone wants a copy! (I haven't accepted responsibility for that one, yet.) For years, we videotaped and saved religiously and never missed adding a concert to the year before, but then we got a new Principal, had a huge influx of new teachers, and unfortunately, the idea got lost in all the changes. LeAnn and I have decided to start it again and keep it going – hopefully establishing a tradition! In the past, I stored the tapes in the school's main video library where everyone could have access to them, but I will be keeping all of the program tapes in my room now. I will have easier access to them, I won't forget to add to them, and it might help keep them from drifting into the hands of "non-returners," prevent others from copying over previous performances, or someone from adding non-performance video to the tape so the space is used up before completing the full six years of shows.

26. ***I OFFER A MORNING AND AFTERNOON PERFORMANCE IN ADDITION TO THE EVENING SHOW*** whenever possible, inviting family and friends to the assemblies. This TRICK provides a larger audience for the performers' dress rehearsal and makes all the hard work seem more worthwhile when we get to perform it more than once. Next, some people who ordinarily could not make it for an evening performance because of health, work schedules, and other conflicts, are able to make arrangements to see their child on

stage during the day! Teachers appreciate it, too, because they get to choose which performance time best suits their busy schedules. I also schedule two evening performances of our big musicals, not the little PTA shows. Typically, one begins at 7:00; the second is at 8:00. Stage crew has to reset props, I have to rewind tapes, some costumes have to be changed, and students have to stay twice as long – but everyone seems to love it and that has been a successful addition for many years now. There are always a few who complain that they don't want to sit through it a second time but they actually survive and are definitely in the minority. Then, of course, there are those of us who would sit through 961 performances if our own kid was in them! Just FYI, we used to have a packed audience, standing room only, for both performances. That is no longer the case...more and more parents are bringing their kids and dropping them off. ☹

27. ***COOKIES AND CAKE, PUNCH AND POP*** either after or in between *evening* performances is always a nice extra treat. Recently, our *incredible* PTA has provided this special "extra" at our December performance! This gives me a chance to hob-knob with parents, family, friends, and performers after the show. Parents tend to flood out of the building as soon as a program is over if we don't offer goodies. I really enjoy getting to connect parent-faces with kid-faces, hear comments, and just visit. It's an awesome way to build those so-important relationships! (Oh yeah...don't forget to write a thank you to the snack providers and hosts!)

28. ***WRITE PERSONAL NOTES*** to as many students throughout the year as possible but make sure to write to your performers! Take the time to write a note to every classroom that participated in a performance and jot an individual note to each of your "stars" in appreciation for their extra practice and willingness to do a special part. If you're willing, please write to each student...not just the stars. Often, it's non-stars who benefit most from your words of kindness, thoughtfulness, and attention. Not only do kids treasure your thoughts, parents absolutely love it. It takes time...oh so much time, but it is so worth it! If you're not a writer – learn to be one. In the words of Nike advertising: JUST DO IT!

29. ***LOUD LINES:*** When you are rehearsing for a play or musical and you're having the eternal problem of **getting the kids to speak their lines loud enough**, here's what you can try. (It only took me about

22 years to figure it out – but when it finally hit me, it worked like a gem!) I add one extra character to the cast (knowing full well that I'll probably have to create a line for him or her) just to have hangin' around during auditions, blocking, and rehearsals. Then, I tell them that I will be standing a really long way away from them to see who I can hear best. If I can't hear…it's not a big problem at all – I explain that I will just give that particular quiet line to the loudest speaker of the two. Then, to their surprise, I take them and rehearse <u>outside!!!!</u> That's right…outside…no matter what the temperature is! We've even had practices in the snow – it was so much fun! (Please realize though, that my play rehearsals, blocking, and auditions are after school hours.) Anyway, I put the kids on the sidewalk and three-step-high porch area closest to the building and then I walk clear across the parking lot to the other side – about 20 or 30 yards away. It is absolutely amazing how nice and loud they speak in order to make sure I can hear them. After that, I seldom have to mention volume again – only inflection.

30. *<u>ADDRESS THE AUDIENCE:</u>* I used to say "toes out" all the time to **keep the kids from turning their backs to the audience.** I knew it didn't work too well since I was saying it all the time. Well, after 22 years of saying, *"toes out,"* I discovered a more effective TRICK! Tell the kids to pretend the words I'M A DORK are on the back of their shirt and that they sure don't want the audience to see it. There were only three times (as opposed to a zillion with the "toes out" routine) I had to say something like, *"What's that shirt of yours say?"* or *"What's on the back of that shirt?"* With a smile and a sense of humor, it's amazing how the kids relate better to that than *"toes out."*

31. *<u>BLOCKBUSTERS:</u>* Another simple **blocking TRICK** I've figured out is to place students in three areas of the stage: front, middle, and back. I encourage them to move between the three different positions but to remember: If they are in the front area closest to the audience, they are supposed to sit on their pockets. Performers assigned to the middle area get to be on their knees or seated on a chair. The back area kids stand up. This gives a natural three-tier effect that keeps them from upstaging anyone and blocking the audience's view. I use this tactic anytime I have a bunch of kids on stage who are extras or have small speaking parts. The main characters can then move around these other students without worrying that someone will give whole new meaning to the word BLOCKING!

32. ***MIRROR, MIRROR ON THE…SHIRT?*** There are times when I want my choir **kids to face completely to the left or right, and other times when I want them facing out but leaning left or right.** It's always been a little awkward and confusing to know what WORDS to say to get that look without a big explanation. I've learned to tell them that they need to pretend they have mirrors on the fronts of their shirts. Sometimes I want to see myself in the mirror other times I don't. So now I say…"*lean left*" or "*lean right*" if I want them completely facing and leaning. I say "*mirror left*" or "*mirror right*" if I want them facing the audience but leaning in a given direction. For some reason, they can imagine a mirror reflecting to me easier than they can remember "*face me and lean….*"

33. ***RISER RULES:*** Performances can mean **getting kids on risers!** Getting little people on and off the risers can waste you away and fry your brain unless you plan ahead and practice. It is one of the most stressful aspects of preparing for a performance. When you place older students on the risers, for the most part, you can count on them remembering where they should stand the next time they return to them. However, it's probably not the best idea to expect little people, *especially* Kindergartners, to remember from one hour…wait, rephrase that….one MINUTE, wait, rephrase *that*…one SECOND to the next - where they are supposed to stand. Not only will they be clueless as to whom they are supposed to stand by, they probably won't know which step of the risers or to which side of the risers they have been assigned. Although my hair is gradually growing back in after our February Kindergarten concert, there are several ways I've found to help that situation move more fluid :

- WRITE IT DOWN! Actually, have someone write it down for you while you're holding rehearsal. Don't expect the kids to stand still long enough for you to write down 100 names! Yeah…it won't happen. Make a standing chart rather than a seating chart of where every single person has been assigned to be.

- GET HELP!!! Don't try to do it alone.

- ASSIGN STUDENTS THE NUMBER THAT COINCIDES WITH THEIR LOCATION IN LINE. You *can* incorporate the words "first, second, third," etc. into their learning for the smaller ones but the words "one" "two" "three" are just easier. (And "easy" is exactly what you crave during Kindergarten program prep!)

- ASSIGN LINE LEADERS AND CO-LINE LEADERS SO RATHER THAN SAYING ROW ONE, ROW TWO, OR ROW THREE ... or...TOP ROW, MIDDLE ROW, FRONT ROW.... Just say: BEN'S ROW...COOKIE'S ROW....KAITIE'S ROW. Younger students seem to associate with **names** and friends much easier than with a row they have to envision in their heads or a number they have to remember.

- WHEN THEY'RE LINED UP TO ENTER THE PERFORMANCE AREA, HAVE YOUNG STUDENTS PUT THEIR HAND ON THE SHOULDER OF THE PERSON IN FRONT OF THEM. The next time you can ask, "Who's shoulder did you touch?" (This has the potential to be disastrous, so be sure you've got kids who can handle touching shoulders. Some years it has worked for me, some years we had to call in the S.W.A.T. team to re-establish order.)

- It is easier if you ALWAYS HAVE THE SAME LEADERS ON AND OFF THE RISERS. Example: You have Katie on the left side of the risers (facing you) and Kirt on the far right side. Rather than having Katie lead the kids *on* the risers and Kirt lead them *off*, decide on one of them (for the purposes of this example, I will choose Katie), and have Katie ALWAYS lead her row on and off the risers every single time...no matter where the exit is! Essentially, they are just making a big circle – in from the right, out to the left.

With my older students, I have a leader enter from one side and someone else lead the row off and out. Two different leaders works just fine with the *older kids*; the little ones can do it, too, especially if you have plenty of time to practice getting them on and off.

34. *PRACTICING IN PERFORMANCE POSITIONS:* I work with my students **in the classroom, with them standing in their performance places, for days before we ever move to the gym and on to the risers.** This way they know which row they stand on, who they stand beside, between, in front of and behind, and have practiced lining up and assembling in that location until it's a no-brainer.

35. *<u>IN AND OUT, UP AND DOWN:</u>*   Don't leave mounting and dismounting the risers until the end of rehearsal. As amazing as it may seem, getting little people on and off the risers is much more time-consuming, energy depleting, and patience interfering than actually putting the whole program together. Practice it every single day you practice the show. Dismiss classes by riser row or **however you plan to have them exit in front of their audience.** And do me a favor... during the show, don't stand up there or have someone stand up there putting kids in their places! Parents didn't come to see you, their child's teacher, or any other adult! Practice it enough times so no one has to physically move anyone into position. Unless I am at the piano, **nobody in the audience ever sees me during a performance.** I sit on the floor – out of the way – run my accompaniment music, and I do not physically adjust kids on the risers. I may ask them to scoot or give them signals, but I do not touch them or parade around in front of the audience. It's a pet peeve of mine...probably because I've gone to so many elementary performances where a teacher is up there in front directing traffic like a cop after a Chiefs game! Practice until they can do it <u>without you</u>! Give them worse case scenarios and how to react in the event one of those plays out. I believe it is our job to make them independent rather than dependent on us.

36. *<u>UH OH! WHAT "WORSE CASE SCENARIOS?"</u>*   Let me just say that in my 24 years of programming, I have experienced, *<u>during a program</u>*, electrical failure, vomit, fainting, wet pants, poopy pants, bloody noses, tears, *gushing* tears, *wailing tears*, accompaniment recording failure, a blackout, microphone feedback, me forgetting how many verses to play, scenery tipping over, props shattering, a sixth grader driving a Barbie Corvette right off the end of the stage and into the audience, a fifth grader falling off the back of the riser and snapping her arm in two, a fire *drill*, a tornado *<u>warning</u>* – complete with sirens and "take cover" announcement, and even a goat leaving the wet *and* solid remnants of his pre-show snack on the stage shortly after digesting poor Joseph's coat! *You can never plan enough.* You can *never* imagine all you must anticipate – but do your best and make sure your kids know what you want them to do if something like one of these things happens in the middle of their performance.

37. *<u>UP AND AT 'EM: HOW TO ACTUALLY GET KIDS TO STEP ONTO THEIR RISER STEP?</u>*   Everyone has a different way to get students on the steps. I've seen teachers nod their head when their performers are to step up, but that works a little funky when the kids aren't facing the direction of the nodder. Some teachers play a chord indicating it is time to step up or step down. That works pretty well, too, but some people think it seems regimented and control-freaky. Many times, the kids just go up spontaneously rather than in unison. That works, but looks a little disjointed. I've seen kids walk clear across the front of the risers on the floor then step up to their positions and I've seen kids step up the steps as soon as they reach the risers, then walk across the risers on the step where they will be standing. I don't think there is a cut and dry, right or wrong, easy or tough way to do it. I've done it all of those ways...but I'll share with you another way I do it sometimes, and then you can go from there.

Our first concern, I guess, is getting them to know when to enter the room. I use the accompaniment to be their cue. The second they hear music, they know it's time to start. My line leaders and their row of little followers walk <u>on the floor</u> clear to the end of the risers, standing shoulder to shoulder, and face the steps. The line leader waits for everyone to arrive and the line to stop moving, then he or she leads the step-up process. The same way works for stepping down. The entire line follows only that one assigned person who is their line leader. This is repeated for each row. The only trick to this is to make sure you select line leaders who are totally responsible, smart, have good memories, are great leaders, and are sure to be there come performance time.

Two additional TRICKS: #1. I assign one center person to a spot right in the middle of the risers. When walking in, they are to go to their center spot and <u>stop</u> – everyone else on either side then has a way of judging where to stand so they're evenly spaced between the middle person and the end people. This little TRICK helps keep your center person from being off center and one side of your risers being all smooshed and crowded while the other side has enough room for twenty-three more people. #2. When the kids are cued to step up with a piano chord, I have them remain facing the back until the entrance music for the next group begins...that's their cue to turn around all at the same time. It looks cool but takes practice, for sure!

38. ***MIKE, MAC, OR MIKE ON MICS***: Before rehearsals begin, I usually need all or a combination of microphones, stands, sound system, extension cords, music, music stands, pencils, notepads, remote control, risers, stages, steps, props, and maybe even scenery. Rather than doing all that by myself and stressing over it on a daily

basis, I meet with hand-selected helpers or "stage crew," place them in teams of two (in case one is absent, the other can handle the job alone), and teach each partnership a specific job. I teach them exactly how I want things set up before and returned after rehearsal. I go over safety procedures, proper handling of the equipment, rules regarding set-up and striking of the set, time frame for set-up/tear-down, adjusting the sound board, and any other information pertinent to the chore. Then I totally relinquish all of those duties related to the mechanics of a performance to my trained student helpers. They are also responsible for their equipment when we travel for our performances. My assignment of such enormous responsibility gives those kids incredible self-esteem and I can honestly say, I have never once been disappointed with this process! The kids are so reliable, it's unbelievable! One of the coolest things I want to share with you is that three of the many kids who've been crew members over the years, have gone into the professions of sound technology, studio recording, and acoustic design! Just how cool is *that*?! The best part for me is that I never have to give it a second thought – it's a done deal every single rehearsal. I walk in with my mass of musicians and everything is perfectly set up, waiting for us to use. When I first started enlisting the help of students, I just used fifth graders. I got so spoiled by their help, I moved down a grade and started asking for help from fourth. This little process has been going on long enough now, that I have learned that first graders can be just as responsible to do this task as the big kids – if I choose the right ones, of course. I haven't and probably won't assign Kindergarten a stage crew role…not that it's too much for them to handle, I just don't know them well enough by the time the K performance rolls around to know who I can depend on.

39. **_COSTUME CONCEPTS:_** Since I do math far better than I can sew and I'm clearly THE *worst* mathematician in the entire universe, I quickly learned I was going to have to conjure up some very simple explanations for parents who call expecting *me* (ha ha) to help them with costume ideas. I typically suggest second-hand, consignment, Goodwill, Disabled Veterans, and Salvation Army stores for purchasing costumes. It's not uncommon to find a nice, Robin egg blue polyester double knit suit or a June Cleaver dress – complete with pearls and pumps for your 50's dress. These types of stores are relatively inexpensive and limit costuming only by creativity!

I am most proud of my elf costume directions, though, for our Christmas musicals! I'll share it with you as long as you promise you will tell people you read about it in my book and write me a note about how much you liked the idea!! Oh ok...you don't have to, just kidding. This costume can be whipped together with zero talent accompanied by nothing much more than scissors, a hot glue gun, a sweatshirt, sweat pants, and some garland, glitter, or grosgrain!

- Cut the sleeves off of the sweatshirt then cut it right *down the middle in front*, so it resembles a vest. OR...you can cut the sleeves off and cut it *down the sides*, removing about four inches of fabric under the arms – so it resembles a slip-over-the-head tunic. Then put a belt around it. A wide, black, Santa-style belt looks best; but a string of garland, some rope, chord, or just tied-together strips of the fabric you've just cut out of the sides will work.

- Hot glue garland, tinsel, or faux fur down both sides of the front, around the bottom hem, and around the neck.

- Cut the pants into shorts and glue garland around the legs to cover up the fact that there's no hem.

- Use one of the sleeves for a hat by gluing garland around the large end (that was at the shoulder before it was cut off) and tie the cuffed end with a hair tie or rubber band and glue some garland or a yarn ball on the end of it.

- Use the pants legs to make elf shoes by cutting them to size then gluing them together with some garland on the toe. I suggest gluing some sandpaper or rubber band strips to the bottom so they're not slick.

- Stick a long sleeved shirt and tights underneath and voila` you have a great little elf costume for little or nothing. It could be Peter Pan, a leprechaun, a cherub, an angel, or just about any other little character if you choose the right colors!

40. *__MOVE IT, MOVE IT, MOVE IT!__* I make up tons of **choreography** for songs we sing in class as well as for my show groups! I think it adds extra dimension and quality to any performance...but it does great things for class, too! I use it just as much, maybe even more during regular music time than I do in shows, simply because it gives

my little friends an advantage in remembering lyrics, it helps them behave because they're active, it keeps their energy level elevated so they don't get bored, and that keeps their interest piqued so they can learn more. Get those kids moving every chance you get! Kinesthetic learning benefits everyone! And, if you don't get many chances, then start planning them into your lesson format! It's fun – for everyone *AND* when you DO want to teach choreography for a performance, the movements, directions, experience of having done it before and the confidence that experience breeds, will make your teaching a zillion times easier!

41. ***LORD OF THE DANCERS:*** Choreography doesn't have to be fancy – it doesn't even have to be good – the important thing is that you include it – for the kids' sake. I just collect/steal ideas from television and other places where people move to music. I suggest avoiding tons of footwork if your show will be performed on risers and just stick to leaning, arm and hand movements, head turns, body turns, sectional movements similar to "the wave," and one-step moves left or right, forward or back. Whenever I work choreography into a show, there are a few TRICKS I've figured out that help me:

- ***ALPHABETIZE*** I have found that assigning movement by class works great! First, I make sure I assign riser location by class in *alphabetical order* from left to right, front to back, or bottom to top if on risers. I do this whenever it's practical, possible, and appropriate. I realize that sometimes it doesn't work best that way, but if you can, it will ease your memory on who is doing what and when. Here's an example: my third grade kids were lined up from the left with Mrs. **B**asinger's class, in the middle was Mrs. **C**aywood's class, and on the right side of the risers was Mr. **T**rober's class. I kept kids from the same class all on the same row with the Kindergarten and First grade performances, but they were still in alphabetical order. Ms. **B**elgiere's class was in front on the floor, Ms. **B**ritt's room occupied the first riser step, Mrs. **F**iedler's room stood on the second or middle step, and Ms. **G**reene's little cherubs were at the top. I never have to remember or refer to a standing guide to see who I put where with this set-up....it's a great TRICK that de-stressifies a potentially stressful situation. Also, when there are different entrances or different actions, it is easier for me to remember who goes first, second, third, etc. without having to stop and refer to notes or depend on my virtually non-existent memory. When we practice without the other classes in the room, the kids still stand on the left, middle, or right side of the room – pretending the others are there. Repetition is your friend when it comes to getting kids on the risers and perfecting choreography.

This may seem rather obvious, but that's *only* if you've done it before...the class or group assigned to the top row must enter the performance area first. You have to work from the back to the front – which makes the kids enter top row, first – front row, last.

- ***LEFT IS ALWAYS RIGHT*** My kids know, "...*when in doubt, go left.*" That just means that if they are to face a certain direction, use a certain hand, arm, or foot, or turn a certain way, it will *always* be toward the left, first. You can make your standing rule either left or right, I just chose left because their left is my right...I'm right handed...and that feels most natural for *me*. With that same thought...it is always beneficial to exercise and develop their left side since most students are righties. When I'm playing the piano, I prefer using my right hand and keeping the bass and steady beat going as opposed to the melody if I have to cue them. It's a natural thing for me and I've learned that having one direction they can *always* count on...they get in the habit of thinking that way and they will always know which way to move. They never have to ask which way to turn, which hand to raise, which eye to wink, which way to tilt their head, etc., they just know the answer is always left! They move, tilt, bend, and face right, of course, they just always *begin* left. Of course, sometimes there are exceptions, but they are so rare, I can't even think of one to offer as an example.

  Oh yes...one other thing pertaining to this left and right business. I always use the words *left* and *right*. I typically have an L and an R somewhere on the wall or the back of my piano for them to refer to, and I use the old trick of holding your hands in front of you – *palms away*, then, making a letter L with your thumbs and pointer finger. The L that looks correct – or - isn't backwards is on your left hand. This might be a TRICK you can introduce to help those who seem to stumble over this concept or for when they're away from the prompts.

42. *1,2,3...WORDS HELP ME:* Rather than teaching choreography moves by counting, like most dance instructors do, I match moves with the lyrics. For example, rather than telling them to lean left on

85

beat four, I might say, *"Lean left on the word 'roll,'* or *"Lean left when you sing the word pow-er, make a fist in the air on "pow" and pull it down to a muscle-showing pose on the 'er' part of the word."* This works great because they don't have to think numbers while they're thinking lyrics along with concentrating on the next move. Actions are easier for them and end up being much more precise.

43. ***PRECISION POINTING:*** When choreographing movements or posture, I have a user-friendly TRICK to share that works perfectly all the time! Use the point where wall and ceiling intersect or meet for students' eyes to focus if they are "at attention" for a Patriotic piece, or as the perfect height when raising their hands in unison. Instruct them to align their hands to that particular spot on the wall, no matter what room they are in, gym or small classroom, all arm lifts will be parallel! The same TRICK works for hand drops, hand lifts, or side-facing-focus. I use the corner of a room as our imaginary line to follow when raising or lowering arms. It is easy to model, it's easy for the students to do, and it makes the vertical movements nicely parallel.

44. ***PRINTING PROGRAMS:*** When designing the souvenir programs for each performance, I ask each classroom teacher to have their students **sign their name** in a single column, then I reduce the lists to fit my program page before printing them. Not only does this little TRICK prevent me from inadvertently leaving someone out, misspelling a name, or getting in dutch for using the wrong name, it is a nice keepsake of their signature at each grade level.

45. ***REMIND PERFORMERS TO NOT WEAR PERFUME***, lotion, or sprays with fragrance. Odors combined with nerves, warm temperatures, and standing for awhile can lead to upset stomachs, headaches, and sometimes even fainting, so it's just wise to leave the smelly stuff at home.

46. ***REMIND PERFORMERS TO WEAR DEODORANT.*** Speaking of smelly stuff – this is also a good one to leave at home. Don't be embarrassed to mention it and require this – it's good for everyone! Though rare, this can be a noticeable problem, beginning as early as second grade.

47. ***REMIND PERFORMERS TO WEAR COMFORTABLE SHOES.*** They will be standing on risers and moving on the stages. Comfort is

more important than looks, under these conditions, and assure them that the audience doesn't look at feet, anyway.

48. ***REMIND PERFORMERS TO WEAR COOL CLOTHING.*** It gets warm under the lights, warmer with nervous energy, and even warmer with the crowd and audience...so ***cool is cool!***

49. ***REMIND PERFORMERS TO EAT A SMALL MEAL OR SNACK BEFORE A SHOW.*** Attempting to go all evening without nutrition can lead to some bad endings. Even soda crackers or some fruit can get them through without having a sugar-low take them out of the show. On the flip side of that, eating spicy foods, or a heavy meal has a track record of inducing awful tummy trauma when mixed with nerves, standing a long time, and warm temperatures.

50. ***REMIND PERFORMERS TO PACK THE HOUSE!*** I offer a pack-the-pew type contest as an incentive for the kids to invite hoards of people and ensure we have a standing-room-only crowd. Granted, the "winner" is chosen based on the assumption that he or she tells the truth regarding how many people came to the show for them, but I give them the benefit of the doubt and award the "winner" a package of a dozen cookies or doughnuts from the bakery to take home and share with their family. Of course, they have the option to devour them totally and completely solo!

51. ***TALENT SHOW TIME!*** There are *many* challenges associated with talent show time. The first formidable task is selecting who gets to perform. Some schools require that everyone who *wants* to perform *gets* to perform. Send me your address if that's your school and I'll send you a sympathy card! Under those circumstances, talent show is an **all-day marathon** performance full of pantomimed songs to the latest inappropriate hits interspersed with some *actual talent*. But then, I'm not telling you anything you don't already know! Some schools hold auditions and narrow it down to a few top performers. Good luck holding auditions. I suggest you either delegate the audition job to the person demanding auditions in order to narrow the numbers, or take your sleeping bag and a bullet-proof vest because it's going to *take forever* and you're going to come under fire for who you pick and who you do not pick to perform. It's a **lose – lose** situation. Been there, done that, and have the holes in my heart to prove it. (But that's yet, another story.)

The TRICK I share is a combination of the best of both worlds and it has worked beautifully. The only catch is, it takes cooperation and willingness to help from every single person on staff.

Simply put, every grade has a grade-level talent show! Every student gets to perform for his or her peers, no one is left out of getting the chance to show off, parents are invited to attend, it is emceed – usually by the grade-level chairperson, and unless teachers place restrictions on it, the kids can do just about anything they want, from gargling on pitch to hot rodding around on their roller blades. (Words of advice from yet another experience-rooted story, if a student is doing talent that has the potential of being injurious – like skateboard tricks, gymnastics, sports-acro, roller blades, or bike tricks, it's smart to require a parent to be in attendance. If a parental guardian or chaperone is unable to attend, then I do not allow the act to take place. If it gets ugly, I refer them to my Principal who does an excellent job handling it.)

Because grade-level shows usually need the piano and gym space, the teachers sometimes schedule their show during special class time. The only thing special class teachers do then, is sacrifice their class time and set up the microphones, mats, sound system, chairs, etc. for the performance. Being extraordinarily **careful not to imply that the grade-level** <u>**Talent Show**</u> **is an audition,** the names of three or four acts and an alternate are selected by *anonymous staff members* ☺ from the grade-level shows, and then given to me to be included in the All-School show on the last day of school. A discreet note is slipped into the child's folder or back pack informing mom and dad that we would like their son or daughter to perform in the All-School show.

With this method, everyone gets to perform, some just get to perform twice. If you do get a complaint, you simply remind them that their child has had the opportunity to perform for their talent show.

Once I receive the names from every grade level, I start writing a script for introductions. I enlist the help of our four Student Council officers to emcee the show – giving them some much-deserved attention, as well! I make sure they have the script a full week ahead of the show date so they can read, memorize, and practice their best show host/hostess personality. (I shifted from me doing the introductions to student introductions because my hands were always full with technicalities: searching for CD's, keeping performers calm and in order, keeping things running smoothly, etc.) Officers also are directed *in writing* on their scripts, when and where to move mics, mats, set up desks, remove props, etcs. The officers are instructed to look at me periodically and listen for a "tss tss" sound indicating I need to see one of them for some reason. THEY then nonchalantly cross over to me to retrieve information rather than me yelling instructions or doing it myself. This way, I don't ever have to parade in front of the audience and the necessities are covered.

I also have incredible help from the physical education teacher, art teacher, and librarian. I give two of them the list of acts/performers, have them seat them in order of appearance, in chairs, at the back of the gym. That way, the performers don't have to miss the show just because they're performing AND nobody has to supervise a room full of anxious entertainers before and after their act! Another special staff teacher plucks the performers, a few at a time, from their seated spots, keeps them in performance order, and makes sure they get to me by the door (in the wings) so they can hand me their CD or tape, talk about last-minute concerns, and be ready to perform the instant they're introduced. After students have finished their act, they get to go sit with their parent if available or return to their class and be seated with them for the remainder of the show.

One of the other many challenges at talent show time is establishing a student's performance time. Parents often insist that their child is scheduled at the beginning or at the end of the show because they want to run in, catch one particular act, and head back to the office rather than sit through the two-hour long show. If I can accommodate them, I sure try, but it's obvious that everyone can't perform at the beginning or the end. So...I've figured out a reasonably fair way of handling the barrage of *"What-time-will-my-child-be-singing?"* questions. *I assign the performance order according to entertainment and variety value, then list and number the names in order of appearance. I send that to every parent connected with a talent show actor or actress, with the following message included at the bottom of the page:*

Student Council Officers have been given a script to introduce each act.
They have been instructed to **memorize the script**
so our order of appearance is pretty much *inflexible*.
Thank you very much for your understanding in this!

You, your family, and your friends
are cordially invited to attend the All School Talent show on
Monday, June 4th.
The show will begin promptly at 9:00.

If you are going to have to slip in just to see your child, you might like to guesstimate the time he or she will be performing. Generally, if you figure approximately three minutes per act, you can estimate your child's performance time. (I would allow myself an additional 10 minutes on either side of the estimation time just to make certain you do not miss the performance.)

If your child is using a cassette tape, please make sure the tape is in it's starting position – I will not have time to locate the beginning of a song.

Finally, you guessed it, I write notes to each performer (ahead of time – based on what I've found out about their act from the grade-level shows) so I can present it and they can take it with them as soon as they've completed their act. I typically hand them the note as they leave to return to family or friends, right after they perform, so I don't have to track them down afterward.

52. ***MAKE FRIENDS WITH YOUR CUSTODIAN(S)!*** This is a *very important* **relationship** to cultivate! He or she can make your job at program time either relatively stress free (as far as stages, scenery, sound, and risers are concerned) or that person can make you wish you'd opted for that burro-riding tour guide job we discussed earlier. It's up to you. Win them over!! Make them **know** you notice and appreciate every little thing they do! Even comment on things they do that don't pertain to you or the music department – like shoveling a path in the snow, fixing an overflowing toilet, carrying packages to people, repairing faucets...those poor people have such a thankless job – let's change that!

• ***WRITE THANK YOU NOTES***...LOTS of thank you notes, not just one...not just two! I make the time to write to our custodian twice a week, after every practice that he has to set up risers for me. I leave anything from a Post It Note to a full-blown letter on stationery, just gushing over him, his help, his efficiency, and his responsibility. (If you've always had an extraordinary custodian, you might not realize how rare a luxury that is. I think I may have taken our first custodian for granted. It wasn't until after he retired and we salvaged through a bunch of people trying to find someone who could handle all the various skills they need to do that job, that I realized what a treasure a good custodian really is.)

- **_WRITE NOTES TO HIS/HER FAMILY_**...Take a minute to tell your custodian's spouse or parent how much you appreciate all the help they give you. You need to <u>be sincere</u> so if you're pretty sure his wife thinks he's a lazy bum, better not write a letter speaking of his energy and enthusiastic help, unless you mean it. (It'll be up to him to do the explaining to her!)

- **_WRITE A NOTE TO HIS OR HER SUPERVISOR_**...Your Principal needs to know how much your custodian helps you. List specific things he/she does that help you do your job better for the kids. (It's funny how some people are so quick to report failure or laziness but never think to go to the Head Honcho with a *compliment*.) Be the person who does that! And don't stop there! Write a letter to his superior at Central Office – find out who is the head of Buildings and Grounds or who is "in charge" of the Custodial crew and tell that person how well his employee is doing.

- **_DON'T FORGET THE NIGHT CUSTODIAL CREW!_** They may not have much to do with your programs – but they have feelings that need to be lifted just like the rest of us! In my building, it's the night crew who get to fold and stash all the chairs, pick up all the programs that have been left behind, clean the bathrooms that wouldn't have been used had it not been for our show, and clean up the inevitable mess from our punch and cookie soirée. They deserve not to be taken for granted.

- **_COME BEARING GIFTS._** There are lots of easy, inexpensive ways to show your appreciation. Anytime I make cookies or buy snacks, I wrap a special little bag for my custodian – just to let him know that I appreciate all he does. Every once in a while, I throw an extra steak, chop, or Kabob on the grill for dinner, toss it in some plasticware, and surprise him with something a little tastier than a school lunch from the cafeteria! When you're in the department store and one of those always-gorgeous-and-perfectly-presented fragrance models offers you a test spray, ask for a sample – and turn it into a treat for your helper at work! Just build a relationship and then seal it with thoughtfulness.

- **_FAKE IT!_** You know...there are going to be custodial staff members who drive you cotally trazy! You recognize the type...they are teetering on terribly intolerable and trip your temper time after time! You are familiar with the kind..."*I'm too busy to bother with that,*"

91

or "*I'll try but I doubt if I can,*" "*I forgot,*" or anytime you need help they're nowhere to be found! **They are the ones who disappear into the *woodwork* when you wish they _WOULD WORK_**! As difficult as it may be, those are the ones that are the most important to flatter, fake out, and fuss over! You *have* to make them believe that you think they are the most important element to your success. In a way, they really are. You see, I wouldn't be devoting this much space to this particular topic if I wasn't totally convinced that your life at work will be better if you have your custodian on your team! They can be so incredibly helpful. They know where the extension cords are, where power sources and fuses are, most of them know how to do everything from repairing microphone cables to striking sets, setting up risers, repairing anything, and, firing up the kiln! The bottom line: they have to *want* to help you. Appreciate them – they are just as important to you as your administrator!

> **"The secret to success is sincerity. Once you can fake that... you've got it made!"**
> *~Jean Giraudoux*

During my second month of college, my senior year, our professor gave us a quiz. I was a conscientious student and had breezed through the questions, until I read the last one:

"What is the first name of the man who cleans the school?" Surely this was some kind of joke. I had seen the man all the time, every day. He was a short, black gentleman, always wore a smile, and in his 50's - but how would I know his name? I handed in my paper, leaving the last question blank. Just before class ended, one student asked if the last question would count toward our quiz grade. *"Absolutely,"* my professor said, *"In your careers, you will meet many people. All are significant. All deserve your attention, your kindness and care even if all you do is smile, say 'hello and use their name.'"*

I've never forgotten that lesson. I also learned his name was Sam.

Chapter 4

GOBS O' GOOD GUNK

Many things happen during a teaching career that simply don't fit nicely into any category and, more than likely, weren't ever addressed in Methods class. They are just remote, isolated, random occurrences that I decided to discuss. I'm going to cover lots of issues in this chapter but don't look for any beautiful literary segues. I'm just going to tell you how I handle smaller issues like recess duty and tattling while delving into some of the life-changing things that can happen to any of us at any time. I think you will find some very useful TRICKS and ADVICE in this section.

1. <u>*UNCERTAINTY*</u> is inevitable in every phase of life, whether you are beginning or have been beginning for years. There is uncertainty in everything we do, from what to wear in the morning so the kids don't think we're a total geekazoid, to how to reach that poor little guy who hasn't been reachable for five years straight. Rather than letting uncertainty get to you – and it can – it probably will, eventually ….

> **"Let uncertainty spark a sense of adventure and mystery in your life and your career."**
>
> *~ Deb Holt - Univerself*

Convince yourself that it is OK for your future to hold a bit of uncertainty and, as odd as it sounds, that it's good that life has some mystery! Look at uncertainty as fortuitous! Mount up with courage so you don't get discouraged!

> **"Courage does not always roar. Sometimes courage is the small, quiet voice at the end of the day saying, "I will try again tomorrow."**
>
> *~ Anonymous*

> **"History has demonstrated that the most notable winners usually encountered heart breaking obstacles before they triumphed."**
>
> *~B.C. Forbes*

2. **_PRINCIPAL OR PRINCIPLE PROBLEMS?_** So what is the problem? Could it be that no matter what you do, it's never quite enough? Is it useless to try to reason with him? You say you just can't please her? You think he's never satisfied? She takes all the credit for your accomplishments? He gives you no recognition. He won't admit mistakes? You've caught her in lies? He won't help you? She is inappreciative of your hard work? He is mean-spirited? She has favorites and it's obvious? He is vindictive? We first must decide if it is the *person*, the *principle*, or perhaps a bit of both?

> **"In matters of style, swim with the current;**
> **in matters of principle, stand like a rock."**
> *~ Thomas Jefferson*

Solutions some see:

➢ Get a different boss. (Good luck!)

➢ Change jobs. (Probably not.)

➢ Change your boss. (Yea, Right.)

➢ Ignore him (Don't think so.)

➢ Avoid her. (Works for awhile.)

➢ Gripe and complain until your foul attitude ensures the message is obvious. (Ummmm…How do you spell guillotine?)

> **"Those who complain about the way the ball bounces are usually**
> **the ones who dropped it."**
> *~ Anonymous*

Some solutions I see:

➢ Pray *about* what is hurting you but especially _for the person_ who is hurting you. (I don't take credit for this suggestion, by the way, check out Luke 6:28.)

➢ Always remember, he or she is your boss and you either work the way the boss wants, like it or not, *or leave.*

Never insult an alligator until after you have crossed the river.
~ Cordel Hull

➤ Learn your boss's schedule and moods. Figure out what time of day is best for conversation and then remember that the real art of conversation is not only to **"…say the right thing at the right time but also to leave unspoken the wrong thing at the tempting moment."**
~ Ben Franklin

➤ Learn your own moods. Figure out what time of day is best for you to approach your boss. Some of us are morning people; others of us function better in the afternoon. If your wick is lit at both ends, the earlier you instigate conversation, the more successful the outcome. On the opposite end of that spectrum, if you are grumpy and cranky first thing in the morning and don't really start running on all four cylinders until after you've had some lunch, then afternoon is, without a doubt, your best time to approach all issues that need attention.

➤ If your Principal is a talker and monopolizes your time, schedule appointments during your break time so you have a limited amount of time to be a captive audience.

➤ If you are concerned about being rushed when presenting to your boss, it is better to meet with him or her outside of school hours so your time together isn't structured around responsibilities to your students.

➤ Choose your moments and choose your battles.

➤ Endlessly prove that you are responsible, professional, and a master teacher in *everything* you do.

➤ Listen – with an open mind and an understanding heart.

**"It is the mark of an educated mind
to be able to entertain a thought without accepting it."**
~ Aristotle

➤ Be wise.

**"The difference between a smart person and a wise person is
that a smart person knows what to say and a wise person knows
whether or not to say it."**
~ Quote found on the wall of a recreation center office in Berkeley, California

➢ Be brave. Stand your ground on issues you're not able to compromise, but control your temper. People admire non-threatening strength.

"Courage is fear that has said it's prayers."
~ Dorothy Bernard

➢ Be smart. Once it's said, you can't take it back. Don't let your mouth move as much as your thoughts.

➢ Face it…you will not change your Principal. You can, however, change the way *you* look at the situation that seems to be the obstacle.

"Every obstacle presents an opportunity."
~ Jack Canfield

➢ You may disagree; you may even say so, but avoid being disrespectful. A word of caution: It is easy to get in the <u>habit</u> of agreeing to be disagreeable.

➢ Smile all the time…well, as much as possible. The *absence* of a constant smile can speak louder than words.

➢ Avoid confrontations; say that you value his/her opinion but that you would like to share yours. Making certain your boss knows you value his or her opinion may build or patch a relationship.

➢ Ask for your boss's advice. Ask for suggestions on how to improve your work.

➢ Invite your boss to your classroom…*often*. Send both verbal and written invitations. Ask for your boss' impressions of the visit. The more your Principal is in your room, sees your work and the kids' success, the more his or her respect for you will grow. (That's the theory, anyway.)

➢ Give him or her reports on your progress. Include student successes plus your own personal musical, professional, and educational accomplishments.

➢ Admit your mistakes and explain how you've learned from them.

➢ Continue your education! The more you learn, the more you understand, the more you can substantiate your beliefs, and respect your boss' perspective.

➢ Resign yourself, *simply to endure.*

"Hold yourself responsible for a higher standard than anyone else expects of you."
~ Henry Ward Beecher

"Those who make the worst use of their time complain the most of it's shortness."
~ Jean De La Bruyère

"Nearly all men can stand adversity, but if you want to test a man's character, give him power."
~ Abraham Lincoln

"What you are speaks so loudly that I can't hear what you say you are."
~ Ralph Waldo Emerson

"They say God only gives you what He knows you can handle... I just hope He doesn't have me confused with someone else!"
~ Anonymous

"Giving up or giving in doesn't always mean you are weak, sometimes it means that you were strong enough to let go."
~ Anonymous

"It is sheer waste of time to imagine what I would do if things were different. They are not different."
~ Dr. Frank Crane

"Learn to write your hurts in the sand and carve your blessings into stone."
~ Gladiator

"Some cause happiness wherever they go; others,
whenever they go."
~ *Oscar Wilde*

"Intelligence is when you spot the flaw in your boss' reasoning.
Wisdom is when you refrain from pointing it out."
~ *James Dent*

After the game, the king and the pawn go into the same box.
~ *Italian Proverb*

Turn your wounds into wisdom.
~ *Oprah Winfrey*

"You can easily judge the character of a man by how he treats a
person who can do nothing for him."
~ *Malcolm Forbes*

"You can easily judge the character of a man by how he treats
the waiter or waitress."
~ *Anonymous*

"God grant me the serenity to accept the people I cannot
change, the courage to change the one I can, and the
wisdom to know… IT'S ME."
~ *adapted version of the Serenity Prayer*

3. ___HEY YOU WITH THE HAIR!___ Learning all your students' names
can be quite a challenge, especially for those of us who teach every
kid in the entire school. Trying to manage behavior or discipline
without knowing names, can be one of the prime instigators of major
crankiness for any teacher, rookie, or veteran. I used to be fairly
decent at remembering what to call every little person, but as I grow
older, for some reason I have to blunder through "Jeremy, Jared, Josh,
Jordan, Jake, Jason, Jonathan, James, Jeron, and Jamal" before I can
finally get out "Justin." By then, I've completely forgotten why I was
calling on him in the first place!

I've had an Emily in class for five years. Now, along comes a Kindergartner who is a spitten' image of Emily – and her not being an Emily absolutely messes with my brain! I must say...*her parents just named her wrong.* Her name is not Emily, it's Hannah! No matter how hard I juggle my thinking prior to calling on her, I have yet to call her the right name. Worse than that, I have a third grader named Harmony and even though I wrestle with it every single time before I say her name, I still call her *Melody!* Wait...maybe it *is* Melody and I call her Harmony. Argh!

Just out of sheer necessity to accommodate my Alzheimer-ish thinking, I've figured out several TRICKS FOR KIDS to introduce themselves and help me remember the names that their parents anguished over for nine long, anxious months, trying to decide on the perfect title for their little sweetie. (Just between you and me, though, Hannah's mommy and daddy messed up!)

➢ **Yes to a Yearbook.** You can connect a name to those little angelic faces if you have a school yearbook on hand. I actually use it quite a bit. It really helps refresh my ailing memory at the beginning of the year and after a long vacation. I also send one home with my student teachers so they can study and start matching names with faces. Granted, they're a year behind and the kids are usually in different classes, but it's the face-to-name matching that's most beneficial.

➢ **Itemized Intros**. Sequencing or patterning are two skills students work on in every core curriculum class. Here's one thing we can do to support those skills and integrate learning while helping ourselves not have to say, "*...you with the red shirt!*" Before a beanbag musical activity, explain and model: "*As soon as you catch the beanbag, say your name in a loud voice, spin around, and fall down.*" Or, depending on the age, extend the itemized directions: "*As soon as you catch the beanbag, say your name in a loud voice, say your name in a whisper voice, spin around, and fall down.*" Or, "*As soon as you catch the beanbag, toss it in the air, say your name in a loud voice, say your name in a whisper voice, spin around one time, and fall down.*" You can continue increasing the length of the sequence to stretch the ability of the kids. You'll find that a three-part sequence (say your name, spin, fall) is quite a challenge for most Kindergartners until they've practiced it awhile. You can add rhythms, location changes, sound effects, jumps, handshakes, sing a phrase, slap your knee, make the top of your head touch the floor, make a goofy face, or just about anything to the sequences. This adds fun, increases their heart rate, wakes up sleepy heads, forces concentration, is appropriate for all ages, and is a great way to review names. Asking students to stand up until they've had their turn tends to make it much easier for you to keep track of who has had a chance at the game. (This is a particularly perfect warm up activity on the day of your unscheduled observation when your nerves are helping you struggle to remember everyone's name!)

➢ **Dynamic Difference.** Quickly go around the room asking students to say their name – focusing on saying it with different dynamic levels. First time, everyone may say it fortissimo, then forte, and eventually to pianissimo (without whispering.) You may tell the students which dynamic marking to use, either in English or Italian (eventually, both), or you can show the symbol and they not only have to process it's meaning but how to say their name in that way.

➢ **Silly Sounds**. *"When I point at you, please say your first name."* Then you repeat the student's name in a different voice. (high, low, screechy, with an accent, with vibrato, slow motion, really fast, staccato, glissando, growl, monotone, whisper, giggling, pitched, whiney, baby style, holding your nose, tapping your lips – just be silly and creative). Next, invite the student to echo the silly way you said his/her name. You'll be surprised at how many kids have never experimented with making silly noises.

➢ **Point and Pronounce**. The most difficult names for me to remember are the new students and, for some reason, the boys whose names begin with the letter J. I ask all of them to point to themselves and say their name every single time they see me outside of the music room. I do the same. It typically takes less than a week for me to get the *new names*, but I still go through all the J-names, in spite of the hall TRICK. (There must be a moral to this story.)

➢ **Willowby Walloby Woo who?** Willowby Walloby Woo is a cute song where everyone begins standing....one at a time, they drop to the ground at the end of the verse and point to the next person.

The lyrics: Willowby Walloby Woo – an elephant sat on you (point) Willowby Walloby Webbie – an elephant sat on Debbie (fall down with glissando.) I heard it, learned it, use it all the time, but have no idea where to help you find it. Sorry. At least you know the title so you can keep your eyes open for it!

4. *RIGHT-GUARD? GOOD PROTECTION!* When you are caught off guard and presented with an unscheduled conference, new information, or a request to do something, **ask for time** to review the situation or document and to prepare a response if necessary. Spur-of-the-moment decisions, haphazard responses, pressure-laden acceptances, peer pressure, administrative coercion, and all other unprepared reactions are not good for you or your career. Ask for time. Take time to prepare. You will be glad you did.

> **"It is better to remain silent and be thought a fool than to open one's mouth and remove all doubt."**
> *~ Voltaire*

5. *EVERYTHING'S UP-TO-DATE IN KANSAS CITY!* **Keep a calendar** and include all the meetings you attend, conferences you are involved with, programs you perform, performances your students give, extra rehearsals you hold, parties you're invited to, birthdays you remembered, appointments you made, appointments you've cancelled, doctor visits, absences, test days, concert dates, field trips, assemblies, everything that makes your year YOUR year! Then, save your calendars! Save them year after year. Put them in their own little file folder and don't throw any of them away! You should probably condense information to only one per year if you keep different information in different calendars - but please save them! They can be a wealth of information, a great resource, and a very motivating look at the you you were and the you you've become. You will be amazed at all you have accomplished and it will be very satisfying!

6. *LESSON PLAN BOOK:* There are many different styles, shapes, and formats of lesson plan books you can purchase, but I have found that if I spend a little time with my trusty ol' ruler and pencil, I can design one that suits my purposes more than any on the market...and I make it on plain ol' typing paper. The best part though, I've yet to mention! I fill in my schedule, complete with classroom teachers' names, class, recess, break, and lunch times, do a front/back copy on the copy machine, punch some holes in it, stick it in a three-ring notebook, and

I have my own personalized plan book with the entire year completed. I never have to write my schedule again - until next year! It takes a little extra time and effort at the beginning of the year, but in the long run, it's an awesome time-saver!

7. *I HAVE NOT YET BEGUN TO PROCRASTINATE.* Don't be efficient and enter your class lists into your grade book right at the beginning of school. Give it a few days or class times until the late enrollee's arrive and receive placement, kids are switched to other classrooms, and kids drop. It really does settle in a little bit after the first couple of weeks. Then, enter your names and your alphabetical order will last a little longer than it ordinarily would if you did it as soon as you get the lists. Plus, your grade book will look much neater. Er...umm...can you tell I am speaking from experience?

8. *ANNOYING SOUNDS:* Most people would assume that a musician would love having background music playing during test time – to soothe and ease the anxiety. However, take it from someone who loves music, but *hates background music*; conversation and concentration for *me*, don't mix well with compositions! Music playing while I'm trying to concentrate is the single most distracting thing imaginable. I would much rather people be talking while I'm trying to test than have music playing. So...just keep this in mind, particularly if you are one who enjoys a little Mozart while you work: Not everybody does...so use background and mood music sparingly...or provide ear plugs. ☺

9. *MUSICAL MONOTONY:* When students are forced to repeat something to polish it or to master the lyrics, it can get really boring and the kids will shut down, quit thinking about it, and your rehearsal value disintegrates. The younger the student, the more obvious it becomes. Rather than letting that happen, let your kids play the tambourine or other rhythm instruments to different patterns in the song. Or...have them sing it facing different directions, while holding on to their tongues, while rubbing their throats fast – to sound like a munchkin, let them spin in circles while they sing, or sing it *staccato* or "robot style." You could have them smash their lips together with their fingers and say the words or tell them to sing it upside down – and just see how they follow that directive! Ask them to jump to the steady beat while they sing the lyrics, or let them change positions for each phrase or verse – your choice. Turn repetition into fun and

memories by being silly. As ironic as it may seem, you will get much more accomplished.

10. ***MEET 'EM!*** Greet your students at the door every single time they come to see you. Your smile, a touch, a pat on the back, and a welcome can start every class time on a positive note! The times when I can't be there for some reason – like I'm working on the last few words of an email I need to shoot off before class begins, has become a game. This typically happens only with the same classes – because it's the one that comes to me right at the end of my plan time, so they've kinda caught on to our "game." They sneak in, I keep working – acting like I don't see them or know they're entering my room. (Exactly like the receptionist at my doctor's office!) Because they're little second graders, this works beautifully – it'd totally bomb probably, if it were fifth graders. Anyway, they sit down and don't make a peep – believing they've fooled the 'ol gray mare into not realizing they're there. When I've completed my quick, last second task, I exaggerate my surprise, jump like they've scared me to death, and gasp that they'd come in and I didn't even know they were there! They burst into giggles just because of the anticipation of my reaction – so my lack of greeting at the door upon entering is made up with the silliness of our "game."

11. ***HUMOR – FUNNY HOW IT WORKS!*** Humor is an awesome de-stressor, no matter what the situation. Don't take yourself or music too seriously. Smile – put a sparkle in your eyes. Put a smile on someone else's face by sharing a joke or silly story. Notice new hair styles, new glasses, new shoes....If you don't have a natural sense of humor, grab a joke book and offer a joke of the day. Kids love corny stuff like that! I even stick ridiculous questions in the middle of a test or make one of my multiple-choice answers completely absurd. It's a nice way to break test-taking tension for some. I have to admit, though, I've had students mark the completely absurd answer as the correct answer. That's the point where I am the one who feels completely absurd and stressed! (Not really.)

12. ***SIESTA TIME!*** The people of Mexico had a great idea with their siesta tradition. Afternoon has a way of bringing on sleepiness, boredom, and an overwhelming urge to take a nap. Full tummies, warm rooms, and having had to absorb information all day long has a very real affect on our kids' ability to learn! Knowing this siesta-yearning

is inevitable, and knowing that a siesta is not the typical way America deals with this feeling, afternoon teaching requires much more energy from us, more activity and movement for the kids. It's so much harder to concentrate when you're sleepy – so movement wakes 'em up, gets their hearts beating faster, and the blood circulating, again. It also has a way of momentarily distracting their thoughts of getting to go home soon. Don't be surprised if they're droopy – just get 'em moving. I tell them, "*It's time to de-droop!*" (One of my Kindergartners came up to me after I said that and whined, "*But Mrs. Gray, I don't have to poop!)*

13. ***DO IT LIKE THEY DO IT!*** Learn to print exactly the way your Kindergarten through second graders are learning so whenever you write for them, they see exactly the same kind of printing in music as they see in class. The same goes for cursive. This is hard because by the time we're our age, we have created some personal writing habits that are, more than likely, not the official way to make certain letters. Go to your third grade classroom – or whatever grade introduces cursive, and find out how to make all the letters, both upper and lower case – then use that when writing for third graders and older.

14. ***METHODICAL MECHANICS.*** Anytime I have a writing assignment planned, I explain the assignment *first*…then indicate that I've placed the pencils on the file cabinet on one side of the room, the slates are on the shelf beneath the clock along the opposite wall, and the paper on the piano by the chalkboard. I ask them to retrieve all three but to begin collecting materials at the spot that is closest to them. This TRICK keeps everyone from clogging up, all at once, in the same place or trying to be the first to get a "good pencil." It offers them a little more freedom and tends to disperse the crowd so things tend to move more quickly.

15. ***CLEARLY UNCLEAR!*** How we say it can make or break our instruction time. Do not tell your students they will be working in groups, with a partner, or moving to a new location until *after* you've thoroughly explained your intentions and given your instructions! Otherwise, you will find yourself wondering what happened because they *will*, upon hearing they will not be working alone, instantaneously wallow into a frenzy of friend-finding. You will become utterly frustrated with them because they're not listening to you and the whole

fun idea resembles a five-year-olds' birthday party with 25 five-year-old guests!

In actuality, it's the teacher's fault that they began searching for the perfect teammate, partner, or place to sit before knowing what to do. For example, if you say, *"Stand up when I point to you."* All they are going to hear is *"stand up."* They will be clueless to everything else you may mutter, yell, or put in neon lights. Instead, say, *"When I point to you, stand up."* Another perfect example is, rather than utter the words, *"Get a partner and list five instruments in the string family...."* say, *"Think of five instruments in the string family...now tell a partner what they are."* It seems so simple, but I still get irritated with <u>myself</u> because I get my instructions out of sequence, lose their attention, and the lesson plan has to be salvaged instead of it going smoothly, like it would have had I been more careful when wording my instructions. Sometimes it's not the sequence but *the way we say something* that complicates the lesson!

Let me share with you about the time I told my fifth graders to *"Take out VOICEMAIL MADNESS "* just like I'd heard all through high school and college choir. What I didn't realize until I heard all the three-ring binders snapping open, was that they were literally taking the music out of the notebook! I just intended for them to open it but I didn't say that! I said, *"Take out...."* Little people take the things you say and do so literally. If you tell your Kindergarten class to, *"Do what I do"* during a Fingerplay and you get an itch, don't be surprised when 20 little mimics scratch their itch right along with you. Be careful what and where you scratch!

One of the songs we were singing had the words, *"spin around – touch the ground."* I cracked up when I saw little Devin back there by the door, perfectly positioned in his personal space, working as diligently as any five year old could possibly work, spinning in circles, and ***spitting all over the carpet!*** I stopped the music and asked him what he was doing. He answered, *"It said spit around – touch the ground."* Clearly unclear! ☺

16. <u>***HOLIDAY HYPE***</u> I let the holidays help me with my lesson planning. Use them every chance you get to supplement your song repertoire! You can add to the big celebration days of Halloween, Thanksgiving, Christmas, Chanukah, Kwanzaa, Valentine's Day, and Easter with President's Day, Groundhog s Day, St. Patrick's Day, and Columbus Day. It's so easy for special days to sneak up on us, especially if we only see students once a week – so plan ahead. SNIGGLES,

SQUIRRELS, and CHICKEN POX by Jackie Weisman is a super fun additional resource for nearly all of these holidays! Sometimes, I have the kids write their own lyrics to a familiar song, building a new song with a holiday theme. Other times, rather than teaching lyrics to a song for a holiday, I teach a dance – like an Irish Jig and the Hora. http://www.students.m.csbsju.edu/mkbrooks/Social%20Studies/horadanceresources.htm

17. *SAY IT AGAIN SAM!* Repetition and recall are incredibly efficient ways to store information inside a brain. This is a fun way to review, recall, and repeat after the kids have been sitting and listening to you introduce a concept. They're getting fidgety but you're not quite finished. Say, in a syncopated rhythm, *"Repeat after me, 'syncopation.'"* Usually, they will dutifully echo. Then say, *"Say the word 'syncopation' five times, touching one fingertip at a time to a friend's fingertips."* The first time you try it, you may have to model students assuming the high-five position, but instead of slapping hands, they touch thumb-to-thumb, index-to-index, etc. until all five fingertips are touching, one touch each time they repeat the word. With each touch, they both say *"syncopation."* Then have them rotate to someone else and tell that person what syncopation means! You can extend that with the older students by having them "play" the word "syncopation" with a syncopated rhythm on their partner's fingertips. (Starting with the thumbs touching thumbs on the *long* first syllable, SYN, then the index fingertips touch on the *short* CO, the middle fingers touch on a *long* PAY and, finally, the ring fingers meet on a *short* SHUN.) Search for various other ways to extend your lessons this way. It gets kids moving and thinking. If you do "social" activities like this once in awhile, they are sure to respond weird for you, but if you include them in their regular activities, it eventually becomes customary and they don't go whack when you try new "social" TRICKS.

18. *IT THEMES THEY THIT TOO LONG* (Don't think tho hard – jutht thay it.) While listening to a piece, give them something to listen for and they'll be better listeners. You'll probably still have to get after Jeremy, uh - Jered, no - Josh, I mean - Jordan, er-Jake, ooo is it Jason, mmm - Jonathan, James, Jamal, I mean – Justin, but it can help the majority of the listeners. Let me share an example with you. After I've talked about Dvorak's NEW WORLD SYMPHONY, I play and sing the theme, then play the recording just long enough for them to hear the theme. They are then instructed to sit quietly on the

floor and listen for the theme. As soon as they hear it, they are to stand up and move – making their movements match the slow, *legato* sound. They should sit down again when they no longer recognize the familiar theme. It is fun to use a variety of musical styles and tempos so their movements are as different as the sounds they hear. I wouldn't do more than one exercise like this per class period – but doing one each time they come in would be ideal. Please don't expect little people to sit through anything for very long! Even for fourth and fifth graders, anything longer than five or six minutes should probably be accompanied by movement. They'll start squirming and talking which will force a reaction from you that you and the kids would be better off not having to face. I'm not saying they *can't* sit still that long…I'm saying they shouldn't *have* to in a classroom situation where learning and having fun is the key to a successful, entertaining, and memorable experience!

19. ***THIS IS SOME GOOD STUFF!*** Develop and extend lessons by sneaking information in about tempos, styles, cultures, registers, dynamics, timbre, etc. in <u>every single song</u> you teach! The majority of teaching methods introduce *songs that support a concept.* For example, they find every possible age-appropriate song that is *legato* and place it in a chapter about *legato* music. Rather than doing that, I incorporate <u>*every possible concept into every song*</u> I teach. It's kind of a back door approach, I guess, but it works like a charm. I introduce the song as written, but once learned, students then sing it *staccato, legato, fortissimo, pianissimo* and every volume in between; in a major key and a minor key, with a steady beat and *rubato*. With this "in-the-back-door method," the student learns to recognize the differences and effects on any song. The song is the "control group" song, if you will…and incorporating the various concepts to the song are the variables. When exercised regularly and accompanying vocabulary is used consistently, concepts become every day terminology, familiar, and mastered far better than when introduced in a unit study, then not used again until you happen on to it, again. You can teach form in each song by assigning actions to the introduction, interlude, and ending. Then ask students to move a particular way on the A section of the song and to move another way on the B section - freezing in their personal spaces when the music stops. You can also add rhythm sticks or instruments to play while they move to the different styles and tempos of music, all the while playing along with the steady beat. It is fun and challenging for you, too, to see how many concepts you can

attach to every single piece of music you teach. It becomes so obvious and clear in their minds that it's possible for all of these musical terms to apply to every song in music! This is your next step, by the way, to Variations on a Theme!

Even if there is no possible way to MAKE a song demonstrate a concept, use it in your lesson, anyway. For instance, let's say the recording has no interlude – rather than omitting the opportunity to use that term, use that particular word by saying, *"Notice that there is no interlude in this song,"* or *"…can anyone tell me what was missing between the verse and the chorus of that piece?"*

20. ***TRANSITION TRANSFORMATION:*** Be accountable for transition time. I was taught by my high school English teacher, when writing, to repeat a "theme word" from the previous paragraph in the first sentence of the next paragraph in order to make a strong, easy-flowing transition. I concentrate on applying that same TRICK to my music class transitions. For example, if we are talking about *instrument timbre* and the kids are seated, my next concern is to get them up and moving as soon as possible, so we might do a movement activity from John Jacobson's, HOP TIL YOU DROP. Rather than just plunking in a new activity, I think about transition or segue. The goal is to tie their thoughts together; perhaps by repeating a word from the last concept builder – again in the new, so I might say, *"Listen to the timbre while you dance so you can tell me what instruments you hear in this recording."* (I could have said, *"While you dance, listen to the timbre…"* but I chose the other way around so they're thinking about listening first – the dancing will take care of itself. When they listen, they don't have to think much about dancing but when they're dancing, they don't automatically concentrate on listening. Plus, had I said the word dance, first, they probably never would have heard me say *listen* or *timbre*.) The suggestions for better writing from English class have helped me to do a better job transitioning my kids from one lesson section to another. Give it try – you'll get better at it the more you concentrate and practice.

21. ***IT'S PUZZLING.*** I created a modified word-search bulletin board to help trigger reminders of all the concepts I want to remember to include with each song. I have the words: TEMPO in one color with the defining words FAST and SLOW in a contrasting color. The T of TEMPO is the **T** of FAST, the O of TEMP**O** is the O of SLOW. I try to do the same thing with every concept word. PITCH has the

108

words HIGH and LOW above and below it. DYNAMICS has the
words LOUD and SOFT next to it, with **D** of LOU**D** being the **D**
of **DYNAMICS**, and the **S** of SOFT being the S of DYNAMIC**S**.
The word FORM has the accompanying words INTRODUCTION,
INTERLUDE, ENDING, VERSE, CHORUS, A, AB, ABA, and
ABC in the same vicinity to help students make term and definition
associations. Having those words on the wall right in front of *me*, not
only keeps them in the students' minds eye and in a reference place for
them, it reminds me constantly of what *I* must make sure I include in
every piece!

<pre>
          L O U D
              Y
              N
              A
              M
              I
              C
          S O F T
</pre>

22. *VARIATIONS ON A THEME BY DEBINNINI.* Another way
I incorporate concepts with a song is practiced every time we sing
HAPPY BIRTHDAY. We sing it in different styles: <u>fourth-grade</u>
<u>style</u> (or whatever grade they're in – and it just means sing normally,)
<u>country style</u> with syncopated *ostinato* (requires a quarter rest between
the words "*Birthday*" and "*to you*"), <u>baby style</u> (high vocal register),
<u>monster style</u> (minor key), <u>robot style</u> (staccato & teacher directed
when to begin next phrase), <u>underwater style</u> (finger rubbing up and
down on lips), <u>Marching style, Munchkin style</u> (fingers rubbing on
their neck – which has no intrinsic value other than fun), <u>Speedy</u>
<u>Gonzalez style </u>(fast or *presto* tempo, of course), <u>Slug style</u> (*largo*),
<u>Kitty style</u> (meow), and I'd be remiss if I left out <u>opera style</u> (sustained
and *legato* with *vibrato*). This is fun and it is a great lead-in or
reinforcer when introducing or discussing style, theme, vocabulary,
and variation! These are awesome to refer back to when introducing
minor key (monster style), *staccato* (robot style), *vibrato* (opera style),
etc. because it is very familiar and they have actually USED the term
in action! The key to mastery is repetition – or...I prefer the more
contemporary term, ***recycling***!

23. _CONNECT THEIR CONNECTORS!_ Students relate to things so much quicker if they can tie them to something familiar. There are many examples so I won't be able to give you a surplus of illustrations. When talking about the clarinet – most will remember it because that's what Squidward in Sponge Bob Square Pants plays! *"Fill in the blank: Angels play _____."* (Yep, they'll get it. They'll say baseball, probably.) Use the connection to help them! When helping to remember vocabulary words, give visual cues for each syllable. As you review, you can gradually eliminate cues, first by not saying each syllable with the students, then by just showing the visual cues, next, by showing only the first of the segment of cues, and eventually by not offering any help at all. I try to use this trick for every word possible, but it takes some out-of-the-box thinking and a willingness to be perceived as "totally weird."

> **COME-POSE-HER:** a person who writes music. COME = hand upside down – palm up, index finger straight, bending, then straight . POSE = strike a pose like a model or statue. HER = point to a girl.

> **TIME SIGNATURE:** TIME = point to your wrist-watch area on your arm. SIGNATURE = mime signing your name in the air or on your hand.

> **PIZZA-CAUGHT-TOE:** to pluck a stringed instrument with a finger, making a light *staccato* sound. *"What do you order from Dominoes or Godfathers?_____* *"What is the past tense for catch?"_____* *" What is at the end of your foot?"_____* pizza + caught + toe

> **TIM-PAN-KNEE:** A large, brass or copper, kettle-shaped percussion instrument that can be tuned. *"I have a little turtle. His name is tiny _____."* *" The little boy who will never grow up is named Peter _____"* Point to your knee. Tim + pan + knee

24. _TAPE ON TAPE._ This dates me, I know…but…just in case you have a collection of oldies…anytime I purchase an audio tape, I always **cover the title and song titles with clear tape**. Thumb oils will eventually rub off the print and then the cassette becomes a mystery tape with no title and no song list on it – this makes for an interesting lesson. Having no clue what tape you have is definitely an obstacle rather than an asset! You'll save yourself frustration, stress, and tons of time by not having to search for each tune.

25. ___SAY WHAT?___   Speaking of saving things...I have a file called **MEETING MORSELS**. Every single piece of paper, including agendas, napkin notes, and personal doodle droppings, of every meeting, inservice, or conference I attend is held captive within this file. You can purge the file once a year if you're so inclined...but often times, those little notes can become great, insightful quotes, thoughts, or information fragments for when you're nominated for Outstanding Educator, Disney Teacher of the Year, or tackling that National Board Certification and need words and ideas for answering the plethora of questions on the applications. They're also nice for when you decide to write a book!

26. ___DON'T THROW IT BACK.___   I also have a file simply called **KEEPERS**. After 20-something years, I now have a KEEPERS 2 file, too! This file is crammed full of inspirational stories I receive over the internet, magazine articles, quotes, brochures, cartoons, anything and everything that qualifies as a KEEPER. I refer to them often when asked to speak or write, but mostly, I open them and enjoy on a rainy day or a day I just feel blue and need a lift. Try it – you'll like it!

27. ___TIMELESS TREASURES.___ Save the notes you receive from students, friends, family, cohorts, and administrators. Save anything that is good and has to do with you as a teacher. Trust me....there will be days when you will need this personal cheering section to get you ready to face the day. That's just the way it is, sometimes. It will also help you remember why you are doing this job – wow! They become treasures of your heart!

28. ___CRUISE THE CLASSROOM___ While you are teaching, always **move around** the room and call on the people who are furthest from you whenever possible...or at least as often as you call on those who are close to you. That reinforces the distance and encourages them not to coagulate around your feet. If the kids think you always call on the kids closest, front and center, (and many of us tend to do that), they'll make sure they plant themselves right at your feet and if they do not want to be a participant, they will venture as far from you as humanly possible. If you use chairs or desks, this gives them proximity and a barrier, but if they're standing in the room, they'll gather as close as possible

unless you make an exaggerated, conscious, obvious effort to alternate calling on those farthest from you with those closer. Especially with Kindergarten, I find myself pointing to or calling on someone far from me and saying, *"You can answer, you're in a great personal space."* Instantly, all the little ones disperse into their personal spots so they, too, might be noticed.

Also, join in with the students when they move around the room – don't be a spectator…march along with them, skip, jog, hop, spin - - whatever it takes to be a part of the action and show them you're never too old to have fun and respond to music! *While you're moving, be a trout.* That's right, move upstream, against the "current." This little TRICK will help you keep a better eye on your "school." There are always a couple Beta fish placed together in the same class that, for their own sakes, need to be separated. If you see them, face to face, eye to eye, toe to toe, you can usually prevent conflict without uttering a word.

29. **_LADIES AND GENTLEMEN, I COME BEFORE YOU TO STAND BEHIND YOU TO TELL YOU SOMETHING I KNOW NOTHING ABOUT!_** Lately, there have been an inordinate number of research studies on the topic of **gender equity** and **gender bias**. Without delving into those findings, let me just suggest that you have a little mental chat with yourself each time you are planning to call on a student. Say to yourself, *"Self, last time, you called on a girl for the answer, this time, make sure you call on a boy"* and just keep alternating until you get the answer you want to hear. That's all I will say on this subject or I will have to cite references, include a bibliography, and do all those things that would clearly set me up for becoming yet another topic of research study or statistical data. I just have to stick to my own personal opinions, throw in an I've-heard-that comment and all is good.

When you do call on any student…don't let the silence between question and answer make you squirm. Be patient, give the child ample time to process and answer. If you see they're struggling or getting anxious, just ask, *"Would you like me to come back to you again later?"* That gets them off the hook, saves face, and helps build that relationship of trust, respect, and security.

30. **_THE GREAT PRETENDER._** Remember that respect thing we discussed earlier? A little suggestion on the **respect-while-talking-to-kids topic**. I've mentioned this once already, but it bears repeating.

I have found that a great way to manage what comes from my mouth during class is to imagine one of several things happening: the intercom is on and the entire office staff is hearing my every word, the Principal or Superintendent is observing my classroom, or there is a parent visiting music class. It is truly amazing how carefully I choose my words (that's "choose" although it really could be "CHEWS") and how calm and gentle-spirited I can be when some little feller is stomping on my last nerve...WITH CLEATS!!! Don't forget... intonation, body language, facial expression, and attitude can speak louder than words!

> **Let the words of my mouth and the meditation of my heart**
> **be acceptable in Your sight, O Lord...**
> **~ Psalm 19:14 *~NIV***

31. ***SING LOW, SWEET HARRIET.*** Increase your students' vocal range by repeating songs up or down a half step each time you sing them. This works especially well for the younger kids - for two reasons, they don't realize they're singing higher and secondly, their I, IV, V songs are *much easier* for a below-C-level pianist (like me) to transpose!

32. ***IT'S A HIT!*** We have so much fun singing warm-up exercises made from local radio station call letters and numbers! Not only does it make for a more entertaining vocal warm-up, it opens the door to discussions about musical styles, careers in music, technology, instrumentation, and all kinds of other radio-related information. An example of one I use is from a radio station I saw advertised on a billboard near Topeka, Kansas. We sing: WIBW on one pitch, UNISON, then move up and down by ½ step intervals. Eventually, we sing it in thirds, moving by ½ step. That then springboards me into yet another concept to teach: HARMONY. Use radio and television station jingles, commercials, and familiar sitcom theme songs for warm-up exercises, too!

33. ***THE LONE REARRANGER.*** Rearrange the room *every single time* the kids come to class. I am on an ABCD rotation, so every A day, if it's possible and appropriate, I move my piano to a different wall so they're facing a different direction when they sing. Sometimes I move my desk, a lamp, my "big chair," decorations, the record player, or something that will add change. I enjoy having a candle burning when the kids aren't there – to fill the room with a nice fragrance. I change that from time to time and they *always* notice that difference, too.

Expect them to comment and to be a little noisy when discovering the differences – but that's OK – they are learning and we have to not only tolerate but encourage curiosity and perception.

34. ***MIX IT UP!*** Keep your kids interested, on task, and entertained by alternating movement, activity, or standing with sitting and concept or song introduction. Change their positions from sitting down to standing up or up to down every four or five minutes. This time can be extended maybe a *little* with the older kids, but there are ways to keep them moving, too, and we should. For example, instead of them raising their hands to answer your questions, try one of these TRICKS:

➤ *"If you know what the form of this song is, stand on your chair."*

➤ *"If you can tell me what the next rehearsal number is, turn your chair upside down and stand on it."*

➤ *"If you can find the second ending, balance on one foot."*

➤ *"If you know who composed this song, lay down on your back."*

➤ *"If you remember what this symbol means, take off your shoes and put the toes of them against one of the walls."*

➤ *"If you can name the instrument family you're hearing, jump up and down."*

➤ *"If you remember the lyrics of the next phrase, spin around and then sit on the floor."*

➤ *"If you know the name of this note, jump up, spin around, and sit back down."*

➤ *"If you can tell me how to pronounce this word _____, turn your shirt around backwards."*

➤ *"If you said, 'one-ee-and-uh, two, three-and-uh, four-ee-and-uh' you were right. Walk backwards to a personal space, run in place until you count to twenty, spin around twice, touch the top of your head to the carpet, and then walk back here and sit down."*

Get the idea? Be creative when offering ways to indicate they know the answer to your question or reward them for answering correctly with some bizarre kind of movement . This not only gets them moving and breaks the doldrums that can hit, particularly when "woodshedding" on parts, but it also tends to keep them from yelling out the answers and to try harder when offering an answer.

35. ***YELL OUT YOUR ANSWERS!*** Honestly, more often than not, I ask a question and give them the directive to do something out-of-the-ordinary to show they know the answer. Then I quickly peruse the crowd, take inventory of who knows (or thinks they do) and who doesn't, then ask everyone doing the out-of-ordinary thing to answer the question at the same time. Sure…it's noisy and chaotic – but only for a few short seconds, then we settle back in to our working mode and accomplish some more learning. I used to be in a rut by insisting that kids always sat quietly and raise their hands to give an answer. Amen. Then I got de-rutified! It's much more fun for the kids and I don't stress out because someone blurts out their response without being called to answer! In fact, next time you ask a question, try one of these fun ways to get everyone involved in answering your discussion questions, *"Tell your neighbor the answer, then sit down on the floor back to back,"* or *"Take three giant leaps in three different directions, then tell the person standing closest to you your answer." "If you know the answer, stick out your tongue." "If you know the answer, balance on one foot and tap your head." "If you know the answer, touch someone's elbow with your shoulder."* You'll notice that even kids who normally refuse to get involved in answering questions, will ease into participating with fun, goofy activities like this. The kids who were clueless of the answer, might even hear better when a *bunch of people answer* than if only one person says it. They listen to rock music, remember? They're used to noise. ☺

36. ***LESSON-PLANNING LESSON:*** Bombard their brains visually, aurally, and kinesthetically. Search for brain "inlets" where information can enter with the least amount of resistance for the most amount of children. Just like me, many students have trouble comprehending verbal directions and have difficulty with short and/or long term memory. These delays often hamper their ability for success with verbal expression, written expression, and following directions. Far too many of us teach primarily auditorily – meaning we talk more than we show or demonstrate. We may be leaving the struggling learners

behind by teaching this way. We can change that though, just by making certain that with every *verbal* directive or concept we include in our lesson, we provide the same information *in writing* for the visual learners. This is easy. Just write it on paper, point it out in the text or on the music, write it on the chalkboard, use the overhead projector, have it included in a bulletin board design, spell it with magnetic letters, or any way to make it visible and helpful. Also, for the little folks with receptive language delay and auditory processing problems, along with the visual aids, just speak slower, move closer, and give shorter sequences. Bi-lingual students and all others with auditory discrimination problems and special needs, *need our help, patience, compassion, and understanding* just like I needed help, patience, compassion, and understanding in Algebra, Geometry, Statistics, Trig, Calculus, Counter Point, and Composition classes! (That list was dramatically abbreviated - due to lack of space...oh yeah... and also because it's pretty self-incriminating and self-deprecating.) ☺

37. *SCANNING, SCANNING...* Anytime I introduce a new text book to the kids, I love to give them a few minutes or so to scan it and satisfy their curiosity, their eagerness to look at the illustrations, and their interest in seeing what songs are included. This opportunity dawned on me after thinking about what *I* naturally want to do the instant I pick up a new book. I figure if *I* like and take the time to flip through the pages to see what's inside, my kids would probably like having that same opportunity.

38. *ROUND AND ROUND WE GO, WHERE WE STOP, NOBODY KNOWS.* Scheduling is always a challenge – sometimes a nightmare, but thank heaven above, I don't ever have to do it! Our grade levels have different numbers of sections so a regular rotation of ABC doesn't work with four or five on a grade level and only three on another...so we've tossed around many different possibilities to see what works best. One **rotation** we have tried was Monday-Thursday SET schedule and our Fridays rotated from week to week. I used Fridays as **Music Ace** day, **FUN FRIDAY, FLASH BACK FRIDAY,** or sometimes I called it **RETRO FRIDAY.** Regardless of what we called it; they looked forward to it and had a great time. "Flash back" or "retro" just means we sing any song they remember ever learning in music class. Sometimes, we turn it into a contest to see who can think of the most songs. We even dig out entire musicals and perform them on retro Friday. It's so fun for a fifth grader to reach back to second

grade and sing a whole performance done when they were eight years old.

Another good activity for you if you have a similar single rotation day, is **Music Ace**. Music Ace is a computer program series teaching steady beat, rhythms, and a huge variety of good stuff. (If possible, invest in this program – you will have as much fun with it as your students.) I am not one of the fortunate ones who can afford to have a copy on each computer in the lab, but I do have it loaded onto my computer at my desk, so the kids, sitting in personal spaces right on the floor in front of the television monitor, each have a tennis ball they hold (not bounce) and hit the ground with the bouncing ball that's on the screen. (I am fortunate enough to have my computer screen hooked up to a larger TV screen so more students can view it.) I tell them, *"I'm watching for kids who can really bounce the ball on the steady beat and the ones I discover doing a great job will be the ones chosen to come to my computer and actually work the mouse or the space bar."* I have had tremendous success turning that into an all-class fun and learning time. They love to be student leaders, so almost all are motivated by the opportunity to come up and work the "master controls." It is a tremendous assessment tool, too. While they're tapping the beat or answering the questions, the teacher has the opportunity to evaluate their ability and being hands free, can easily record their progress.

39. <u>***DO THAT TO ME ONE MORE TIME, ONCE JUST ISN'T ENOUGH!***</u> Incidentally, you will notice that when you are giving every child a chance to do something special (and they get to do it by earning it with behavior, attention, or mastery), once they have had their turn, their focus wanders and they have a miniscule amount of motivation to continue paying attention or participating. They figure they've had their chance – why keep working? I avoid that by simply making certain that I choose at least one child who has already done it once, to do it again just because, *"Mindy is STILL doing a great job ____, so I'd like for her to come back up here again and try it another time. Don't give up just because you've already done it…you might be like Mindy and get chosen to do it again!"*

Let me share another little TRICK of encouragement that works well to eliminate pouting. This works most effectively when you have to remove instruments, game participation, manipulatives, beanbags or anything fun and special, from *at least two people* for not following instructions, and you get a POUTER! You'll find them in every grade level, but the littlest ones and the biggest ones seem to be the most well-versed pouters. ☺ Hopefully, only one of the two will be pouting so when the other accepts the mistake and continues to pay attention and participate, you can make a comment like, *"Jonathan, you have had such a good attitude! You haven't pouted and have done everything I've asked since you lost your beanbag! Why don't you go get another one – thanks for not being cranky or a poor sport."*

Usually, this will have some amazing strategic effects on your POUTER and other potential pouters. If not, let him pout – and do something not even planned, but extraordinarily fun, so you can say, *"You'll have to wait while we do this one since you didn't join us on the last activity."* I know…it's pretty brutal, manipulative, and sad to do that to them – especially when you want more than anything to let them join in…but I guarantee you, if there's an ***emotional element*** connected to the behavior or misbehavior, there's a better chance that the behavior won't happen again- at least not in the near future. Before feeling too sorry for them, remember they are the ones to make the choice to do whatever they did to lose the equipment in the first place.

Just a day or so ago, a new-to-our-school second grader came in begging to do a particular song. I explained that we would sure do it, but not until after we did something else first. He huffed and went over to the opposite side of the room, plopped down, buried his head and pouted the whole time. Instead of forcing him to join us, I just let him sit there in his huff. When he heard me play the introduction of the song he'd begged to do, he smiled and jumped up from his clump, ready to play the game song. In my most apologetic, sad-to-have-to-say-this voice, I told him he'd have to sit back down during the game song since he'd chosen not to participate in any of the other activities so far. Now…you tell me. Do you think he'll join in the next time or will he plop in his pout, once again?

40. ***IT'S HOW YA PLAY THE GAME.*** There are some songs and games that are designed to find a winner. That means they are also designed to establish losers. It is good if you can have something for your "losers" to do while the "winners" are being determined or you have an increasing number of students with nothing to do but get squirrelly. I'm thinking of chants like, DOWN ON THE BANKS OF THE HANKEY PANKEY or ONE POTATO, TWO POTATO, THREE POTATO FOUR, and songs like LONDON BRIDGE IS FALLING DOWN. Each time someone is "out" in an activity, I have that "out" kid start a new group and begin play again – along with the winners, just in a different area of the room. Another successful and fun thing I've tried was asking the "out" students to predict who they think will be the "winner" and then to go and stand behind their predicted champion. If their prediction proves false, then they are to move behind one of the other remaining players, making a "revised prediction." This game adds a game to the game – and helps develop vocabulary and terminology that is used in science and other subject areas. The words *predict, hypothesis, outcome, proof, revised,* and *results* are all science and math vocabulary builders.

41. ___*HAVING ONE OF THOSE DAYS*___ when the kids are gloomy, low-keyed and hard to wake-up? Pitch sagging? Interest plummeting? Energy deficient? Have the **kids remove their shoes** and place them next to the wall. (I join them, by the way.) Spend the remainder of the class time sock-footed. Trust me on this one, they'll perk up. Just remember to allow a few minutes at the end of class to get those shoes back on - especially with younger grades, 'cause **you are** going to have to tie a few laces and de-knot a few knots. Don't do it very often though, maybe once a semester, or the fun and novelty of it will wear off. Any TRICK like that used too much loses it's effectiveness.

42. ___*THERE WAS AN OLD WOMAN WHO LIVED IN A SHOE, SHE HAD SO MANY CHILDREN SHE DIDN'T KNOW WHAT TO DO!*___ Tying shoes, untying shoes, pinning on ribbons, removing pinned-on ribbons, etc. can be so time-consuming and attention hampering **when *you* have to be the one to do it for every child in the class.** Instead of heroically attempting to do it all yourself, use the helper/buddy method: *"See if your neighbor can help you tie your shoe."* Or *"If you can help your friend take off his ribbon, that would be great."* It seems so obvious, but when you have all these little people needing your attention and help, it is easy to be overwhelmed and not realize or remember that there are probably some capable helpers in the group. It also makes for a very positive experience for the helpers, so be sure to honor them for their good work.

43. ___*PULL OVER BUDDY!*___ Be sure your kids know to stop *next to the wall* to tie shoes or effect a repair on something. When kids are moving down the hall or around the room – the fastest way to form a catastrophe is for one of them to stop mid-stream to fix something. I

draw the analogy to cars on the highway. I ask: *"If your daddy needs to fix a flat, does he do it right in the middle of the lane? Where does he go? Why should we not just stop and do it right where we are, wherever we notice it?"* You should probably make this one of your concept lessons early in the year.

44. *BANANA SPLIT SPLIT.* This little TRICK works with your own kids as well as your students! Sometimes we split something in half when we have to share. I will use a PIXIE STIX as my example. Joey and Kevin are to share the treat. If Joey splits the PIXIE STIX in half, then KEVIN, the recipient of the other half, *gets to choose* which half he wants. (You split, I choose.) It's amazing how evenly something is broken or torn in half when the other person gets to do the choosing. (If I use food as a reinforcer, I like to use powdery PIXIE STIX rather than chewy candy or hard candy so I don't worry about someone choking.)

45. *DUST MAGNET.* If your chalkboards hold magnets, use round, flat magnets as music notes. Some of you may have permanent lines painted on your boards, but if not, use your staff writer to make the staff with chalk, then when the students are working at the board, rather than writing the notes and getting a chalky, dusty mess and having to re-draw the staff each time, just have them place the magnet "notes" on the correct line or space. My chalkboard is black and the only magnets I could find were black so I bought some googley eyes from the craft store and Super Glued them to the magnets so they were more visible. Plus, I added a, *"Somebody's watching you…"* note above the board covered with googley eyes as a little reminder to be respectful to others.

46. *STAFF STUFF.* It took me *years* to figure out why kids get confused with what I *thought* was a simple concept of identifying a note on the space or on a line. They kept doing it incorrectly and I kept trying to figure out why it was so complicated for them. *Finally*, with the help of a particularly bright first grader, it dawned on me that since they were in Kindergarten and learning to write, they have been shown and told to write their name *"on the line."* *"On the line"* in Kindergarten looks like <u>Debbie Gray</u>. In music, *"on the line"* looks like: ~~Debbie Gray.~~ Once I figured out the glitch that was confusing their sweet little minds, it was easy to fix. Now I show them what *"<u>on the line</u>"* looks like when they are writing words and letters and how it is different

when they are writing "~~on the line~~" with music notes. As soon as that is pointed out to them, the little light bulbs begin to click on, they are no longer confused, and the task becomes much easier for them.

47. ***LASER TAG*** Many times when using an overhead projector, I like to be at the piano playing the melodic line that is being shown as an example. Rather than walking back and forth between the screen, the piano, and the projector or standing beside the projector all the time, I use a laser pointer to guide us through an exercise. Lending it out to "experts" in class who can take over the well-supervised pointing responsibility while we are reading rhythms, adds incredible incentive to do well and prove it! Of course, check with your district guidelines; laser pointers are not allowed in some schools.

48. ***COLOR CODING CUSTOM FOR THE CRANIUM!*** There have been times when I needed to send an entire packet of papers home with students. Some papers in the collection were strictly informational, some required memorization or study, and some needed to be signed and returned. I use colored paper as indicators for these different requirements. This way, I can say, "*...let's go over the yellow sheet together, be careful to remember to let your mom and dad see this and help you study. The green sheet is a go ahead and keep it page just so you have the information at home. The red page reminds you to stop and have it signed by mom or dad.*" Instead of saying look for the page that looks like this (and hold it up), it's just easier to say, "*Turn to the hot pink page,*" or "*fold the orange page....*" You can use any associations with the colors, but I've sure found that whatever the color, whatever the topic, it helps immensely when little people are sorting through several pages of information!

49. ***COLORFUL CONNECTIONS:*** I have several fun and simple pieces of two-part music I like using as introductory songs to help the often-difficult transition from reading music out of the text book to an octavo that includes the written accompaniment. Because reading from a two-part piece with accompaniment can be *amazingly* confusing for newbies, I mark the girls' part with pink highlighter and the boys' part with blue. I'm not set on girls having to sing part one and guys always having to sing part two – I mix them up quite often, actually - but for the beginners' sake, I use this TRICK just to help <u>train their brain</u> and eyes to follow their own part from one line to the next. After learning a few songs with these colorful cues or prompts, I gradually wean

them off the highlighter help and onto music with no color to help them make connections.

When reading from an octavo, I also refer to the pattern a heart monitor makes with a flat line followed by a tent-shaped cone, followed by another flat line. After drawing it, I explain that this is exactly the way their eyes need to move when jumping from the words to the notes and back to the words. Training their eyes to move up and down as well as from left to right is something that takes verbal coaching and a picture model so they don't just look at the words when they sing.

50. ***PUNCH PURCHASE:*** Hopefully, you will be able to purchase a few office or desktop supplies sometime early in your career. One item you will use quite often is a three-hole punch. That's not news. *The news is…*don't waste your money, like I did, and buy a small, inexpensive one. *Order a heavy-duty punch* so you will be able to punch more than one or two sheets at a time. Awhile ago, I started putting my sheet music in three-ring notebooks for the kids. I'd spent a fortune, over the years, on regular cardboard choral folders and they just didn't last long enough to suit me, but the three-ring binders, so far, work nicely. The unfortunate thing is, my El cheap-o, three-hole punch won't punch through the multiple pages of an octavo, or when it does, it gets jammed! So, I *always* have to borrow one from someone smarter than I, who made a better punch purchase than ol' DG!

51. ***BOOK 'EM:*** I so wish someone had suggested this TRICK to me when I first started teaching, I would feel so much more organized and efficient had that happened. Buy yourself some standard three-ring notebooks and a three-hole punch. Label one for COMPUTER AND TECHNOLOGY, one should be for PRINCIPAL NOTES AND MEETING AGENDAS, one for MUSIC MEETINGS, one for saving all of your IN-SERVICE notes and handouts; label one for INSURANCE, CONTINUING EDUCATION, CAREER LADDER, CORRESPONDENCE, and one can be titled, DISCIPLINE LOG. I even have one called KEEPERS. This is the file where everything that does not fit into a category but is too good to chuck is kept. You will probably discover other categories that you would like to organize, but this is my list and it'll be a good starter for you.

52. ***RECYCLE.*** Sometimes, the music companies will send short excerpts from their new music for your ordering pleasure. Once you've listened

and extinguished the use of those **cassettes**, use them for copies. Just take Scotch tape and cover the square holes at the top, narrow edge of the cassette and you can record right over them. I use them mostly for copies that I send home with kids, for recordings of oral tests, to practice a solo with accompaniment, or for memorizing parts, etc.

More recently, they have been sending their samples on **CD's**. As you know, some CD's are CD-R which means they are recordable, but can't be erased or overwritten. Some are CD-RW which means they are rewritable and can be written on thousands of times. If you receive some that are reusable, recycle them and save yourself some money. If not – use them for decorations! CD's reflect light like a prism. When hung from the ceiling with clear fishing line or pinned to a bulletin board like wallpaper, you can add dimension and reflection to your room. I also use their excerpts as a teaching tool for concept examples of style, timbre, rhythm, rhyme, solo-duet-trio-quartet, musical form, major and minor key, expression, texture, dynamics, tempo, male/female/adult/child voices, accompaniment instruments, and many other teaching concepts.

53. *IS THAT RE-CORD OR RE-CORD?* Anytime we do listening assessments, I **record** what I say and play so when kids who are absent return to make it up, I have a **record** of it and can send them to the library, hallway, or even home with the taped recording and they can take the test with the exact same information their classmates received in the classroom. It is an awesome way to help our special-needs students, too. They can take the tape back to their self-contained classrooms and practice or complete, with the help of their Para-professional, for mastery. The tapes are also immensely helpful tools for the easily-distracted students who just do a better job indicating what they know when they are isolated from the commotion and distractions of the classroom.

54. *ORIGINAL OR CRISPY?* Every single time you make copies of lyrics, scripts, or a note to be sent home to a grade level or large group, always **file a hard copy of the original.** Sooner or later, you'll be so glad you did! It sounds so basic and obvious, but, I can't tell you how many times the original has gotten stacked with the stack and the stack got distributed, then someone came for a copy and the stack was gone and so were the copies. Computers help with this because the original is usually saved, but I still like to keep that hard copy on file – just in case my computer is down, something happens to the hard drive or the

server and I can't access it, or it's not booted up and I need a quick copy. It is also not entirely out of the realm of possibility that I'll crash and lose everything. Heaven forbid...but it happens. Unfortunately, that is experience talking, yet once again.

55. ***STASH THE CACHE.*** Since we mentioned the topic of computers **crashing**...I know you've had this preached to you over and over and over and over and over....but I'm going to write it one more time just to even out the "and over's." When you are doing any kind of word processing, SAVE after every few minutes. I have lost more important things than you or I can even imagine just because of electrical failures, power surges, hard drive virus attacks, server freezes, network demons, lightening strikes, and a variety of other plagues that seem to attack just as the final few words are finding their way to my fingers. Though *I'm* going to have to learn how to do this, I understand we can set our word processor to save automatically. (How cool is that?) Also, it's wise to copy valuable data to a diskette or CD so you will have a backup. If it's something *really* important (like a book), I send a copy to someone else, too. Just SAVE. OK...I'm finished with that little sermonette.

56. ***HANG AROUND UNTIL THEY'RE GONE!*** When you dismiss elementary students from after-school activities, it is imperative that you or another certified staff member stand with every child while waiting for their ride to pick them up! Make mental notes of who left with whom, who walked, who rode bicycles, who's transportation arrangements varied from usual – take notes if you need to – just make sure you can answer to anyone if asked about a particular student. This can be incredibly tricky if you're like me and have 75 kids leaving from choir at the same time; so I solicit the help of another teacher just to make sure all my kids are accounted for and have a safe departure. Two heads are better than one when it comes to remembering, explaining, detailing explanations, and witnessing, if necessary.

57. ***TRANSPORTING KIDS.*** Sometimes I take kids to grab an ice cream cone after school. I've learned the hard way, that even though I have a permission slip in my hands, trouble can happen. Now, I *make sure* I do three additional things before we ever leave the building.

> **First,** I have the student call and remind mom and dad, grandma, and grandpa – whoever they live with, that he/she is going to __

___ with Mrs.Gray, and will be home by ____. Mrs. Gray's cell phone number is: _____.

➤ **Second,** I make sure everyone in the office and our before-and-after-school day care providers know not only who is going with me but where we are going.

➤ **Third,** I make sure I have all contact numbers with me so I can reach someone in the event of an emergency. (What if someone plows into my car? What if the student should need medical attention? – Don't disregard anything. If it's possible, be prepared.)

All this caution stemmed from one disastrous experience when I took someone with me after school. Mom just forgot she'd given permission and when her child didn't get off the bus, she freaked. She called school and no one could help her, the classroom teacher knew, but she couldn't be reached. Before it was all said and done and I drove into the drive-way to drop him off a full ten minutes before I'd established, my Principal, Central Office, the district's Transportation department, *and the police* were involved. Everyone was innocent and had followed all appropriate procedures, but one thing you can't count on is forgetting; so....*don't forget...don't let them forget.*

58. ***TEACH SOCIAL SKILLS:*** Model what these *sound like* and *look like*: listening, sharing, encouraging, disagreeing appropriately, following instructions, not interrupting, contributing, ignoring distractions, offering help, asking for help, tattling vs. informing, complimenting, cooperating, asking permission, responding to teasing, accepting consequences, compromising, being honest, accepting responsibility, respecting others, reacting to failure, ignoring, and working with groups. Verbalize the responses you want to see and teach them what an appropriate-to-you response *looks* and *sounds* like. Then expect the best from them.

59. ***COLLECT CRITICAL CORRESPONDENCE!*** Save notes sent to you from parents. Even though you may remember or think you will remember all the details of the circumstances, it's still good to keep them on file in case you need them for future reference. Notes as seemingly insignificant as, "Susie will ride home with..." can be vital to your liability if Susie doesn't end up where she is supposed to and mom and dad have to know of her status when she left your custody.

60. ***LETTER TO THE EDITOR.*** I have made it a habit to have someone **proofread** every note I send home to a grade level. There is nothing much worse or more embarrassing for a teacher than having one of your notes returned with red marker, check marks, a sad face, or a grade at the top. Check your spelling, punctuation, content, dates, check *EVERYTHING!* Don't give anyone any ammo against you and don't embarrass yourself with an oversight! Believe me...someone out there is just waiting to pounce. Sometimes we anguish over how to say something "just right" so we don't offend, we worry about making sure we say everything we need to cover, and we want to be so positive, clear, and concise that we often can't see the forest for the trees. That is when you enlist the eyes and brain of a cohort and have them proofread your work. Take advantage of their distance from the topic, their education, and expertise so you continue to hold the respect you have worked so hard to earn from your students and their parents.

61. ***CHECK IT OUT!*** Anything I send home en mass I make sure my **Principal sees it and approves.** First, it is a respect thing - he or she will appreciate it. Secondly, it is just a good idea because your Principal has access to dates, times, building availability, etc. that can effect your plans; but mostly because you need to always keep your superior apprised of your plans.

62. ***DUPLICATES IN TRIPLICATE.*** Remember to **give a copy to your school secretary, nurse, and custodian.** They will be fielding calls about times and dates and need to be as well informed as you are about what is happening in the music room or on the music calendar! They will appreciate not having to search you down to get an answer for a parent regarding something pertaining to music.

63. ***WRITE ON!*** I seldom take the time to do written work in class, but there comes a time when it's the best way to get a precise reflection of student understanding. Anytime I assign written work and someone is absent, I **write the absentee's name on a sheet and return it to the folder.** After grading and recording everyone else's work, when I'm ready to return it, I have the not-yet-completed paper(s) right in front of me so I don't have to refer to my grade book and I don't forget to have the student(s) make it up. I do the same thing for **notes that go home.** Of course, I can't do this if I'm sending to an entire grade level (unless I have a volunteer aid who is willing to invest the time to write every name on every page) and, it's not necessary, but if I have notes that go home to a specific group, I write a name on a note for each individual. Then, when I pass them out and have one left over, I know exactly who to track down and put it in their little hands. Another way I make sure everyone receives a copy is by typing all the recipients names on the page, much like the To: ___, ___, ___, on an e-mail. After making copies, I highlight one name per sheet. It's one of those things that take a little extra time in the beginning, but it's a great insurance policy that everyone gets what they need!

64. ***GRAFFITI GRAY!*** When I am introducing a new song by rote, I write the lyrics on the board to use as my **cheat sheet**. I try to have the kids *facing me*, with their backs to my cheat sheet, so I have it right in front of me, but the kids aren't preoccupied with reading what it says. It keeps me from forgetting the words and it keeps me from having to look down at a book for reminders. Also, it's there when I'm ready to include the visual for them and let them brush up on their reading skills.

65. ***JUST HANGIN' AROUND.*** I place key **vocabulary words around the room** and then sing songs with new lyrics using them. (I use traditional construction paper words on bulletin boards, but I also use foam-cut magnet lettering and stick them to the drop ceiling metal dividers.) For example, The French Folk song, CHUMBARA (arranged by Dave and Jean Perry. *Sing Out Series* – Heritage Choral Series 15/1548H – Two part) is fun to sing the words "*minor key*" (while singing it in a minor key) "*major key*" (same), "*fast tempo*" (and sing it really fast – same with "*slow tempo*." "*Staccato*" and "*legato*" are great words that fit, too so you can practice the vocabulary words while singing what they mean. "*Sing high voice,*" "*sing low voice,*" "*vibrato,*" "*sing forte,* " "*crescendo,*" "*clear diction,*" "*whispering,*" and "*dynamics*" are also fun words to sing or say to that tune to stretch the reinforcement and recall. If you want and are not of a formal heart, add the dynamic marking "*piano*" and have the kids sing softly. It's a little outrageous when they realize that they're singing "*P P P P P P P P P Piano*" on the descending scale in the middle of the tune, but even the fifth graders get a chuckle out of it and I know they'll always remember the fun.

66. ***PARENTHETICAL PARENTING.*** When I first started teaching twenty-plus years ago, *parents had lots of kids. Today, kids have lots*

of parents. This relatively contemporary family component tends to affect us in more ways than you might imagine. Don't be surprised or disturbed when both parents request copies of report cards, papers, homework, daily grades, weekly reports, and *all* other school-to-home communication sent to them. This will mean you must remember to duplicate copies for their child(ren), remember to send those copies home with the kids, and mail a copy to the other parent.

Different last names and the name the parent prefers their child to use in a program, signed permission forms, attendance and transportation for before/after school activities, and conferences can all be affected by these family divisions - so just be aware. *Forgetting* to do as wished after being asked to accommodate the parents on all sides of a separation, divorce, and/or relationship...can mean big trouble for the *forgetter.* Trust me, *I haven't forgotten what I forgot* or *what I got for forgetting!*

67. <u>*BACH TO THE FUTURE.*</u> I have a **"MAIL BACHS"** in my room that provides a communication network for myself as well as those students who don't yet feel comfortable visiting directly one-on-one or have chosen to remain anonymous. Recently, I've extended the use of my MAIL BACHS to faculty and staff. Every day at lunch recess, two of my pre-appointed, responsible, extraordinary, fifth graders deliver the mail. Everyone knows that any correctly-addressed mail that is in the box will be delivered every day at noon. This saves me soooo much time and becomes a high point in the day for many students and staff throughout the building when mail arrives! It's a great time of day for deliveries, too, because all grades are either preparing to go to lunch or recess or returning from lunch or recess, so deliveries rarely interrupt learning. Having someone deliver mail gives me more time for writing more notes and other things I need to do. (Don't be too impressed or gagged-out, because I'm just like everyone else. When I am swamped, the amount and frequency of my notes don't change, but the volume and content definitely face some reduction!)

68. <u>*KETCHUM BEIN' GOOD!*</u>   On that same topic, but venturing from the mechanics of mail delivery for a minute or perhaps only a handful of seconds if you're a speed reader; if I have a child I predict I might *"get"* to contact parents about a concern, I <u>*always*</u> **write a complimentary note** addressed to parents, family, and friends about that child the second I can catch 'em being good. If that opportunity is non-existent, I make sure I write a note to his or her sibling. I do this as

soon as possible so that when mommy and daddy hear from me about their troubled child, it's not the first time they've heard from me and I've already made a positive contact with them *prior* to having to visit about problems. It's another relationship-strengthening opportunity and it's very beneficial to the recipient of your note. Sometimes, that sibling note and the attention the recipient receives from getting the note is all it takes for "wittle bwother" or "siwy sistuh" to get the message and straighten up their act.

Unfortunately, this won't always alleviate repercussions for reporting poor behavior – in some cases, no matter *how carefully and fairly you discipline*, you become a **victim**. As long as you know it happens to every teacher, maybe you won't feel so devastated and miserable when you get shot down by an angry, defensive, irrational parent.

Just one last comment and then I'll put this writing topic to rest: I have always missed (and misunderstood) the lack of written expression of appreciation *from* others, *to* others, *by* others! I realize some people aren't comfortable expressing their thoughts, some don't like to write, others don't always know how to compliment, and some just don't see the importance of it. Nevertheless, I *know* that **everyone** enjoys receiving a letter brimming with compliments or nice comments noticing something otherwise overlooked. Think about it. Have you ever received a letter of thoughtful expression and deemed it a waste of the writer's time? I doubt it. Words expressing kind thoughts or appreciation are treasures to *everyone* whether they believe in note-writing or not. The notes don't have to be elaborate. Even a scribble on an index card can do great things for someone having an icky day. Everyone loves to receive them. So…I urge you to begin placing note writing at the top of your list of priorities and communicate those little things that others forget to take the time to mention! **Email gratitude is nice. Written gratitude is memorable!**

> **"The smallest act of kindness is worth more than the grandest intention."**
>
> *~ Anonymous*

69. ***CHECK IT OUT!*** Check your check stubs to make sure all your payroll deductions are correct. These may include taxes, insurance, professional dues, retirement, credit union, automatic bill payment, and anything else that has the potential of being complicated later on if they've been figured wrong. It's far better to nip it in the bud than to

have to retrace paperwork on down the road. Be proactive and avoid that kind of unnecessary stress.

70. ***SIGN ON THE DOTTED LINE*** When it's evaluation time, remember that when you're asked to sign the evaluation sheet, you are only signing that you read the information, *not that you agree with it.* (Unless, of course, it's a glowing, walk-on-water evaluation, then you definitely want to *agree with it!*) ☺ Incidentally, save all copies of your contracts, salary schedule, evaluations, supportive documentation, and any professional responses you may have made regarding job targets. Keep everything in the same file so it's easily accessible. It's not a bad idea to keep this information at home rather than at school.

71. ***VERY SPECIAL STAFF!*** Some of the most important, significant people in your profession are the *secretaries and school nurse!* Go out of your way to **honor them and compliment them regularly.** Befriend them and *appreciate them,* for the jobs they do are ones that help make your busy life as a teacher tolerable. They will be taking and forwarding phone and email messages, they will help you disseminate information via staff, newsletters, phone calls, and announcements! They will be the ones who "front" you when sales people call, and they manage your orders, billing questions, and dozens of other headachy things that otherwise would plague you if they weren't there intercepting them. Don't miss Secretary's Day and don't miss School Nurses' Day! They often have the most thankless job in the community! Can you imagine trying to keep Central Office, Administration, Principal, Faculty, classified staff, bus drivers, parents, grandparents, businesses, students, the community and who knows who else...happy? What a job they have! Notice – they'll be glad you did.

72. ***THE CHAIN GANG!*** The chain of command is essential to follow! Let's examine a hypothetical situation. Let's say a parent has a problem with something you said or did, so he goes to your principal. You find out there's a problem only when you get called in to the office and discover you've been accused . Wouldn't you be less defensive, less surprised, and more appreciative had the parent come to you first to resolve the conflict, rather than *tattling*? (After all, that's what it is, isn't it?) Of course, you would. We *all* would!

  The same holds true with co-workers. If you have a disagreement with a fellow staff member, go to that person directly and resolve the dispute. Only if that fails to solve the problem do you resort to the next step, your assistant principal, principal, counselor – or whoever is next in command. The goal is to settle disputes at the lowest administrative level possible. Resist the urge to "go over someone's head" for it might just cost you yours. ☺

73. *A THREE HOUR TOUR...* Do you ever get a song stuck in your head...? It just reverberates through your mind all day long and drives ya nuts? Wanna know how to get rid of it? Just sing the Gilligan's Island Theme song. It'll work every time! If it doesn't for some reason, sing something else. ☺ (That one came outa left field!)

74. *SCOPE IT OUT!* Keep a bottle of mouthwash in your room...and use it. We *do* want to make memories...but, Scopeless memories can be stinky memories.

75. *TAPE CATASTROPHY* Almost any kind of tape can and will leave it's mark. I've used tape on painted walls and when I removed it, turned them into need-to-be-painted walls. I've used tape on the carpet to mark a spot, and when I removed it, discovered that the tape can be removed but the stickiness sticks, resulting in a dirt-collecting permanently marked spot. Instead, I either write on the carpet with chalk or I use the rubbery tape the PE teachers use on the gym floor and put it on the ceiling to mark where to line-up, where to stand, etc. This works well for *me* because I have a drop ceiling with metal brackets and any tape residuals can be rubbed off with alcohol. If you don't have the drop ceiling and your ceiling is painted, you could use colored chalk on the ceiling, which can be wiped clean. Or you can either hang something from the ceiling to mark your spot or use a small piece of the looped side of Velcro. It will attach to carpet and provide a nice location indicator. Be sure to test it somewhere in a corner, though, to make sure it doesn't prick, pull, or fuzz the fabric when it's removed. As far as the walls are concerned, I either hang things on bulletin boards with staples or pins, on glass or wood with a hot glue gun, on metal with magnets or clips, from the ceiling with string and paperclips, or inside a poster-sized picture frame that is hanging on a nail. Announcements, decorations, reminders, etc. can be easily tucked inside with little or no difficulty. Those wonderful new-fangled wax machines for hanging posters may be your ticket to hanging things worry-free.

76. _WRITE SITE_   http://www.teachertools.org/forms_dynam.asp is a website providing a wealth of information! The site provides free letter templates for every imaginable topic a teacher could ever need!

77. _WRITE IS WRONG_ My good friends, Melanie Caywood and Carol Windler, taught me a lesson I *have* to share with you. *There is a wrong time to write!* Here's an example: mommy sends you a note: "Dear Iamtorquedwithyouagainyouworthlessteacher, My precious little Priss has been *very* upset all morning because she said you did not give her a chance to tell you what happened or allow her to explain why she...." You instantly grab your TI84 in an attempt to calculate just how many times you actually pulled Miss Priss aside so she could tell you what was bothering her. Then, you sit down with your red ink pen to respond to Mrs. Allyoueverdoiscomplainbut I. Stillhavetobenicetoyouandihate it. Your letter is decorated with capital letters, a few underlined words, some bold explanation marks, and rage-induced shaky lettering. It's alright to go ahead and write it and get it out of your system, but then, **DON'T SEND IT.** Ya see...we tend to think we *have* to respond to everything sent to us. We want to defend ourselves and let mommy know, by golly, how the story *really* unfolded! But the fact is, if we read it again, we realize that this kind of letter doesn't even require a response. If we are asked questions, we are obligated to respond, but be sure to check for that. If you get a letter that is just chewing you out for something, read it, file it, and realize that in some cases, to **write is wrong**.

78. _SNEAK A SNACK!_ The first thing I do when I get home from school or work is grab a snack. Back in grade school, I remember grabbing an apple or banana before I even took off my coat! Keeping that in mind, I figure my own students aren't much different from me when it comes to being hungry, tired, and needing a nutritional shot in the arm at the end of the school day. So, anytime I have after-school meetings, rehearsals, or events with kids, I *always* offer the first ten minutes for munchin'. Kids may bring a snack from home, share with a friend, or purchase something from the snack machine. I can *definitely assure you* it is not time wasted! In fact, it's proven to be a good time for us to talk through music, take attendance, review performance schedules, answer questions, and do just about everything else that needs attention while the kids refuel. You see...after being in class all day, the afternoon siesta-need broadsides them, lunch was three or four hours earlier, and consequently, their blood sugar levels plummet through the pavement! A light snack gives them just the boost they need to revive and be ready to work, again. Compared to before I adopted this little TRICK and we started practicing immediately after school, I've found that rehearsals go so much better, kids are far less cranky, far more congenial, have much more energy, pay better attention, smile a lot more, and we accomplish *so much more!* Give them just a little bit of time at the beginning of practice to fill their tummies, and they will fill their time more wisely and be much happier kids!!

79. ***FACE IT!*** **"If you're happy, please tell <u>your face</u>."** *~ Hal Urban*

80. ***THE LION, THE SCARECROW, AND THE TIN MAN:*** There are so many ways to help kids understand what good character looks like. For starters: Students can show their **COURAGE** by raising a hand when they're not sure of the answer. Students can show their good **BRAINS** by considering possible consequences and making the right choices. Students can show they have a **HEART** by sticking up for someone when other people are acting ugly, being rude, or making fun. Just think of the possibilities of extending this lesson! Isn't it exciting!?

81. ***TRANSPORTATION TROUBLE:*** It's always a problem with elementary kids, having to wait on parents who can't or don't pick up their children on time. (You are fortunate if you have a site-base or district policy to handle situations like this.) It's nearly always for a great reason: *"...the traffic was terrible," "...there was a bad wreck," " I got off work late," "I forgot...," "I had an appointment... "* but the fact remains, regardless how good the excuse, you're stuck with supervision. You will find, too, that it's usually the same ones who are your repeat offenders. I finally solved the problem this year with the following note or some variation thereof:
Dear Parents of Concert Choir Members:
    Thank you for making the commitment to transportation, regular attendance and for making all the other necessary arrangements it takes to be in a group that practices twice a week. That takes a lot of dedication! Also, thank you to those of you who have made the commitment to be on time to pick up your child(ren)! I really appreciate that – more than you can imagine! In the past, we have had some problems with transportation.

There were times when I was not able to leave school before 5:30, sometimes as late as 6:00, because someone did not arrive on time to pick up one of our singers. In order to alleviate the problem, I have established a policy that goes into effect October 4th, 2003. Please look over the SAMPLE document below so you will know and understand what to expect in the event of an unreasonable delay in picking up your child(ren) at 4:30 from Concert Choir.

To the parents of: _____, Date:_____

Your child's participation in Concert Choir after school is very important to me. I am delighted to have him/her attend and be a part of this awesome group. However, the pickup time for this after-school club is 4:30 p.m. and he/she was picked up at

_____.

This may be the first time he/she was picked up late. However, if your child is not picked up on time in the future, it will result in him or her not being able to attend any further rehearsals or performances. The policy must be followed to ensure the safety of your child who will not be left unattended and respect to the sponsors when he/she stays after school for rehearsals or attends performances.

Thank you for your cooperation. Please sign & return to me tomorrow so I know you have seen this information.

Debbie Gray   _____
                                                    Parent signature

Concert Choir Membership Transportation Termination

Dear _____,

Date:_____

Your child's participation in Concert Choir after school has been very important to me. I have been delighted to have him/her attend and be a part of this awesome group. However, the pickup time for this after-school club is 4:30 p.m. and he/she was picked up at _____.

This is not the first time he/she was picked up late. You were notified on _____ that if your child is not picked up on time in the future, it will result in him or her not being able to attend any further rehearsals or performances. The policy must be followed to ensure the safety of your child who will not be left unattended and in respect to the sponsors when he/she stays after school for rehearsals or attends performances.

In accordance with the policy, I regretfully inform you that Concert Choir membership, rehearsals, and performances are now no longer a part of _____ 's after school activity.

Debbie Gray

This may seem harsh, and if it is, just *delete it or dilute it* anyway to suit your needs and preference. I only offer the note template to help point out the need to inform *ahead of time* what your intentions are and how you plan to handle specific situations. Hopefully, this covers you from any misunderstandings, hurt feelings, or other trouble that can occur when you are left responsible for a student after school hours. It's not always about inconvenience. It can turn into a liability for you – particularly if you are the only one left in the building with a student. Just cover your tracks – and if it takes something as strong as this transportation policy several of my friends and I finally had to devise, then at least you have one idea of how to approach the issue. Good luck!

Debbie Gray

Chapter 5

REINFORCER ROUND UP

AND

M_{mmmm}OTIVATOR M_{mmmm}AGIC

"Nothing has a better effect upon children than praise."
~ Sir Philip Sidney

"Nothing has a better effect upon *PEOPLE* than praise."
~ Sir Debbie Gray

"I can live on a good compliment for two months."
~ Mark Twain

Boy, if *that's* not the truth! If I could say that and mean it, *and I can*, then my students can say it and mean it, too. The positive results for managing students, increasing confidence, and building relationships through *compliments* are endless!

"But encourage one another daily, as long as it is called today...."
~ Hebrews 3:13 NIV

1. ***PERFECT PEOPLE POPPERS*** bulletin board. The board is used to reinforce the behaviors I hope to see continued by allowing students to "*go pop*" one of the large, quarter-size, plastic, packing bubbles that are stapled to a bulletin board. I slide appropriate colors, pictures, or decorations behind the clear poppers for a simple seasonal or thematic change. For variations on the same idea, I titled it POP STARS and another time I had POPular behavior written above it...both had posters of contemporary groups behind the poppers (and I had "pop" cans hanging from the ceiling. FYI for you non-mid-westerners, "pop" is what easterners call "soda." It's a west-of-St.-Louis generic term for a carbonated beverage or soft drink.) When I had a MOOsic theme with all cows, my poppers board said: KIDS WE CAN COWnt ON. I once cut logos from familiar soda cans, tacked them behind the poppers and titled the board COOL KIDS *CAN* POP! One of the most

popular was when I hung a large, empty picture frame and surrounded it with popper bubbles, encouraged the kids who got to "pop" to bring a non-returnable picture of themselves to place in the frame. The title was: PICTURE PERFECT POPPERS. Several years I put my PICTURE PERFECT POPPERS board out in the hall for all to see. **Parents were pretty proud of their picture perfect people poppers pictures!** POP ROCKS candy is a fun decoration to connect with the poppers board and so is PICTURES OF OUR POP...when the pop star gets to bring a photo of his/her daddy. Finally, you could hang a mirror in the middle of the poppers and write: MIRROR MIRROR ON THE WALL...WHO HAS POPPED MOST OF ALL?

2. *"SUPER STAR BOARD"* is another great reinforcer! Kids are asked to "autograph the board" when they earn a compliment. They get to be a "Superstar" for every class visitor to see and admire! Two different times I used this theme and heard rave reviews...particularly from parents who were brought in after PTA programs to see the board with their child on it. One variation on the same theme was to have the kids sign-in on giant foil stars I purchased at Paper Warehouse. Another time, I had a nautical theme going throughout the room, so I sketched a big ship and they "signed-in" on the "Star board" side of the ship. (I know...I know....) Another variation on that is, once school pictures are taken and returned, you can have them staple their picture on the Superstar board. I tried a "HERE'S ANOTHER STAR" board. I cut out pictures from magazines of current pop stars, then mingled my student's pictures in with the big name, famous stars! That can add some current events topics to your reinforcement opportunity idea, especially at Grammy time. It actually looked pretty cool, too!

3. *OH SPRAY CAN YOU SEE?* I have a travel-size hair spray bottle (about three inches tall) that fits perfectly in my hand and sprays an ultra-fine mist of **"THANK YOU SPRAY"** on kids needing some attention or deserving to be noticed. This year, I changed *"THANK YOU SPRAY"* to *"COOL KID SPRAY."* I'm just telling you...kids will line up without a word, total non-participants will participate, yackers will hush, and naughty kids work to be nice kids just to get *"COOL KID SPRAY."* Crazy but true. Maybe it's all in the way I make a big deal about it – maybe it's because it feels so good, maybe it's the surprise of getting something sprayed on their faces, maybe it's the novelty of it, maybe it's just because they feel special – but no matter what the reason or the catalyst, I know there is some miracle in the tap

water I put in that little bottle! It's better than a Genie! (I tell students who prefer not to be sprayed, to simply cover their faces with their hand, and I'll not squirt water on them.)

4. *"THANK YOU SPRINKLES"* go to kids who impress me. "THANK YOU SPRINKLES" are just the contents of Pixie Stix. The kids tip their heads back, open their mouths like little birds, and I pour in a little flavored sugar to thank them. If they deserve a really big compliment for doing something like *anticipating need* (i.e. someone drops something and they pick it up for them; someone opens the door for someone who has their hands full; without being told - someone picks up art work that has fallen on the floor in the hallway; someone moves out of the path of the rolling piano without being asked, or someone picks up something on the floor that three classes of kids have stepped over during the day...) they get to go to my dolphin cookie jar and keeper of the "THANK YOU SPRINKLES," (the Dolphin is our school mascot) get a Pixie Stix, and enjoy the *whole thing* rather than just a dusting on the tongue. I also have something on hand for those kids who can't have food reinforcers. Go to a carnival supply store and buy something by the gross like erasers, badges, pencils, stickers, magnets, mini slinkies – miniature things that'll still fit in the bottom of your KEEPER OF THE PIXIE STIX. 99% of the time, kids will choose the candy over the inedible treat, but they're there for the taking and it avoids issues that may come up when offering candy as a reward.

I can't emphasize this enough: If you choose to use food as a reinforcer, stick with something that is **_safe_** for all ages to eat! Hard candy, chewy candies, and nuts are just too easy to choke on and are better avoided. My experience is talking, again. My Jess choked on a jaw breaker when she was nine. I'm not talking about coughing and gagging...I'm talking *about not breathing, turning purple, and falling unconscious* in my arms while waiting for the ambulance! Who would have ever thought a *nine-year-old* would choke on a piece of candy?

5. **_CATCHY, CRUNCHY CEREAL_** is another fun way to give the kids a treat without worrying about them choking. I used this idea when I was teaching summer school reading. We used Fruit Loops and Sugar Pops, each representing a musical note. Fruit loops were whole notes, Sugar Pops were quarter notes if there was only one, two eighth notes if they were side-by-side. We then threaded them onto yarn in a rhythmic pattern, and made a necklace for a fun, first-thing-in-

the-morning activity. Throughout the day, the kids got to "*crunch a compliment*" right off their necklace when I caught them doing something "*NOTEWORTHY*" like: working hard, finishing a project, saying thank you or please, anticipating need, etc. If you send a "NOTE" home explaining the process, hopefully the kids will receive even more accolades when they get home with an empty, Fruit-Loops-free piece of yarn around their neck. The important people at home can know they had a "NOTEABLE" day because all their decorations gratefully got gobbled. Of course, some of the had-a-rough-day kids could eat their necklaces before they get home, but not to worry, if even one great kid gets more attention for his or her good student behavior, you have made your point. Plus, if you're concerned about it, you can collect the ungobbled notes, drop them in a labeled zip lock bag and pass them out again the next morning.

6. ***LAY IT ON THICK!*** I bought clear, peppermint-scented fingernail conditioner (not polish) from Avon. Boys and girls love it when they get to come up and get a finger "*painted*" because they "*nailed that one!*" It smells so good and is an all-day reminder that they were caught being great!

7. ***THINK OUTA THE BOX*** It does not have to be food, extra recess, or even something tangible to reward and reinforce the behaviors you relish! Think up something *weird!*
"You get to wear my I'm-stinkin'-awesome T-shirt."
"You get to draw on the chalkboard for five minutes."
"You get to come in during Kindergarten and help me teach."
"You get to play a glissando on the bells (or piano) at the end of each phrase."
"You get to choose one friend and tape your thumb to his/her thumb until the end of music."
"You get to watch and decide who gets COOL KID SPRAY and then you get to spray them." I have some other TRICKS, too, so keep reading...

8. ***LET THE CHAIR DO IT*** I have an overstuffed arm chair from my x-living room in my music room. Sometimes, when I notice something extraordinary, I just ask, "*Would you like to go sit in that big ol' soft chair?*" They love it! (Typically, the chair is saved just for me.)

9. ***TEACHER'S THRONE*** Once in awhile, I invite a student to sit in my teacher's chair, which is behind my desk and otherwise off-limits. I know it sounds goofy, but they actually consider it a big deal to sit there, for some reason!

10. ***"TOES TO THE WALL"*** means spending the remainder of class time without shoes, just socks, with the toes of their shoes to the wall! You join them…you'll have as much fun as they do and it will compound their fun by seeing their teacher traipsing around class in sock-clad feet. You're making memories that will last a lifetime, and I guarantee you, they will work toward getting to do that again every time they return to your class! Incidentally, I don't *require* them to remove their shoes – it can be embarrassing to some. I just offer it as an option.

    You can also use this to your *"manage advantage."* They love being sock-footed, so much that if someone is interrupting or not participating, you can quietly ask them to put their shoes back on. The others recognize *that* a lot faster than you might imagine and tend to keep their noses clean so they don't have to put their shoes back on prematurely.

11. ***FIDDLER ON THE ROOF*** Pick a nice warm day and **have a picnic on the roof** of the school! Just make sure you get it cleared with your boss. We did it, now other grade level teachers have adopted the idea, so come spring, it's not a bit unusual to see kids eating lunch on top of the school. Like all other fun activities that are unusual, establish your guidelines first and make sure they know exactly what will happen if they mess up while on the roof. Stick to your guns, too. Don't get soft-hearted, feel sorry for someone, and give in and offer the fun even if he/she didn't meet the criteria for winning your reward.

12. ***THROW IT IN REVERSE*** I have **"backward days"** where we all turn our shirts around and walk backwards while in the music room. You can extend the fun (and confusion – so make sure you're in the right mood and frame of mind for this) by having them do *everything* backwards – or opposite. You tell them to sit when you want them to stand, you say quiet when you want them to sing, say *"talk"* when you want it silent, you say, *"fortissimo"* when you want them to sing quietly, you say, *"staccato"* when you want them to sing *legato*, etc. It's crazy, to say the least – but it's a blast! The older kids like it just as much or more than the wee ones. It probably has little educational value, unless you are working on opposites and vocabulary, but it

induces smiles, builds lasting relationships, associates music with fun, and makes crazy-but-good memories. After all, isn't that what we want?

"Growing up happens in a heartbeat.
One day you're in diapers; the next day you're gone.
But <u>the memories of childhood stay with you for the long haul.</u>"
~ Kevin Arnold

13. *<u>LET'S DO LUNCH</u>* Have a **Bach's Lunch** (box lunch - get it!?) and invite students to join you for lunch in the music room. If you want to provide the meal, your Bach's Lunch menu could include: Bassoon burritos, violin veggies, piccolo pizza, piano pudding, tuba tuna, treble clef candy and bass clef cookies. Just put the ideas on a bulletin board if you can't or aren't interested in providing the meal. I used to provide the lunch snacks, but now, because time is so tight, I just invite the kids to bring their school lunch or home lunch to eat with me and share time together. While you're munching, get to know your kids by asking them questions about themselves, their families, their pets, *anything* that will help you build a relationship, understand what happens in their lives, and help them know you care about them. You'll be amazed at what you can learn about a child during fifteen minutes of munching!

14. *<u>BUBBLICIOUS</u>* I love to use **bubbles** and a small bubble wand to let the kids who are right on task give a gentle blow to release the bubbles into the room. Actually, this idea struck me after a wedding where small bottles of bubbles were handed out to blow toward the bride and groom. I kept the tiny bottle thinking, *if it spills, I won't have too big of a mess*, and gave my mid-wedding brainstorm a try. It turned out to be a simple, very inexpensive, really popular reinforcer for the kids. I am the one who places the wand in front of the kids' lips rather than letting them touch it, so they're not actually handling anything that could spill.

   I am amazed how many kids have never blown bubbles before! I constantly have to remind them, blow gently, and hold it up while they blow! Try it...you might like it! The kids sure do!

15. *<u>WET YOUR WHAT?</u>* If their schedule permits, our city's fire department will bring a pumper truck to our parking lot or playground and create an educational, wet and wild break in the day. They came during summer school last year and extended their hook and ladder,

attached a water hose on the end so the entire parking lot was showered in a fine mist, and had various other "stations" for the kids to visit. The kids who earned the fun, were invited to bring towels and swimsuits so when the first hot spring day arrived, they got to play. Although we've only had the opportunity to do this activity once, it was an incredible hit and made memories they will never forget!

16. ***IT IS BALLOON!***   If you do a lot of movement in class, dancing, skipping, jogging, etc., like I do, you may find it fun to add a **helium-filled balloon** to float around the room in the air current. I try to get one with a face on it, give it a name (I call ours, Smiley), and the kids love him! He will actually move around the room and the little kids think he is following them because they are doing such an excellent job. (Wonder where they got THAT idea?) This really reinforces participation and singing. I should probably mention though, it's awfully crushing when Smiley floats out the open window and heads for another school. (He can usually make it back by afternoon, if you have a lunch break and there's a balloon store with a twin Smiley close by.)

17. ***CATCH A STAR.*** Sometimes we want students to answer questions individually. If you need a reinforcer for students who remember to raise their hand to answer a question or participate in class, **KOOSH balls** are tremendous helpers! They also come in handy if you're having trouble with students not participating or refusing to answer questions they know. The added element of getting something tossed at them, getting to catch it, and feel that individual sense of pride will often encourage otherwise non-participants, to become involved in class. Instead of *calling* on someone by name, just chuck him or her a KOOSH ball. The ball only goes to those who raise their hand without a word. Be sure to establish some guidelines before using this TRICK or you could make more trouble for yourself than it's worth.

➤   The ball is tossed back (to me) gently or it won't be used again.

➤   The ball is not to be intercepted in the air by another hand. This prevents the big dive for the outside pass - everyone wants to be a Marcus Allen, Dante Hall, Tony Gonzalez, or Marc Boerigter! (Ahem…can you tell I'm a Chiefs fan?)

143

> If you don't have a KOOSH BALL, a bean bag works well, too. KOOSH BALLS just <u>feel</u> so cool and <u>feel</u> softer if you bean someone!

> I have them throw it back immediately so it doesn't end up being a distraction.

18. ***DOUBLE OR NOTHING*** A good individual reinforcer with older kids, especially boys, is to let them **sit on double chairs.** It's amazing how hard they will work if you just let them sit on a chair that's stacked on top of another one! Make a big deal about allowing them to do it because they deserve something extra. Also, don't overuse any reinforcers or they become boring and ineffective. Try to be random in your rewards and reinforcers!

19. ***GO WET YOUR WHISTLE!*** *"You are so awesome! Why don't you go down the hall to that drinking fountain and get yourself an ice cold drink of water! You definitely deserve something special!"*

"A great manager has a knack for making ballplayers think they are better than they think they are. He forces them to have a good opinion of themselves. He lets them know he believes in them. He makes them get more out of themselves; and once they learn how good they really are, they never settle for playing anything less than their very best."
~*Reggie Jackson*

(Teachers are managers, ya know!)

20. ***BE SPECIFIC:*** I'm going to crawl on my podium here a minute… (hold on a sec – this "crawling" could take a little while.) Bear with me! …almost…there…. Ok…I am poised, positioned, and prepared to preach. (Hopefully, I'm preaching to the choir!)

<u>Too many teachers *PUNISH EVERYONE* for the mistakes of others!</u>

I have the unfortunate job of nearly an hour of recess duty every day, all year long. It's not that I mind recess duty so much, and I don't mind making sure kids who owe time for not doing as told – pay up. But let me just say, I HATE having to punish a ***whole class*** by making them <u>all</u> miss recess, stand on the line, or *anything* that punishes every child. Even if it's "*...only for five minutes...,*" even if "*...it doesn't happen very often...,*" even if "*...I've never done it before.*" I think **it is just plain wrong!** (I, like most parents of kids who are punished for the actions of others, draw some serious conclusions about those who carry out punish-the-whole-class discipline plans. This consequence definitely has the potential of damaging relationships and respect!)

Before jumping to any conclusions and you get grumpy with me - the out-of-touch old hag - let me be straight up with you. I believe it is *very important* for us, as teachers, to stick together and support one another. So...I *always* follow through with the teachers' assigned consequences, even if it's blanket punishment. But this is one issue I will passionately resist until the day I die. It is a management plan that is inappropriate and grossly unfair to *everyone* involved! I hope to present a powerful enough defense that I convince you to hate it, too! Even if you don't adopt anything else from this book, I beg you to *please* let this one leave a lasting, career-long impression!

Just like with kids, stories that put the situation into a personal perspective add emotion to it by changing the frame of reference. Creating a familiar or potential conflict *may help us to empathize* and see the situation from another viewpoint. Let me draw an analogy or two, if I may. I'm not sure these are particularly good analogies, but they are what come to mind.

Let's assume *you* are a proud part of an eager, efficient, people-pleasing, always on-time, go-the-extra-mile staff of master educators; but *several* among you keep neglecting directives by making too many personal phone calls during school hours. Another arrives late every morning and someone else manages to stir up trouble in the lounge every time she's present. In response to these responsibility infractions, your Principal, in frustration, makes a blanket statement that affects you and all of your fellow staff members. He or she establishes that **1.** *"Now no one is to ever make or receive personal calls during school time – only before and after school is it permissible."* **2.** *"Everyone's required arrival time is moved earlier by a full fifteen minutes"* - which plays havoc with your already-established morning routine of transporting kids to the sitter; and finally, **3.** *"All teachers are restricted to their classrooms for lunch, rather than the lounge, for the duration of the year until all rumors and backbiting stop."*

YOU, ***through no fault of your own***, are **punished for the choices of others!** You can't deny there was or is a problem. You can't really do anything about the problem because **you have no power or control over the choices of your cohorts**, and more than likely, some pretty __*serious animosity*__ has been established between you and the actual offenders as a result of their behaviors and *your Principal's reaction to them.* So, it's highly likely that this blanket punishment creates yet another management issue: Hostility among the ranks!

Here's another example that might fall closer to home. Let's set up a scenario where you and all of your fellow staff members are allowed to run out and grab lunch if your break provides adequate time. It's not something you get to do very often because of your schedule, but you enjoy and look forward to that once-a-month privilege! Sometime during the course of the semester, however, someone takes advantage of the privilege, is detained, and doesn't get back to school in time to cover her regular responsibilities. Even though you *always* did everything possible to make sure you were 100% responsible and appreciative of the opportunity, your privileges to grab a fast food lunch were revoked right along with the person(s) who failed to follow the expectations that had been clearly established!

To make matters worse, in spite of the blanket restrictions, you find out that *some* staff members are still allowed to go out for lunch, while the majority concedes to the blanket policy. Don't you wonder why the one(s) who didn't follow directions weren't the only people punished? Don't you want to know why those of you who did what was right are exempt from the privilege? And mostly, don't you feel like there's a double standard? After all, for some reason, some distinguished select still have the privilege of slipping out and grabbing lunch – so leaving isn't the issue. It's human nature to wonder these things! It's also human nature to expect consistency, **fairness**, and lack of favoritism.

Wouldn't you have preferred that your boss deal with those offenders on an individual basis rather than making *you* pay for *their* misconduct? But, you say, *"The Principal couldn't tell who it was."* I say, if the Principal knows someone is arriving late – then that could easily be identified. I say, if someone is making personal calls on school time, then monitor the phones and find out who it is and deal with *that* person specifically. I say, if someone is being a "spoon" and stirring up trouble, wait and trace – you'll get your perpetrator with patience, determination, and a vigilant eye. I say, if someone fails to follow procedure regarding lunch, then *that* person is the *only one* who should be held responsible for his/her actions and denied the privilege. Don't punish those of us who met expectations!

There are at least three issues involved here: punishment, rewards, and *specificity*. Can you see how being specific fits into this equation?

We have to be just as precise in identifying those who are doing what we want them to do as we are those who are not meeting expectations!

On a side note, when it comes to consequences, *whether they are punishment or rewards and recognition* of commendable behavior, **what is fair for one is not necessarily fair for another** (OK...I heard that *harrumph*!) I'll explain what I mean.

Don't hesitate to say to a **repeat-offender**, a parent, or another teacher who challenges you on your choice of consequences "*...you know, had this been a first time offense, you probably would have only received a warning, just like Quinton, instead of missing recess.*" But also, don't hesitate to answer to a challenge, "*...the two people who were following directions are being shown my gratitude because they are not serving consequential time like the offenders.*" Let your punishment increase in severity and be directly proportionate to the frequency and intensity of the rule violations. In other words, if two people make exactly the same mistake, one has never caused trouble before, and the other is in trouble *constantly*, please don't assign the same consequences. Give that great kid the benefit of the doubt – give 'em a break! (That's what we'd want if we were the ones who goofed, right?) Also, make sure your rewards and recognition are commensurate with the quality conduct you notice and desire.

Now, back to *punishment*...the faculty lunch saga would parallel a classroom event where an entire class receives consequences because of the poor choices of a few. There is a gross lack of consistency and fairness when non-offenders remain blanketed beneath the punishment specs. This opens the door to damaged relationships, jealousy, tainted morale, and trouble between those involved who caused the trouble and those who were entirely innocent. Again, I remind us to,

Do unto others, as you would have them do unto you.

Whoo-whee! *Can you tell this is a pet peeve of mine?!* OK...even if I still haven't managed to convince you that it is counter-productive to punish the innocent or hold them accountable for the choices of others, let me offer what can be a better solution.

Here's all you have to do to TURN PUNISHMENT INTO GRATITUDE. When your classroom is getting out of hand, **stop** what **you're** doing and **take inventory** of the situation. While they continue doing whatever it is you wish they wouldn't, either **make mental notes** or if you're old like me and can't seem to remember your name without looking at your I.D. badge, **write down names of the kids who are doing <u>what you want them to do</u>!!** There is

ALWAYS, without a doubt, at least one little person who doesn't deserve to be punished with a class-wide punishment plan!!! Find that kid or those kids, and write their name on your list or…if that's not possible, ask them to stand (or sit if the others are standing), or silently walk by and touch their hand. Once you know who is doing what pleases you, simply announce for all to hear, *"If you are one of the kids I asked to stand up,* (sit down or touched your hand), *I want you to know you were doing exactly what you were supposed to be doing and **I NOTICED!** I appreciate you so much that when the other kids – the ones who are sitting down right now – are not allowed to play during recess for making some bad choices – you, my awesome friends, get to play. Remind me to write (*or call) *your mom and dad a note, too – so they know how responsible and reliable you are!"* It's as simple as that!

Still not convinced? Tell me this…

What motivates a great kid to keep working to be great if he or she is going to be *punished*, even if he or she is wonderfully behaved, just because…
he or she has been assigned to a particular class of students, because people in close proximity choose to be naughty, or because…
their teacher can't figure out who is misbehaving?

Once you're blessed with kids of your own and they have to serve time or miss out on something special because of the bad behavior **of others**, I suspect you will become as adamant about this detail as I am. Until then…just trust me--

It is not fair to be in trouble for the actions of others, particularly when your association with them is not voluntary!
~Debbie Gray

Amen. (Pass the chicken, please.) I will struggle down from my podium now and return to my regularly scheduled programming.

21. ***YOU ROCK!*** I glue googley eyes on a bunch of washed rocks, draw on a smile with magic marker, and pass out ***YOU ROCK!*** rocks for exceptional students! Luckily, we all know which ones we can give a rock to and not have to worry about them stoning someone.

22. ***JUNK'LL DO IT!*** *"Whoa! You were a great singer that time through! See this amazing quartz rock I found on vacation last summer? I'd*

love for you to hold it or put it in your pocket and keep track of it for me. Then, when you see someone else in the room doing as good as you just did...walk over to that person and give him or her the quartz to hold. Oh yeah, and don't forget to tell them they did a great job - just like you!" As silly as it may sound, I've used bracelets like this for girls, an Inspector Gadget watch for the boys, and even a picture of our cat caught in a funny position! Everyone wants to see the picture, so they'll do anything to see what I've just secretly shared with someone else who has just impressed me with their participation. Getting to pass the compliment on to another student has dual purpose. Other students try to do their best and earn the attention of their peer, but equally as important, they are learning to share in their successes, be more aware of those around them, and give compliments! You don't have to limit your TRICK reward to one bracelet, a single piece of quartz, or a photo – you can spread all kinds of junk around the room. Fools gold, a flower, a chance to push the button on the dancing flowers, a daub of hand lotion, a scarf, a belt, (avoid hats – we don't want to share head lice), a stuffed animal, a swatch of soft satin material, a stress ball, even a piece of tape works amazingly well! I've even used a rabbit pelt as a pass-around piece. Anything works, but the more novel and out-of-the-ordinary it is, the more they will work to receive it. Kids love tactile things. The more you can provide them with sticky, soft, silky, gooey, or smooth items to touch, chances to be noticed, opportunities to compliment and be complimented, the more you will have good participants and kids striving to do their best!

"Give the other person a good reputation to live up to."
~ Dale Carnegie

23. <u>**STUDENT SPOTLIGHT**</u> time can be fun. Jaime, my former student teacher, special friend, and very successful music educator shared this cool idea with me. She selects one student each class time to sit in the "hot seat," while the other students sit on the floor around him or her and share their thoughts on specific things they like about the student in the spotlight. Jaime says it's a great morale-builder and encourages students to think of positive things about someone.

I happen to have my own student spotlight: When I found out Jaime resigned from her position as a music teacher, my heart crumbled. She says there are several reasons for leaving, "It's partially because I want to be with my family who all live in Alaska; partially because I know God is leading me into a new career and this new place, but also because of the frustration I felt doing this job." Jaime inspired me to pull out and complete the not-touched-in-a-year-or-so manuscript for this book with hopes of helping others feel less frustration with their music job. Thank you, Jaime. *I dedicate this book to you, my dear friend.*

24. ***CONNECTIONS MIGHT HELP!*** I had one class of fifth graders who were particularly unconcerned about completing work. Grades didn't seem to matter a bit to them. So I tried to think of something they could relate to that *did* matter to them. I had these students select their number one, most **favorite kind of car and then I applied that information to my grading system.** For example, when asked, Ferrari's, Lamborghini's, Porsche's, BMW's, Corvettes, and Mercedes were chosen as their A or most favorite choice of car for them when they grew up. Mustangs, Hondas, and Mazdas were mentioned in the list for choice B; an Aspire, a Focus, and Saturns were listed in their C column. Someone listed an old beat up truck as his D choice as were plenty of other, less-desirable-to-a-teenager vehicle choices. Among other equally disgusting-to-a-kid modes of transportation, a hearse and a "wiener mobile" made the F list. (Of course, there were some who thought those should be in the "A" category!) Nevertheless, kids, especially my boys, were able to relate to cars more easily than grades.

The next step toward making my point came when I questioned them if they were working toward earning a Ferrari, an Aspire, or a "wiener mobile." The room started getting a little quieter at that point and the silence became deafening when I explained the correlation or "natural cause and effect" of hard work and what a good education can help them afford. From that day until the end of the year, I no longer put an A, B, C, D, or F on a paper – they earned a car-labeled grade for their work.

Whether or not that little exercise was futile or left a lifelong lasting impression, I will probably never know, but if it was the right combination of thoughts to lift even one of those lackadaisical students out of their doldrums, I count it worth it.

25. ***TAKE IT HOME TEACHER:*** Although I don't do too much written work in class, I do when we're working on note names, stem direction, time signatures, bar lines, etc. So...you'll never believe how I got them to work hard for a perfect paper!! I said, *"I'm not taking grades on any of this stuff - it's just for fun and for me to see if we are ready to go on to something else or if I need to re-teach*

*this some more.   Here's the deal: If you can prove to me that you understand this and get a perfect paper - IF (and only IF) you'd like, I've made an extra **worksheet just like yours for you to take home** and teach your mom or dad, grandma or somebody. Now remember, they're probably not going to know this stuff - but IF YOU DO A GOOD JOB TEACHING it to them, they should get a good score on it – just like you. After you've taught them, have them do the work, don't help them, you grade it when they're finished, and then bring it back to me and let me see how they did on the same worksheet as you."* You will be astounded how hard they work to get that blank test page to take home.

The next thing to consider is this...they DO NOT have to get a perfect paper the first time - if I check it and find errors, they get to take it back, "make repairs" and then let me see it again. Some get it the first try, some work on it for a long time, but the reward for LEARNING THE MATERIAL is getting to TEACH THE MATERIAL! It's a workable TRICK!

26. **<u>STUMP THE CHUMP</u>** is a fun game that encourages students to ask questions. Tell them you like for kids to ask questions – that it makes you think they're smart if they ask - and it's even more fun if they can ask something you don't know. Challenge them to TRY to stump you. I only play this "game" when we're singing from sheet music and they're searching for something <u>in the music</u> to stump me – otherwise, questions about butterflies, race car drivers, chickenpox, soap, and hair styles can attempt to veer lesson plans way off course. Stump The Chump will help you learn a great deal about what kids don't know and assess what they do know. For instance, one of my fourth graders asked me, "*What does that crossed out circle mean?*" It was a middle C.

27. **<u>GET AN AUDIENCE!</u>** After working long and hard on a section of a song, I often use the intercom and invite the Principal, Counselor, or someone in the office to come in and listen to them sing. Performing for someone, particularly if that someone gushes over what is heard, is an unbelievably effective reinforcer, confidence builder, and perfect closure to a lesson.

28. **<u>STAND UP FOR YOURSELF!</u>** To break the monotony, energize the workers, and keep some fun in the format after some tedious part-singing practice, the kids are rewarded by me inviting them to **stand on their chairs** while we sing, "*...to see if our hard work has paid*

off." Kids are energized when they are allowed to stand on chairs for some reason – it's typically a NO NO, so permission to do the "forbidden" may be what makes it all the more fun and exciting. I know it probably sounds uninspiring to you – but give it a try – you'll see what I mean. Just like with the KOOSH BALL, <u>make sure you have your ground rules established from the beginning</u> – you sure don't want someone hurt and you don't want standing on their chairs to be a distraction.

Simply make the statement: *"IF YOU COME OFF OF YOUR CHAIR – FOR ANY REASON – YOU DON'T GET BACK UP."* That's it – it's simple, fun, fair, and they'll work hard to be able to do it!

29. *WE'RE IN THE DARK:* Anytime my classes are informally discussing anything, I want to encourage as much participation as possible, so each time a student offers an idea, he/she gets to turn off the ceiling lights in the room. We remain in the dark until another comment or answer is offered and then that person gets to turn the lights back on. This off and on is continued throughout the discussion. It's exciting for all lower elementary ages, keeps them focused on wanting to answer the questions, changes the mood of the room, and is a TRICK way to reward participation. Fourth graders are still inspired by this little motivator but not so much with fifth graders, unless you have an abnormally immature group.

30. *M & M DISPENSER:* I purchased an M & M dispenser that runs on a battery, has a belt clip on it, and is small enough to keep with me. I put the little chocolate candies in it so when they hold their little hands out for a yummy reward for answering a question, participating, or anticipating need…they get one treat. Their reward doubles if the one that plops out onto their hand happens to be the color of the day. The kids seem to like it, but I don't let it lose it's novelty. Once I go through one "load" of candy, I put it away for a week or so before reloading and sharing my "compliment treats" once again. I don't worry too much about M & M's because they melt so quickly and don't pose as much of a choking problem as some other type candies that would fit in the dispenser, like SKITTLES, although I have used SKITTLES and the kids sometimes seem to like those even better than M&M's.

31. *SEQUENCING – AND I'M NOT TALKING DIGITAL!* Rewarding students who read rhythm flashcards correctly has become so much fun since I started incorporating this little TRICK. Kids read the rhythm pattern aloud and immediately after I say, "*If you said... (*and I say the rhythm correctly) *stand up and spin to a personal space, touch the floor with both palms, and spin back to me and sit down."* Each time after that, I add an additional movement to the sequence. This TRICK keeps them moving, encourages them to do their best, builds vocabulary, and is great sequencing or patterning practice which is a cross-curricular skill that we can help develop.

32. ***SPOTLIGHT*** I *love* to carry a small flashlight in my pocket. When students deserve to be "*in the spotlight,"* they get blasted with their very own ray of light! Try it! You'll see – it's a great motivator! I've used the flashlight to call on kids, too. It's amazing how many otherwise non-participants are willing to raise their hands to answer a question just to get a flashlight shined in their face. To make it even more dynamic, I usually close the shades and turn off the overhead lights on my flashlight-in-my-pocket days.

33. ***JUST CARD IT!*** My computer and GREETINGS WORKSHOP help me **design special cards for special people or special occasions** and I make sure to send them often. Here are some silly examples with notes that involve an accompanying treat:

<u>S'mores:</u>

On the front:

You're even s'more special than I can say.

or

I appreciate you s'more than you realize...

Inside:

Kids are special...and work really hard...so I'm giving you candy and this little card....to express my appreciation and thanks for all you do...from your music teacher, Mrs. Gray...

here's s'mores to you!

<u>Junior Mints:</u>

From Mrs. Gray, some candy just for you...they're "mint" to express thanks for all that you do! So as you enjoy them, one bite or a few... remember who it is that appreciates you!

Hershey Kisses:

Whether it's a "kiss" for luck, for thanks, or good bye… I appreciate you and how much you always try! You're a leader, that's for sure… and you sure sound great! I hope these Hershey's Kisses prove I think you're first rate!

Hot Dogs:

(Great snack for BACH's lunches together.)

**There's an old thought that is said when somebody's glad…
they say "hot dog" or "that's not too bad!"
Well, I've been around long enough to say without any doubt –
I know all of you are glad school's almost OUT!
With that thrill in common – I write just to say…
I really appreciate you …and HAVE A NICE DAY**

34. ***COURIER AND I'VES*** got a TRICK for you! Kids of all ages *love* to be chosen to help, especially if it means getting to ditch a few minutes of class! Although I seldom *need* to send anything to anyone on the spur of the moment because of my MAIL BACHS and assigned couriers, sometimes I write a "SPECIAL DELIVERY" note to be taken to one of my friends on staff by a student who deserves some special recognition, a reward, or an ego boost. I'll just jot down a quick:

   ➢ "JUST THINKING OF YOU – HAVE A GREAT REST OF THE DAY!"

   ➢ "MY SPECIAL DELIVERY PERSON DESERVES A LITTLE ATTENTION FOR BEING SO ATTENTIVE THIS MORNING, SO I SENT HIM TO YOU FOR A PAT ON THE BACK."

   ➢ "WOULD YOU PLEASE TAKE A MINUTE TO COMPLIMENT _____ FOR FINALLY PARTICIPATING IN MUSIC TODAY?!"

   ➢ "TAKE A BREAK THIS AFTERNOON. I'M GOING TO TAKE YOUR RECESS DUTY."

➤ "HERE'S FIFTY CENTS. ENJOY A COKE ON ME SOMETIME THIS AFTERNOON."

➤ "ACT ALL SURPRISED AND TELL _____ THAT MRS. GRAY WANTED ME TO KNOW THAT YOU HAVE REALLY BEEN _____."

It doesn't have to be elaborate, sacrificial, or even important. The point is….that child gets to skip class for a few minutes, feel trusted because he or she is walking the school unsupervised, and spending some time alone thinking about how cool it is that he's trusted and getting to do that. You think he won't be extra awesome next time he comes to your class? Oh…yeah…he will…you can tell by his strut and self-satisfied smirk.

35. ___WRITE ABOUT RIGHT!___ It is a goal to write complimentary letters to the parents of every student I can catch doing well. It obviously helps reinforce great behavior and helps to develop that **relationship** that I believe is so important to teaching success. It is a terrific way of letting your students know that you admire them enough to be willing to take the time to write and brag on them, but I've found that there are some intrinsic rewards from it, too. It just feels good to take the time to let parents and kids know that you noticed the positive things they do. It is immediate reinforcement for ME because I _know_ more than likely, that note is going to be displayed on the fridge, saved in the baby book, and will be shared with friends and family. (Becuz of this, its probly knot a bad ideer two make shure you're speeling and punkchuashun is correkt!)

I started making special efforts to write notes of compliment after our district music teachers voted umpteen to four, to resort to a pass / fail format rather than letter grades. In spite of all the persuasive comments I could muster, I could not convince them that it is imperative to make sure students who are extraordinary know they are…with a letter grade. (I have concluded that it is a good thing I did not go into law, because my skills of persuasion are considerably short of stellar.) The "slacker" students already know they are slackers, so an F or D does not come as any surprise to them and usually not their parents. The "average" kids are already passing - or *not failing* (and there is a difference), so this kind of pass/fail grading system is not as significant an issue for them, either. But, knowing that the poor A+ students receive the same credit (grade) in their personal file

155

as someone who's barely holding on by the hair of his or her chinny chin chin, but still passing, *really bothers me*. I don't like it and not a single argument in favor of pass/fail tempted me to lean that way in acceptance, but majority ruled and the vote carried - probably because letter grades are more work and time consuming.

Our newest grading system does provide for pre-programmed comments like, "Pleasure to have in class," "Works well with others," and "Participates in discussion," but in my opinion, these are nice, but quite trite. They are just too generic and even when my own kids received them; I gave little credence to their sincerity. Nevertheless, since my extraordinary students don't find out from their report cards that they really are *extraordinary*, I make absolutely certain they, their parents, family, and *friends know that I KNOW* they are extraordinary kids by the letters I send home!

So what is "extraordinary?" The word "extraordinary" is an adjective that describes something that is exceptional, far above typical or expected; someone who is beyond ordinary or above average. Although there sure isn't anything wrong with "average," (providing average is their best), Dr. Eph Ehly always told us, **"Average is the best of the worst and the worst of the best."** I think this reminder was his motivation to keep us from settling for average and to perform at our highest potential. French dramatist, author, diplomat, and government official, Jean Giraudoux, wrote, **"Only the mediocre are always at their best."** To this day, I teach with these two thoughts constantly spinning around inside my Gray matter.

No matter who you are, when you do something extraordinary and it goes unnoticed, it is human nature to gradually devalue yourself and your effort, at least in your own mind. The lack of positive response tears at self-confidence. Confidence, or lack of it, directly shows in learning and teaching, too. It can't help but affect mood, attitude, and drive. It may not be a permanent response, but the impression that you and your work are not respected become very real, hurtful, demoralizing, and can strangle your thinking.

Anytime I experience this feeling, I try not to let it get me down by remembering:

> **Whatever you do, work at it with all your heart,**
> **as working *for the Lord, not for men*...**
> ~ *Colossians 3:23-24*

For years I was fortunate to work for two principals who knew and understood this inexplicable and complex phenomenon of building confidence and morale with <u>sincere</u>, genuine words of compliment! Although I thank God for their influence in my life, I am ashamed to admit that I did not realize, until they were gone, what a blessing it was to work for them. Their generous words of praise and their steady flow of little notes of appreciation constantly encouraged all of us on staff. I know they sure built *my* enthusiasm and skyrocketed my confidence…enough that I believed I was the best music teacher in the nation! The funny thing is, I taught my kids like I was the best teacher in the nation, too! I wasn't about to let anyone down by being even a borderline average teacher. They thought (or made me think) I was the best and I was determined to prove them correct!

I didn't realize how much I took for granted my former principal's thoughtful introductions before each program, their post-performance compliments to the parents, teachers, kids and me; and their kind handwritten notes packed with superlatives. The saying that hindsight is twenty-twenty is absolutely accurate! Shame on me for having taken Mrs. Johnson and Mrs. Reynolds for granted!

And we know that in all things God works for the good who love Him, who have been called according to His purpose…
**   *Romans 8:28 ~ NIV***

Everything happens for a reason, and in this case, I have become an even better communicator myself, because of these juxtaposed experiences. They have become my catalyst and inspiration to make it a priority to write thank you notes, birthday greetings, notes of concern, and notes of compliment so that every extraordinary person in my life might know that I notice and appreciate their strengths, help, kindness, and talent.

Does that mean that the "average" students don't receive notes from me? No, not *at all!* There are extraordinary "average" people, too! You know them, the ones who work harder than anyone else, have the best attitudes in the world, have enough enthusiasm to fuel a football team, but still only manage to earn average grades, have an average personality, or average talent? Those kids are actually some of the first recipients of my letters honoring them! There are also the low, struggling students who receive "*you're extraordinary!*" notes from me because what may be a small step for one may be a huge step for another and I watch for those tiny threads of progress and write about them. All I'm saying is, writing is another way to translate the Golden Rule. **Just notice**…and then **take time** to let everyone know you did…just as you would like others to do for you.

There always seems to be a reverse side to the silver lining of writing. Unfortunately, if you teach long enough, you will experience how people *do* take the time to tell you AND write if they are *dissatisfied* with something you have done. When you get one of these notes, you are going to *hate it* – I guarantee it! You are going to think to yourself, *"Oh yea...I see how it is! I work my buns off for these kids all year long! I DONATE hours of my own, personal time, I tutor on the side, I give them tons of extra opportunities, I spend hours planning so they're entertained while they're learning, I write copious notes to everyone, and I never hear a word from anyone about those great things!! But, oh baby...let me mess up just once and I receive enough e-mail to freeze the network and enough letters to close down the recycling bin!"* My point is, *we* hate to hear from someone *only* when we've messed up...so let's make sure we don't mimic that kind of frustrating correspondence.

**"Write when they're right
before having to write when they're wrong!"**
~ Debbie Gray

Still not totally convinced writing notes is worthwhile? When *you* receive a thoughtful note, from anyone, think about how totally good you feel from it – and how you think good thoughts about the sender. YOU, as a teacher, friend, cohort, peer, sibling, son or daughter, wife or husband, mom or daddy...need to be the SENDER as often as possible. I guarantee you - you will reap rewards and be blessed right along with the recipients.

Here is an example of a letter I wrote to parents of a group of students deserving some extra attention for making good choices. Please feel free to use, edit, and personalize to your heart's content! I keep a "template" of sorts, on file and then make appropriate changes for all the times I want to send a nice, complimentary note to a group of students without reinventing the wheel.

To the parents, grandparents, family, and friends of:

Duncan Bickilt, Michael Swedin, Skyler Heineman, Kara Kolack, Jess Sprit, Daniel Langerly, Sam Fledston, Nick Rhiles, Brittany Madden, Cody Stintfell, Kayla Liery, Shenae Cabbart, Jake Pentoning, & Thomas Sharley

I have the pleasure and honor of writing to let you know that your child is one of the fifth graders out of the entire grade level, who made some awesome, independent choices yesterday morning during our musical rehearsal! I am so proud of every single one of the kids on this list and I know you will be, too! I made sure each one of them got a compliment and a little extra recess time. But, to me, that's just not enough; so I'm writing this letter to compliment them and YOU and to let you know just how incredibly awesome I think they are! It's kids like yours who make teaching a rewarding, really-worth-it kind of job! Your kids are a teacher's dream come true!

It is not always easy to do the RIGHT thing when you're a kid – especially when the majority of the people around you aren't making the best choices. It's awfully easy to be persuaded to follow the crowd rather than do what is right. Being a mom myself, I know that one of the biggest sources of anxiety during my "mommyhood," has been wondering if my girls would be leaders or followers, good kids because it's the right thing to do or only because someone was *MAKING* them be good! I worried if they'd make the choices that would make me proud of them, make others impressed with them, and mostly, keep them safe and out of trouble. I imagine you're a lot like me…wanting more than anything for our kids to be happy and make good, healthy, safe, and integrity-filled decisions. We know that, as they grow up, it only gets harder to do the right thing all the time.

Making excellent choices is exactly what *your child* has done! Not following the majority and instead, thinking independently, is exactly what we want them to do! That is precisely the kind of thing that will help them in the future to stay away from drugs and alcohol, be excellent judges of character, choose their friends wisely, avoid people who might be bad influences, and make their life journey happy, successful, and full of good opportunities!

What happened today with these fourteen kids is also a very nice reflection on you – at home! Things like this don't "just happen;" you've done an awesome job giving your kids the self-confidence, the conscience, the decision-making skills, the direction, and the inner strength to do what is right – no matter what! Congratulations mom and dad, grandma and grandpa, friends and family!!! Thank you for sharing your incredible sons and daughters with me during music classes week after week and please be sure to extend my appreciation and compliments to *them* for being bold, confident, and RIGHT!

Let them tell you what happened, what they decided to do, and what instigated this letter of compliment to all of you! I'm telling you…these are awesome kids! ~ Deb Gray

Please don't think that notes have to be that lengthy or specific – just jot something…anything down and get it in their little hands, and you will notice such a great difference in their attitude. When kids know you admire them, they won't want to let you down, I promise.

Incidentally, one of the unusually fun kinds of notes I write is on calculator rolled paper! I write the letter from end to end – sometimes making it outrageously long – eight, ten, fifteen feet in length! Then I roll it up from the end to the beginning (so they can unwind it as they read), and paperclip it or put a small piece of tape to keep it from unraveling. Part of the "coolness" of getting the compliment is the medium in which it is received! Give it a try – it's ok to be weird! Novelty is a blast and is a great TRICK for motivation!

> **"People often say that motivation doesn't last.**
> **Well, neither does bathing, that's why we recommend it daily."**
> **~Zig Ziglar**

A FINAL THOUGHT ON

REINFORCERS ROUNDUP AND MOTIVATOR MAGIC.

Many people compare teaching to acting, and rightfully so. Only the *greatest of teachers* realize they are "on stage" every minute of the day when they are with children. That includes in the hall, at recess, during lunch, or even in the nearest Wal-Mart or local café – **a teacher has to turn it on and keep it on.** I also mentioned earlier that being a teacher is much like being a salesperson. I have played both roles for twenty-some years and as a result, I've seen good, healthy changes in attitude, academics, and self-assurance. There's a bonus in it for me, too! Those students who feel pride and satisfaction with themselves are almost always happier, less disruptive, and more respectful students.

"Education is not about filling a bucket.
It is about lighting a fire."

~Yeats

While searching for just the right ways to motivate, inspire, and reward your students, it's important to remember the incredible value of a simple smile and the power of words. Most of us actually forget most of our day-to-day experiences; but words of comfort, encouragement, assurance, compliment, and kindness are sealed forever in our memory.

Likewise, and unfortunately, hurtful words are seared into our memory, as well. Therefore, it is very important for us to control our frustration, avoid sarcasm, keep our exasperation from leaking out of our mouths, and realize that even with an apology, we can never take back the hurt that has been spoken.

When exposed to a difficult situation or trying person, it is good to step away from any circumstances or anyone who has the power to trigger words we might say and later regret. The impact of words, both encouraging words and destroying words, is too often forgotten and underrated. We must be careful to always use words that lift up, refresh, and edify others. I'm not a Bible scholar, but I do find great inspiration about this particular topic in the scriptures:

I tell you that men will have to give account on the day of judgement
for every careless word they have spoken.
~ Matthew 12:36, NIV

When we put bits into the mouths of horses to make them obey us,
we can turn the whole animal. Or take ships as an example.
Although they are so large and are driven by strong winds,
they are steered by a very small rudder wherever the pilot wants to go.
Likewise the tongue is a small part of the body, but it makes great boasts.
Consider what a great forest is set on fire by a small spark.
The tongue also is a fire, a world of evil among the parts of the body.
It corrupts the whole person, sets the whole course of his life on fire,
and it itself set on fire by hell.
~ James 3:3-6, NIV

Words are so easy to utter – let us strive to make sure our words are affirming things that will impact our kids' futures in positive ways.

Debbie Gray

Chapter 6

GIVE YOURSELF AN A+ OR
ATTRACTIONS, AESTHETICS, AMBIANCE, AND ATTITUDE

WHO IS THIS WEIRD WOMAN?
AM I ANYTHING LIKE HER?

At the beginning of the book, I put in a section called DEBBIE'S DOSSIER. It was chockfull of descriptive words and boring facts about me and how I perceive life as it unfolds. You may not be like me, but I can almost guarantee we share some commonalities and personality traits that could make us entertain the same kinds of strategies and décor!

MY CLASSROOM AND MY TEACHING STYLE REFLECT MY PERSONALITY

(YOURS SHOULD DO THE SAME)

GIVE YOURSELF AN A+ OR Attractions, Aesthetics, Ambiance, and Attitude

Beauty and a sense of orderliness in our classroom, just as in our home, are functional. Not only do they give us a sense of accomplishment; they boost our energy and reduce some stress. Neither place has to be spotless or fancy, expensive or professionally decorated, but if they *feel and look organized* and are *comfortable* to you, tension will be decreased and it can create a safer feeling in the hearts of the kids.

The "Grand Central Station" atmosphere makes it obvious that an extrovert occupies my music room. You'll observe your basic hodge-podge of community gathering with people coming and going, former students, parents, and teachers dropping in to visit. *I LOVE IT!* (It's actually much the same way at home, but I opted not to survey the neighbors in the cul-de-sac to see if they love it!)

People will pay extra money to dine at a restaurant or stay at a hotel *just for the atmosphere*. This is dynamic proof that atmosphere effects moods. For the same reason, I like to provide a classroom with an atmosphere. I attempt to match the warmth and security of home with the décor I choose for school.   For instance, rather than always having the bluish-tinted ceiling lights glaring, I turn them off and turn on lamps that are scattered around the room. Sometimes I have white Christmas lights dangling from the ceiling or stapled to the walls and almost always on my silk fig trees. This is cozy, comfortable, warm, and homey light.   The softer, indirect lighting is soothing and helps calm the kids after a flurry of activity, but most of the time, I have them on because I'm simply in the mood for soft, indirect lighting.   Remarkably, the kind of lighting in the room seems to fit the way I present the lesson that day. My thing with "mood lighting" makes *me* happy and probably makes a lot of folks at the electric company happy, too! ☺

On the other hand, when some new explosive idea spins into my head, and that happens a lot, I flood the room with light. Along with the lamps, I add spots pointed toward the center of the room, the shades go to the top of the window, the sun blazes in, and the overhead lights brighten everything! The kids and I are energized and stimulated by the brightness and lighting changes.

In addition to the special lighting and living room furniture, I also have added some plants, ivy, trees, and various other greenery in baskets to make it feel and look more cozy and like home. I remember I'm teaching little kids, though, so I don't want it to look all "adultish!" So...I've decorated in some fun ways, too!

1. ***MY DECORATIONS HANGING FROM THE CEILING ARE ON THE MOVE.*** Fishing line, which will eventually be connected to decorations, is threaded through paperclips attached to the ceiling and then hooked to the door so everything dangling from the ceiling moves up and down when the door opens and closes. If comments are a direct reflection of how fun and unusual it is, then this TRICK makes for the coolest decorating gig, ever!

   Process: With the door closed and a DO NOT OPEN DOOR WHILE I'M DECORATING sign posted on it, tie one end of some fishing line to a coffee cup hook or screw that's screwed into the wood, about twelve inches from the top of the door. Then thread the fishing line at a sharp upward angle, through a paperclip attached to the ceiling somewhere close to the door – then out into the room wherever you want the decorations to hang. Next, thread it through another bent L-shaped paper clip that's been slid under the metal framework of a drop ceiling or you can use a coffee cup hook screwed into a solid ceiling. Let it dangle down clear to the ground, still connected to the spool.

Now, open the door all the way. This will give you an idea of how high you can tie another paper clip to hold decorations. Remember, they need to be close to the ceiling when the door is open, because they're going to drop considerably when the door closes. Be prepared to have decorations dangling about eye level for a 5'6" person. If you try to make them any higher, they will hit the ceiling when the door opens…you don't want that! ☺

It is fascinating for the kids but best of all, it helps you know when someone enters or exits your room - even if your back is to the door! I leave the string up year after year, but change the decorations . I hang seasonal decorations, instruments, candy canes, top hats, fall leaves, Easter eggs, spiders, packages with bows, stuffed animals, hearts, small bags of potato chips, foam rocks, and tennis balls. You name it, it's probably been hanging around my music room accompanied by some silly pun! I buy in bulk when I can. Party prize packages are great for getting a lot of "hangy-down-things" for very little cash.

One of the craziest decorations I thought of went with the motto: SPRING HAS SPRUNG! I bought several party prize packs of plastic, pink and purple Slinky's and hung them from paper clips connected to fishing line, which was connected to the door. When they would move up and down with the door, the Slinky's kept bouncing up and down, even after the movement of the door stopped. It was so cool! I think that's been my most favorite concoction of all!

2. **_I DO NOT OVER DECORATE MY ROOM_** Busy rooms with lots of clutter and color - even if it's *good* clutter and color, can raise behavioral agitation and tension. I haven't done any scientific research to prove this fact, but I've experienced undeniable proof that my ability to discipline becomes a tougher chore when the room *looks and feels* busy. Consequently, I try to keep clean, interesting, but simple walls with a basic color theme running throughout the room. If the room isn't overly animated, the kids are calmer and are less likely to be distracted. If something needs to be up, but looks cluttered or busy, I use pastel colors to help ward off the intensity that breeds restlessness and agitation. Although I haven't been a student of these theories, there have been studies on the effects of color on temperament. All I've heard is that cool colors are purportedly calming colors, while vibrant colors, like red and hot pink, supposedly have the opposite effect. Anyway, I pay most attention to the *amount* of stuff rather than the *color* of stuff in an attempt not to over stimulate their senses with décor.

3. ***WHAT DOES IT LOOK LIKE?*** I think the *arrangement* of my room reflects my personality! One of the chairs is soft, bluish-gray, overstuffed living room furniture and sits by a table with a lamp and flower arrangement. My student chairs are stacked in the corner of the room 95% of the time because kids need room to move! When we do use them, they are in a quaint little semi-circle around the piano, close together and near me, so that everyone can draw confidence from each other, or in "personal spaces" for activities that require plenty of room to move around between them.

4. ***NO SEATING CHART FOR ME!*** Unlike many, I don't use a seating chart or structured place to seat the students. They may be in sections, but they can sit anywhere within that section they choose. When they are allowed to sit wherever they want, by whomever they want, it's deemed a treat and privilege. If trouble begins brewing, that's the first thing I can effectively take from them. If they have to sit where *I* assign them to sit all the time, then they don't realize the advantages of good behavior and excellent participation.

Another reason I never implement seating charts is because they seem to penalize the really awesome kids. Rather than allowing them to sit together and enjoy the perks of being a great kid, they are often forced to sit between troublemakers as buffers or barriers. Some defend seating charts as their way of learning names, but seriously, how long does it take to get to learn names? If this defense was actually true, then seating charts could be abandoned after the first few weeks of school. If teachers were candid and we could examine their charts closely, I suspect the majority of seating charts are set up in a fashion devised strictly to help with discipline problems. I *know* we often have to separate the icky-acting people, but I still think it's wrong to victimize the great-acting people by forcing them to move away from their friends and sit by or between people who are obnoxious and disruptive. Let's face it, the icky-acting people don't give a rip, and the awesome-acting kids hate it.

If you have to separate icky-actors, move them away from their audience, first. If that doesn't do the trick, make them stand by the door. That typically quiets them down, no one else feels disrupted, and the great kids get to stay seated by their friends.

5. ***FUN FABRIC*** I buy lots of thematic, inexpensive fabric, cut it to size, fold over one edge and staple it down to create a casing, run

a spring-loaded curtain rod through it, and voila` - I have curtains! Next, I use the same material, cover the back of my piano so it doesn't look so ugly, and also use it as a backing for at least one bulletin board in the room to repeat the pattern, color, or theme. It creates a nice atmosphere and it's washable and reusable - unlike paper.

Debbie Gray

Chapter 7

BETTER BELIEVE YOU'LL NEED BULLETIN BOARDS!

1. *I SAVE ALL OF MY ELLISON MACHINE-MADE LETTERS AND DESIGNS.* I laminate the paper *before* cutting them, which keeps me from having to trim them twice. It makes them stronger, reusable, easier to remove without tearing, and much longer lasting. I keep them filed alphabetically in an accordion file for quick and easy, organized access. Bulletin boards go up so much faster when I don't have to take time to cut out letters every time. You'll find, too, that when they're easier to do, you change them more often. Eventually, you'll have enough letters saved and filed that you can have color themes – until then - stick to categories like primary colors, monochromatic, or pastels.

2. *BOARD BACKGROUNDS!* I used to always use construction paper for the background of my bulletin boards, then I tried butcher paper – which was nice - but it only came in brown and white. The art teacher buys large reams of paper, but it's about three inches too narrow on either side so I still have to splice it to make it fit; plus, I really don't like to mooch off of her budget items. Consequently, I've switched to some other background products that work really well! Fabric is my favorite! It doesn't show pin holes, can be washed, used over and over again, can be purchased in themes for every holiday, and is relatively inexpensive. I've also used table cloths and sheets. If you have some old sheets or can locate some at a garage sale, spend a few bucks for a tie-die kit and brighten up your board a la 70's style for little or nothing! Another favorite board cover that comes in outrageously cool colors, themes, designs, and even prismatic effects, though not nearly as inexpensive or ecologically friendly, is wrapping paper!

3. *STUDENT-DESIGNED BOARDS.* Turn loose some of your kid talent. Just think what an untapped resource we have in students! Why not give them a chance to team up or work as individuals, create a theme, a design, and with your supplies, make your next bulletin board? Actually, you could assign a different group each month –

so your board could be constantly changing while featuring student work! If more kids want to do it than you have need, you might have them submit their ideas and you can choose your favorite plans.

4. ***BORED? BOARDS!*** How fun would it be to enlist the help of the crafty moms, hobby hubby's, tinkering grandpa's, and groovy granny's who pride themselves in having a knack for creativity and craftsmanship, but aren't sure how or where to donate their time and talent, to design your hallway bulletin board?! It's amazing how many people whose talent has gone untapped only because *we've failed to ask!* So, why not ask? Use your school newspaper to place a nice little HELP WANTED ad. You could try something straight and to the point, like: *If you would be interested in decorating the bulletin board in the hallway just outside of the music room, please phone 555-5555 and ask for Debbie to schedule which month(s) you'd like to display your talents.* Or, you could try a more Grayistic approach and attempt something along the lines of:
HELP WANTED: Bland and boring, bright blue bulletin board seeking clever, crafty creatures to create, cover, and construct a curriculum-centered, seasonal, or program-introducing design destined to delete doldrums, decorate, delight, detail, and diversify. Dial devoted-but-devoid-of-time-and-deficiently-depleted-of-ideas-Debbie at 555-5555.

5. ***LET THE MACHINES HELP!*** Since I'm such a hideous artist, I secure the aid of an overhead projector to help me anytime I need anything, other than words, on my bulletin boards. If I don't, the pictures aren't recognizable. Here's how I make myself look like a master artist: On clear, overhead projector film, I make a copy of the photo, cartoon, instrument, or character I want to use. I scoot the projector closer or further away from the wall in order to adjust the picture to the perfect size I envision. I tape the film to the screen and mark the spot where the projector cart stands – so if something moves, I can easily realign everything. I then staple or pin backing paper to the wall before beginning to trace. This prevents movement which can distort the size or shape. If I work on my project on Sunday afternoons, there's no traffic in the building and I can set it up right in the hallway and put the backing paper right where it will stay. Other times, and more times than not, I have to find some place, get it all glued together, remove the backing paper, and then staple the finished product to the bulletin board. Sometimes I just trace and color, but most of the time, I'll patch it together with construction paper, like a

paper puzzle or quilt, pinning the construction paper color-of-choice in place first, tracing around the shape, cutting it out, then gluing the cut-out shape to the backing paper. For example, I pin a piece of red paper right on the backing paper, trace around the shape of a characters vest that is being projected by the overhead, then I cut it out and glue the red vest right to the backing paper. It's kind of like a puzzle, quilt, or mosaic. I just keep piecing parts together until I've completed the entire picture. When I remove the backing paper, I either put it up as is or cut the whole character out and staple it to a background that's already been hung on the board. It's a fun way to get professional-looking characters on your bulletin boards, but it is definitely time-consuming.

The most recent project I did using this TRICK was for St. Patrick's day last year for a door decorating contest! Give me a little competition based on creativity and I'm in heaven! So...I projected a full-sized cartoon picture of Barney, the big, purple, singing Dinosaur on some backing paper. I made him all GREEN though, instead of purple! The title of the masterpiece was something like: MEET BARNEY'S BIG BROTHER, *BLARNEY*! I didn't win the contest, but the little kids loved him and the older kids "got it" so it was simple and some silly fun for the holiday. Just for added nonsense, I put a Band-Aid on Blarney's nose, right beneath his left eye – to match mine! I'd recently had surgery in that same location and had spent the last week or so answering why I had a Band-Aid on my face. What I didn't realize is, I just invited *more* questions because the little kids didn't make the correlation of Blarney's ouchy and my ouchy!

6. **_MY BULLETIN BOARDS SCREAM, "WEIRD PERSONALITY"_**.
Some of the suggestions in the teacher's manual are a little too obvious for my penchant for novelty! Some of them I liken to setting the kids' minds in concrete; one need not even think to figure out a meaning! Of course, if your objective is to make a board that is an information key, that is a different story. Those kinds of decorations definitely have their place, but nobody needs my help to get ideas for them. They are a dime a dozen in teacher resource guides and text books. My ideas, on the other hand, have messages that aren't at all transparent to most elementary students. I love these kinds of bulletin board ideas and the novelty of them has become quite popular around the building over the years. As you will see, I've adopted some of the ideas from T-shirt slogans, bumper stickers, banners, quotes, and flags.

USE THE TALENTS YOU POSSESS...
FOR THE WOODS WOULD BE SILENT IF NO BIRD SANG EXCEPT THE BEST

or

LIFE IS LIKE A PIANO...
WHAT YOU GET OUT OF IT DEPENDS ON HOW YOU PLAY IT!
~ Tom Lehrer

I like this one:

LIFE IS THE SONG, FRIENDS ARE THE MUSIC

I made copies of front pages of songs about friends for the background paper so it was all black and white. The lettering was all in black. This is fun, too:

MUSIC HISTORY

The entire board is a montage of performance photos dating back to my first year of teaching.

Another Music History theme I did was:

MUSIC HISTORY

And beneath the words, glued or pinned to the board, was, in chronological order:

an old 78 album

a 33 1/3 album

a 45 record

a reel-to-reel tape

an 8 track cassette

a cassette tape

a CD

a mini disk

a computer chip

OR...

You know how a photographer comes in and takes school pictures every year? Well, I have saved all of those pictures of me since I first started teaching in 1980! Placing them in order on a board is another one of my MUSIC HISTORY boards! ☺ Kids are amazed at how the ol' gray mare, she ain't what she used to be!

USE THESE CLUES TO DISCOVER OUR

COMPOSER OF THE MONTH

My own version of TV's game show CONCENTRATION:

- September's composer board had a three-dimensional cardboard cut-out of the Nativity Scene, complete with Mary, Joseph, and Baby Jesus to my bulletin board backing paper, then stapled an arrow pointing to Joseph. With the help of an overhead projector and coloring books, I made a poster with kids peeking from behind trees, covering their eyes, scrunching down behind boxes, covering up with blankets, and one little guy was sitting on the limb of a leafy tree, barely showing his face. Then I stapled these words: "Opposite of:" followed by an EXIT sign next to the poster of the kids.

The composer?

JOSEPH HAYDN

(Joseph Hidin')

1732 - 1809

- My October board had a picture of a pack of wolves. Below that, I hung up a Playskool lawnmower, and below that was a FINE ARTS poster.

The composer?

WOLFGANG MOZART

1756-1792

(Wolf-gang Mows-art.)

- For November's featured composer board, I stapled the following words in small letters: Here we go Looby **(LOO)** with a plus sign (+) followed by the letter "D." Next, beside the blank, in small letters, I wrote the words: *"Rhymes with* (I stapled a **WIG** to the board) *but starts with the letter "V."* Under that, I hot glued an A**VON** bottle to the board with a minus sign (-) followed by the letter "**A.**" I placed a poster of San Francisco **BAY** below that and underneath the picture was a large plastic **TOE** that I excised from a foot bought for a buck

173

from the carnival store. (A photo of a toe from a magazine would work equally well...just maybe a bit less dramatic ☺) At the bottom of the puzzle was a Match Box mini **VAN**.

The composer?

LUDWIG VON BEETHOVEN

(Lood vig Von Bay Toe Van)

1770 – 1827

- The December had photos of Fred (Flintstone) and Ricky Martin to picture the composer's first name, Frederic. Then, for his last name, I made a poster of a drive-in movie theater with: "It's **SHOW** time" on the marquee and I hung a frying **pan** next to it.

The composer?

FREDERIC CHOPIN

1810 – 1849

(Fred Rick Show Pan)

- January brought out another composer puzzle for the New Year. Our board had a single green pea, the letters "TER" On the next line were more letters: "CH," a + sign, followed by a huge eyeball. Next, I attached a large stuffed cow with hot glue and nailed up a full-sized water ski.

The composer?

PETER TCHAIKOVSKY

1840-1893

(Pea-ter Ch-eye-cow-ski)

- My February feature was:

RIMSKY-KORSAKOV

1844-1908

(Rim-ski Coarse-uh-cough)

For "**Rim**" I connected a basketball hoop and put a little arrow pointing to the rim. I used the same water **ski** from Tchaikovsky's board. I bought a package of **COARSE** sandpaper and put an arrow pointing to "coarse." And for the last syllable, I cut out a picture of a man **cough**ing, from a magazine advertisement.

174

• March brought us to Mr. Franz Schubert! There was a light switch nailed to the board, turned to the "on" position. The letters F & R were in front of it and a Z was on the right of it. Then, I hung up an orange and white, *size 20* Nike tennis shoe! (That caught some attention in and of itself!) And right beside it was a doll of the Sesame Street character Bert!

Franz Schubert
1797 – 1828
(FR"on"Z - shoe – Bert)

• The next month, I used the same gargantuan tennis shoe, a picture of a robber plus the letter T, and the photo of a man. Can you guess?

Robert Schumann
1810-1856
(Robber + T Shoe – man)

• The final composer board of the year had a 5x7 photo of one of my students named BEN. I glued a small sample-sized jar of grape JAM next to Ben's picture, and an IN sign. One of our teachers last name is BRITT – so, of course, a picture of her suited the puzzle nicely and all I needed at the end was a +N. Since you're not fortunate enough to have a BRITT in your building, you could revamp and use a photo of Brittney Spears add –EY at the end. It'll take some farfetched thinking, but someone will figure it out.

Benjamin Britten
1913-1976
(Ben – jam – in Britt – N)

• One year, my spring bulletin board said:

PERFECT PITCH!

This board was very simple. I used black electrical tape for my staff lines, a large plastic treble clef sign, and I cut out circles in white paper using a drinking glass for my pattern and some red marker to draw stitching, to make baseballs. The balls (with proportionately-sized black stems) were scattered on the lines and spaces to look like music notes.

• How 'bout this idea: HUGE letters saying:

COME IN FOR SOME GOOD SOUND ADVICE!

- This quirky little idea made a *great* bulletin board and people were constantly touching the foamy lettering trying to figure out what it was. Most people thought it was dough…how fun to fool!

  ➢ First, I covered my hallway bulletin board with basic brown butcher paper.

  ➢ Then…to make my letters, I used foam insulation! I covered a table with aluminum foil and used the foam insulation that comes in a tube to write (in cursive so they were connected) the words **MUSIC ROCKS** and then I made individual, non-cursive letters to create the words **ROCK CONCERT**.

  ➢ Next, I took a large, $3 bag of aquarium rock and sprinkled it all over the foam lettering so as it dried the stones stayed embedded on the letters.

  ➢ I hot-glued the words, **MUSIC ROCKS** across the top of the bulletin board.

  ➢ I hot-glued the words, **ROCK CONCERT** down the middle of the board, from top to bottom.

  ➢ I then bought a bag of shiny flat rocks in the crafts section of Wal-Mart for about two bucks, glued on a pair of googley eyes that cost less than a buck for a huge package, and with permanent marker, drew a circle to resemble an open, "singing" mouth. Finally, I hot-glued all the little rock faces to the board, encircling the words, **ROCK CONCERT** .

The singing rocks, giving a ROCK CONCERT was a big hit!

- ___**LOOK ALIKES:**___ If you are making lettering for a bulletin board, try if you can, to **make the letters look like the <u>word</u>** – that visual clue makes it look cool, more noticeable, more memorable, and maybe even multi-dimensional. For example, when discussing the four families of the orchestra, spell the word STRINGS with actual instrument string - kite string works if you don't have access to the other. WOODWINDS can be written with old reeds that you can collect from a local band director or just use wood chips, branches, or ice cream sticks. For BRASS, cut the letters out of metal or shiny gold wrapping paper that looks metallic. If neither of those are accessible, find some metallic gold model paint or puffy paint and cover your letters. For PERCUSSION, be creative and use mallets for the straight lines, finger cymbals, jingle bells, etc. for the curvy lines. The mental picture is sure to help with memory and you'll get lots of nice comments about your creativity and ingenuity – which is always nice.

- *USE QUOTES TO INSPIRE!* Here are some of my favorites – both for students and adults, public and parochial schools. Sometimes my inspiration is directed to my fellow educators and administrators, sometimes only to the kids or their parents – often, everyone can draw strength and inspiration from these thought-provoking words of wisdom. You can have a QUOTE OF THE DAY or QUOTE OF THE WEEK board to encourage critical thinking, add a quote to the bottom of your programs, tests, or writing assignments, or you might just want to write them in chalk or marker and plunk them in the corner of one of your chalk/dry-erase boards each day. If you're really industrious, you could design a poster for each quote, laminate them, and recycle them year after year.

A PEEK AT PART OF MY QUOTE COLLECTION

1. **"Ability may get you to the top, but it takes character to keep you there."**

   ~ John Wooden

2. **"We are not made rich by what is in our pockets but rather by what is in our hearts and our souls."**

   ~Anonymous

3. **"If everything is coming your way, you're probably in the wrong lane."**

   ~ Garrison Keillor

4. **"Hard work & determination isn't going to guarantee you anything...but without it, you don't stand a chance."**

   ~Unknown

5. "An apple a day keeps the doctor away. An onion a day pretty much takes care of everyone else."

~Unknown

6. "Keep away from people who try to belittle your ambitions. Small people always do that, but the really great make you feel that you, too, can become great."

~ Mark Twain

7. "Good things come to those who wait...but GREAT things come to those who get off their bum and go after them!"

~ Anonymous

8. "The greatest gift you'll ever know is to love and be loved in return."

~ Christian, Moulin Rouge

9. "No one is useless in the world who lightens the burden of it for anyone else."

~ Charles Dickens

10. "Honesty and frankness make you vulnerable; be honest and frank anyway!"

~ Anonymous

11. "The good you do today may be forgotten tomorrow; do what's right anyway!"

~ Anonymous

12. "A part of kindness consists in loving people more than they deserve."

~ Joseph Joubert

13. "What we do in life, echoes in eternity."

~ Maximus, The Gladiator

14. "There is never enough time to do all that you would like. The important thing is to do all you can, while you can, because one day you are not here anymore."

~ Charles Dickens

15. "He who angers you, controls you!"

16. "He who exalts himself will be humbled but he who humbles himself will be exalted."

~Luke 18:14

17. "When someone hugs you, let him or her be the first to let go."

~ *Unknown*

18. "If you tell the truth, you don't have to remember what you said."

~ *Abe Lincoln*

19. "You can put a pig in a castle, but the castle will turn to a sty before the pig will turn to a king."

~ *Anonymous*

20. "He who throws dirt loses ground."

~ *Unknown*

21. "Two things are hard on the heart - - running up stairs and running down people."

~ *Unknown*

22. "How old would you be if you didn't know how old you are?"

~ *Satchel Paige*

23. "Average is the best of the worst and the worst of the best."

~ *Eph Ehly*

24. "When one door of happiness closes, another opens; but often we look so long at the closed door that we do not see the one which has been opened for us."

~ *Alexander Graham Bell*

25. "Suspicion often creates what it suspects."

~ *C.S. Lewis*

26. "Honest criticism is hard to take, particularly from a relative, a friend, an acquaintance, or a stranger."

~ *Franklin P. Jones*

27. "In what other language do people recite at a play and play at a recital? Ship by truck and send cargo by ship? Have noses that run and feet that smell? Park on driveways and drive on parkways?"

~Unknown

28. "How can a slim chance and a fat chance be the same, while a wise man and a wise guy are opposites?"

~ Unknown

29. "You have to marvel at the unique lunacy of a language in which your house can burn up as it burns down, in which you fill in a form by filling it out, and in which an alarm goes off by going on."

~ Unknown

30. "Preach the Gospel at all times; if necessary, use words."

~ St. Francis of Assisi

31. "All it takes for evil to succeed is for good people to do nothing."

~ Anonymous

32. "Never go mountain climbing with a beneficiary."

~ Anonymous

33. "In prosperity, our friends know us; in adversity, we know our friends."

~ John C. Collins

34. "A positive attitude may not solve all your problems but it will annoy enough people to make it worth the effort."

~ Anonymous

35. "Milk the cow 'til it's dry and then make hamburgers and wallets."

~ Jerry Stiller

36. "Even if you are on the right track, you will be run over if you just sit there."

~ Anonymous

37. "In just two days, tomorrow will be yesterday."

~ Anonymous

38. "Some days are a total waste of makeup."

~ Anonymous

39. "The best car safety device is a rear view mirror with a cop in it."

~ Dudley Moore

KRAZY KEYBOARD KORNER

I place my electric piano, complete with headphones, in front of a fun, interactive bulletin board titled Krazy Keyboard Korner. The objective is to allow students the chance to teach themselves, work independently at their own ability level, and learn to play the piano! Most often, kids get to rotate in and out of the Keyboard Korner during regular class activities. Sometimes it is used whenever a student is unable to join in holiday or patriotic songs and activities due to religious reasons. Sometimes I just use it as a reward for great work. The kids absolutely love it and look forward to having their turn.

I copied various pages of sheet music for the background and used black lettering for an overall, black and white sheet music effect. The board has guided lessons that include laminated pages from a beginning piano series as well as plastic keyboards with note names written in marker for reference. The lessons are numbered and advance gradually so students are always challenged, regardless of their musical aptitude and reading ability. I place these step-by-step instructions in a notebook on the piano for kids to follow at their own pace. For students with IEP's or who simply struggle too much to be able to follow the written instructions, I have recorded each lesson on tape or assigned a buddy to team up for help. Here is an example of Lesson One:

1. Play as many keys as you need to decide which side of the piano plays high sounds and which plays low sounds.

2. Start on the left side of the piano (closest to the windows) and play every single white key, moving from left to right. This is the sound of *going up* or *getting higher*. Listen to what *going up* sounds like.

3. This time, start on the right side of the keyboard (closest to the chalkboard) and play every white key, moving to the left. This is the sound of *going down* or *getting lower*. Listen to that sound.

4. All keyboards have keys of two colors, black and white. The black keys are divided into small groups of two and three.

5. Play every single black key.

6. Press two fingers down at the same time and play some of the black keys that are in groups of two.

7. Press three fingers down at the same time and play some of the black keys that are in groups of three.

8. Starting on the left side of the keyboard (closest to the window), play just the black keys that are in groups of two.

9. Beginning on the left side of the keyboard (closest to the window), play only the black keys that are in groups of three.

10. The keys named D are the white keys right in the middle of every group of two black notes. Look at the plastic keyboard on the board if you need help. Beginning on the left or low side of the keyboard, play all the D's. The first D is marked for you with tape.

11. Now you are going to locate and play all of the F's. F's are white notes or keys on the left or lower side of each group of three black keys. See if you can play all the F's. The lowest F is marked for you. They should all sound the same except the ones on the right will sound higher.

12. Now let's combine everything you've learned so far. Begin on the left or low side of the keyboard and play the lowest D, then leap over a few keys to F. (They're both marked for you.) Now leap up (or to the right) to the next D and then to the next F. Continue playing each D and every F until you run out of keyboard on the right side.

13. Now let's go the other way. Reversing the direction, begin on the right (high) side of the piano and play all the D's and F's. Go slowly, be careful and make sure you play only D's and F's – no other key or note should be touched.

Thank you for working at the Krazy Keyboard Korner.

Please return to the class now and quietly select someone to take a turn at the Korner.

If you are a girl, please choose a boy. If you are a boy, please give a girl the next turn.

This interactive bulletin board was easy to make, lasts all year long (so it's a one-time creation), involves every child, allows for success at every level, is fun for the students, and develops reading and processing skills. I actually recycle it by leaving it up from year to year by covering it with a bed sheet over the summer. Sometimes I change the lettering to a different color so it goes with my color theme, but most of the time, it just stays black and white.

A FINAL THOUGHT ON
BANNING BORING BULLETIN BOARDS

Take photos of your bulletin boards so you don't have to re-invent your ideas. Place dates on them so you can recycle them after a couple of years. Take pictures of your room decorations, too. After a couple of decades, you'll be wishing for a new, fresh idea and it's amazing how something you thought of right out of college can look like a new, fresh idea!

I have photos scanned of most of my boards, but they didn't turn out clear enough to reproduce in the book. I'll post some of them on my debbieonethewebbie web page or, feel free to email me and I'll do my best to send some of them to you, if you'd like!

Debbie Gray

Chapter 8

MANAGEMENT METHODS FOR THE MASSES

**When science discovers the center of the universe,
a lot of people will be disappointed to find they are not in it.**
~Bernard Baily

I remember (amazing, isn't it?) my Pediatrician advising me that if my toddler was getting ready to do something she shouldn't, that I should react just as I would if I saw her heading toward a hot burner to touch it. He told me to move with <u>intensity and urgency</u> when correcting her. He went on to say that if I just said, in a sing-songy, mild-mannered way, "No no, don't touch" and sat relaxed in my recliner, she wouldn't recognize that I really meant it, and would probably continue toward her target. Initially, it took a lot of extra time, energy, and attention, because of having to constantly jump up and make a big deal about her following directions and minding - but gradually, I was hopping up less - and she understood, by my words and sound of my voice, that I **meant business. Eventually, my words were effective** without all the *extra* body language, energy, and thespian talent.

I've discovered that the same advice holds true in a classroom full of students – no matter if they're five or twenty-five. We need to move with intensity and urgency when correcting our students. If we establish the ground rules, work hard, tirelessly, and consistently to *enforce them in the beginning*, gradually, we won't have to work nearly as hard because our students will recognize our insistence and know we **mean business** without being hovering, quick-to-react, or overly assertive.

"It takes time to save time."

~ Joe Taylor

It's only fair to mention – this whole theory catapults right out the window come spring when the weather gets nice, the end of school is near, state testing is complete, and "the sap is rising!" Then, every day is much like the *first* day! At that time, just get out your little calendar, mark off the days until summer, keep it in a very prominent place so the X's are quite obvious, and let your countdown help you survive!

Most people outside of the teaching profession drastically underestimate the skills and talent necessary to manage a classroom *full* of students! Many aspiring educators are even shocked when they meet with a class of students and discover the complexities of each having their own interpersonal dynamics, characteristics, temperament, and needs. The most challenging component of managing the masses is dealing with and extinguishing unacceptable behavior. Most of the time, you will be managing individuals or groups in the less-than-twenty-five-at-a-time range. But, there are times when you will be required to manage an entire grade level, sometimes maybe even an entire school. Assemblies, hallway supervision, emergency drills, grade-level rehearsals, and various other situations may place you in a role of leadership that will require you to take control of hundreds at a time! As frightening and intimidating as that may sound, developing great rapport with your kids and establishing good ground rules in your classroom will prove to be your ally both with your smaller class and whenever you're placed in charge of multiple classes. Here are some good TRICKS to help you manage the masses:

1. **_RESPECT_** is a two-way street. **Give it / Get it!** We **teach people** how to treat us.

2. **_TAP INTO EXPERIENCE!_** Seek help from seasoned teachers. Look to them for advice, example, encouragement, and guidance. You're not in this alone. We music people have a distinct opportunity to know which classroom teachers to observe and retrieve help. We get to see every single classroom and it quickly becomes obvious which teachers have compelling, successful, and effective ways of management. Granted, student behavior is not *always* an indicator of their teacher's expertise in classroom management! In fact, typically the best, most-seasoned teachers are the ones who get a roster full of trouble...because it's obvious they can handle it. The dynamics of every class change as different personalities move in and out, but it doesn't take too long to see which classroom teachers have a way of making extraordinary differences in their students' behavior. THOSE are the teachers you want to adopt as your mentors and role models! Get permission from them, then go sit and watch them teach during your break. Do your normal break stuff before or after school – just take advantage of their wisdom and talent! Visit all of their classes,

all year long. There is so much to be learned from observation and experience!

The other obvious concern for beginning music people is that we're typically the only music person on staff. Often, there's no one to be a *music* mentor, unless you're fortunate enough to have a Fine Arts director in your district who can and will meet with you, watch you, and take over where your college professors left off.

Just don't be afraid or embarrassed to ask for help. It does not make you look weak – *it makes you look **smart***! Anyone who has spent any time at all in this profession knows that the learning curve is steep and the trials aren't few.

"I make progress by having people around me who are smarter than I am – and listening to them."

~ Harry J. Kaiser

3. ***RELAX!*** Kids will *always* be kids - ornery, noisy, giggly, silly, and *hopefully*, full of energy. Even if our noise threshold is low, and sometimes it is, it is wise to "bite the bullet" on a regular basis and let kids act like kids. In fact, join in - *laugh with them*, let them know you have a silly side, too. Join the ranks of some undeniably successful people:

"I like nonsense, it wakes up the brain cells."

~ Dr. Seuss

I know…it seems too obvious to even mention; yet, I've known a *lot* of teachers who take themselves way too seriously and miss out on **the fun of teaching!**

"To every thing there is a season, and a time to every purpose under heaven…."
"… a time to keep silence, and a time to speak…"

~ Ecclesiastes 3:1 & 8

When you give yourself time to be relaxed and goofy during class, then, you have the right to let your students know you have a time when it's essential for them to focus and *listen*. Make sure they understand that you expect their complete attention when that time comes. Use the off-task times as a trade-off for work time. **They will respect our time when we respect theirs.** Relax and offer them regular times to be little. Now, more than ever in history, our kids have to grow up so fast! They do that, anyway, without our prodding. It was only yesterday I was buying big fatty pencils and "yucky-tasting" paste for my own Kindergartners. Now, they're nearly old enough to have their own Kindergartner!

4. ***THEY CAN DO IT!*** Have high expectations for your students! Make them stretch! You can expect them to be quiet when someone is speaking. Not only does that keep their input channels open; it is a matter of basic respect that we need to instill from a very early age.

5. ***HOW DO YOU GET THEM TO QUIET DOWN?*** There are times when an entire class or grade level enters a room, waiting for a program or class to begin. Before a performance you may have an entire grade level gathered in the hallway. You will need to get their attention and get them quiet. What do you do? There's always the old blow-the-whistle routine that we sometimes have to enlist, there's the flash-the-lights strategy, and the old standby...teacher look. But these tactics ONLY work if you've taught them and practiced ahead of time how to respond to these signals.

I can get the entire school to stop talking if I stand in front and clap a simple, standard rhythm pattern – typically quarter, quarter, two-eighths- and a quarter. They know to stop talking and echo my clap. If it's too noisy and rowdy for everyone to hear, I just repeat it once. It's a fun, uncranky way of getting kids' attention. I might say, "*Give me five*" and put my hand in the air...they know to do the same and close their mouths simultaneously. Again, in every case, no matter what TRICK you use, in order for it to be useful and successful, the response you want *must be taught* and practiced ahead of time and you must establish effective consequences for not cooperating.

It is imperative for me to be able to get my choir kids attention in a discreet way – many times we're back stage waiting to perform and I can't blow a whistle or talk loudly. They know, without me saying a word, that when I raise my hand, their hands should immediately go in the air, and silence should spread like wildfire! I use that one *sparingly* after we've practiced *abundantly* at the beginning of the year – but they know there are some severe consequences to not following that routine. Because I only use it under certain important-to-be-quiet situations, they know there's urgency in it. Remember, you can overwork anything to the point of being ineffective, so teach a large variety of ways to gather student attention and you will develop a large, industrial-strength arsenal of ways to manage the masses!

6. **_CLOSE YOUR EYES._** This three-word sentence is interchangeable with *"Stop talking."* Try it sometime and see if it works for you like it does for me. I can't explain it but for some reason, if I say, *"Close your eyes, please."* The room gets quiet. If someone talks, he or she has their eyes open and are peeking...**_guaranteed_**. (Okay...okay... there ARE exceptions – some kids talk no matter what.)

7. **_BACK TO BASICS BUBBLES!_** Remember the bubbles I told you about earlier, that I use as reinforcers? I also use them for practicing self-control. After discussing what self-control looks and sounds like, when the kids are lined up to leave music and we're waiting for their teacher to arrive, I bring on the bubbles for closure, reviewing what we've learned. I walk beside the kids, blowing bubbles in the air. Without any coaxing from me, they naturally reach up and pop them. Inevitably, I get to use this exercise to remind them that self control means being quiet and in control while doing any activity. *"We're popping bubbles so make sure you do it without talking or bumping into anyone. Wait until I get to you to pop the ones over your own head – you don't need to reach over others. There's plenty for everyone – just be patient until it's your turn. Notice, they float down – you can wait until they reach you rather than jumping up to reach them."* It's a fun way to practice all the components of the concept lesson of self-control and nice manners.

   You might want to use bubbles to manage a quiet line-up time by asking (before you tell them to line up), *"Let's see who gets to go first and pop bubbles as they go out the door...will it be the boys who are the quietest...the girls...or, if we're really having a great day, everyone will be popping!"*

8. **_DON'T TAKE IT PERSONALLY!_** Some kids will fight, argue, disobey, and a few have the innate ability to flat out drive their teachers crazy. If we can remember that kids *need* to be kids and that a certain amount of rivalry will give them resources they can use later in life, we will be less likely to take their behaviors as a personal affront or disrespect to us.

9. **_BUILD A RELATIONSHIP_**! Invest the time it takes to build a friendly, safe, and trusting relationship with every single one of your little students, on an individual basis, so they *want* to respect you!

10. ___RULES WITHOUT A RELATIONSHIP LEAD TO REBELLION.___
~ *Josh McDowell*

11. ___PRAY EVERY DAY!___ Let's face it, some kids are contentious and there's nothing inside us, short of a miracle, that will make a day with them easily tolerable. So, I pray for the antagonists, the quarrelsome, the argumentative, the belligerent, the mean, and all those other kids who push my buttons. Every day, before I lift my head from the pillow, I pray for patience and wisdom in handling each situation and I pray for kindness when everything inside me is screaming! I urge you to do the same – it isn't a magic formula and it doesn't change things overnight, but giving it to God takes the stress off of you. Pray that you might find an inlet into their lives that will help you help them. Prayer is a powerful helpmate to teachers just because God loves those little ones and wants what's best for them. He'll help us! He obviously already has helped me...or I couldn't still be doing this after all these years!

12. ___DON'T ARGUE___ That's it. Don't argue with a student! Don't lash back at a child who is angry or exploding. Don't say, *"Oh yes you did..., I saw you...."* Those kinds of responses only elicit more argument from the student. Don't argue!

13. ___IF I CAN'T SEE YOUR FACE, YOU'RE IN A BAD PLACE:___ This or *"If I can see your face you're in an excellent place!"* are phrases I use regularly to ensure students are in my line of vision. It rhymes so it is easy to remember – for all of us, it has a little lilt so it's fun to say and hear, and it gets the message across without having to harp at kids about moving to the left or the right, forward or backwards. Behavior management is intrinsic when students know they're directly in sight. And, without realizing it, they give themselves away - that they're up to something or up to nothing - when they try to duck behind someone.

14. ___SILENT WARS___ Sometimes, kids - like adults, just plain don't like one another. Sometimes just being in the presence of one irritates the other. It's not so bad to feel this way. Though I've done it myself and watched other teachers try, we probably *shouldn't* try to make them like someone they don't like. In severe cases, even making them be nice to one another is forcing an issue that is not too unlike shaking a hornets nest. These are the cases when complete separation is not only the best, but often the *only* solution. You see...there are often

lingering anxieties and animosity between kids that we are totally unaware even exist. Some of their baggage goes clear back to before pre-school. Some fuel is added to the fire on a daily basis by angry, grudge-carrying family members. Kids, like adults, react differently when they are aggravated. While one might erupt and show anger in physical, forceful ways, another, being more devious and deceitful, might be sneaky and use teasing and verbal sparring as his weapon. Still others want peace, no matter what the cost and are consequently, often bullied into submission. Trust your gut feelings. If you sense there is something brewing beneath the surface, separation is the secret to *the first step* toward successfully managing the conflict.

15. **_LISTEN!_**   Listen to your students when they are angry. I've learned that sometimes all they need is someone who will listen to them or give their side of the story some consideration. I try not to expect kids to keep their anger in check all the time, I can't do that myself! I try to help them understand why, if I don't believe they have the right to be angry. If their anger is worthy, I try to help them figure out how to manage it and give them permission to feel angry without feeling guilty. I make sure they understand they are never to hurt anyone or anything when they are angry, though. This obviously needs to be impressed upon some more than others. It's also good to give students who've exploded, time alone to cool down and think about what has happened. I try to join them toward the end of their cool down time just to make sure they haven't fed the flames of anger by sitting there building up more animosity toward the offenders.

    It seems like problems arise most often on the playground – probably because it's not as regimented and supervision is not as closely monitored. I've seen the "cool-down" time work better when it involves walking around and thinking rather than sitting and stewing. Sometimes sitting feels more like punishment than time to organize thoughts – so suggesting they walk around, think about it, then report back with some conclusions works pretty successfully. Just keep your eyes and ears open.

16. **_CAUTIOUS APPROACH!_**   If you are dealing with a particularly despondent or aggressive student and you see him stiffen or flinch when you walk toward him, STOP - go no closer. You don't retreat, either, just hold your position and stay calm. Don't let anything *they* say out of emotions trigger yours. Don't take it personally, just deal with the *issue* rather than the feelings fueling the reaction. If the

191

situation worsens, call for assistance – even if that means sending a student for help. Don't turn your back on a student who is irrational; walk backwards to a safer spot and keep other students out of the way. **Don't confuse your role** – your job is to teach and protect your students, not to be an analyst, psychologist, or behavior specialist (unless you are one of those). Leave the tough stuff to the ones who know best how to handle these particular situations. Just use your authority, talent, and expertise to secure the area. That also might mean removing all the other students from the area.

17. ***FRUSTRATION CAN INSTIGATE TROUBLE*** Not all, but many of the kids you will have to manage because of their anti-social, unacceptable behaviors, are often kids who have lived in the shadow of higher achieving siblings or classmates. They often have very low self-esteem and have a chip on their shoulder the size of Philadelphia. These students often provoke others simply because it gives them a feeling of superiority and power over them. While they may perceive their "enemies" as smarter, more athletic, more popular, or "hotter" than themselves, they *feel* dumb, klutzy, very average and even ugly. They feel they can control those "enemies" when they pick on and provoke them enough to make them irritated. In fact, this may be a subconscious objective. Sometimes, their covert methods of antagonizing will successfully get the other in trouble because they will eventually get fed up and resort to retaliation or defense.

We *have* to put a stop to it! Anytime we suspect something like this is taking place, we need to get busy and find out what's going on so we can bring it to a screeching halt! Once the situation is under control, we can then step into help-so-it-doesn't-happen-again mode. We can, *sometimes*, help diffuse this power struggle or low self-concept by affirming our faith in them. We might build their confidence by trusting them with small tasks and then make a big deal about them helping us! Personal adult attention can often settle the angst in an unhappy child – *be the one to give it.*

18. ***GIVE 'EM SOME TIME…OUT!*** While it is our obligation to keep kid-enemies from killing each other, sometimes it is a good thing to let them work out their own solutions. Now…don't get me wrong. I'm not suggesting that you encourage an angry, frothing-at-the-mouth 220 pounder to sit and have a quiet, congenial little problem-solving chit chat with his adversary who happens to be an insecure, passive, non-confrontational, spindly-armed, nervous 40 pounder. But, I do

believe *as long as you stay "all ears"* and in close proximity, you can give them the opportunity to work it out themselves, without your mediation. These are skills they will need throughout their lives – might as well start young.

Your judgement call is the most reliable source for appropriate decision-making, though. If you recognize that these two enemies would rather eat liver and onions with turnip gravy than look at each other, it's probably in everyone's best interest to dictate a separation and mediate later. Wait for a time when their ears are no longer red, their fists are no longer clenched, their jugular vein is no longer quivering, and the veins in their temples are no longer bulging!

19. *TIME-X* When you have kids working together in groups or with partners, **X-out a little x-tra time** just to let them visit a few minutes when they first get together. If you think about it, adults *always* take time to visit when placed in new groups with new people, even if they've been asked to be quiet. (Teachers are among the worst, too!) If you're not convinced, just pay attention to the sounds in the room at the beginning of your next faculty meeting – maybe even *during* the faculty meeting!! After a bit of free time, stop them and say, "*I loved letting you have a little time to visit, now it's time for you to let me have a little time so we can focus on our project...*" You then have the right to demand their attention. This little TRICK will help you manage your group-learning times because you've established a give-take sort of leverage for behavioral expectations. **It's a good thing not to expect your students to do anything you are not willing or able to do.** Keeping that thought in mind will help you build rapport, a relationship, and respect with your kids.

20. *WHETHER YOUR CLASSROOM MANAGEMENT MAKES IT OR BREAKS IT DEPENDS ON YOUR LESSON FORMAT!* Teachers today have a desperate competition going with technology. Kids spend hours in front of television either watching shows or playing games. *Millions of dollars* have been spent by the entertainment industry to study what colors, sounds, shapes, and characters hold kids' attention and how long attention spans last before requiring a break or change of pace. Watch childrens' programming and you will find shows and commercials that are fast-paced, action-filled, dynamic in design, and multi-sensory. Everything they see has a great deal of movement, color, special effects, unusual sounds, and typically, *only short blurbs of dialogue*. The same goes for the computer and video game industry

which has captivated the <u>same audience</u> we teachers greet every day. After being bombarded by television and media expertise, **we expect them to sit quietly and listen to…** *us talk*?

We can take advantage of the research-provided programming and incorporate some of their successes into our teaching practice. Granted, it's easier said than done, but it is easier for a music teacher, PE teacher, art teacher, or science teacher than a math, reading, or social studies teacher! Nevertheless, the goal is to make every lesson fast-paced, action-filled, movement-oriented, colorful, surprising, and with short spurts of dialogue sandwiched between the activities. I believe that nothing we do in class should last longer than three to five minutes before we "change channels." I respect their limited attention spans and I use that to *my* advantage. Of course, that three to five minutes can be extended with older children, but only by a bit. "Changing channels" may just mean standing up after sitting, turning to face a different wall, sitting on the floor instead of the chairs, sitting on the desks instead of the floor, reverting to a question-answer type discussion, have students ask the teacher in Stump the Chump.

Just in case it might help, let me give you a quick rundown of how my typical lesson format goes: My lessons always alternate action concepts with seated work, but we try to always begin class with movement! This is either dancing, listening for called or sung directives, interpretive dance, a speed-singing-with-actions competition, or a choreographed song. We jump, we hop, and we do the Beanbag Boogie. We blow scarves in the air on interludes while we stomp and sing on the verses. We swing our partners, spin on interludes, bounce knees to the steady beat, and fall down on glissando's. They think so much better when their hearts have pumped some good, healthy oxygen to their brains!

The movement activity lasts about three minutes and then they are <u>seated</u> for four or five minutes for concept introduction or review. Soon, they're back up again with another body-moving activity. Usually this is a concept reinforcer like a chalkboard relay with magnets as music notes, playing and moving with rhythm instruments, stomping rhythm patterns while reading from flash cards or the overhead projector, blowing scarves attempting to make them touch the ceiling, playing with beanbags, improvising movements to unusual, a-tonal music, doing a Boomwhacker exercise, playing kazoos and moving, or singing a song that I've crammed full of choreography.

They've been moving, so next it is back down again – but never the same way as the first sit-down time. They may have been in a

194

huddle or a circle, so this time they'll be asked to sit in their *"personal spaces," "face the north wall," "lay down on your tummies by the piano bench,"* or to *"meet me over by the big chair."* At that time, I'll do another concept review or introduce a new song, handclap pattern, or concept. We may use plastic keyboards or lap-boards, play a rhythm game, <u>create</u> a board game or game show of their own, write lyrics or a melody, perform or be an audience member, do written work for practice or evaluation, use a computer program revised for classroom participation, or make a "cool-sounding" experience by tapping, popping, and rolling plastic drinking cups!

The next five-minute time slot usually focuses student attention toward the television for an age-appropriate, music-laden video of sing-alongs, moves-to-music, musicals, musicians in concert, introductions to instruments, or a composer biography. Obviously, the older kids video time can take longer than five minutes.

The visual, auditory, and kinesthetic learners are accommodated with the alternating sessions within your lesson format. The quick changes nearly eliminate behavioral interruptions. The kids rarely get bored and if they don't like something, they know if they just wait a couple of minutes, they'll be doing something different. Everyone learns while they're having a great time...and most of the time, they don't even realize it!

21. *<u>PICTURE WHAT YOU WANT - THEN PUT THAT IMAGE INTO</u>* *<u>WORDS:</u>* Create a mental image of what you want your class to look, sound, and act like. Then, put that vision *into words* – be very <u>succinct,</u> use <u>age-appropriate vocabulary,</u> and then <u>model</u> it for them. It sounds so simple, but it really isn't an easy concept. We have to take every behavior we hope to experience in class, break it down to it's most basic fundamental elements, and then *<u>TEACH</u>* the kids *how* to do it.

We teachers tend to get cranky when our students don't behave according to our expectations. It might be that they are talking when we are speaking. They could be paying more attention to the reflection of someone's watch on the ceiling from the sun than being involved in class discussion. Or maybe they're into the slouch-with-eyes-down-and-dare-ya-to-make-me-do-anything attitude. **If** their teacher has clearly explained what is expected and the students are not following those directions, the teacher has every right to be cranky and respond in an appropriate way; but, the teacher must ask him/herself if the kids have not only been taught but have practiced exactly what he/she expects them to do. If not, the instructor is at equal fault with the students. In other words, TEACH and model the behaviors you want to see. Include them as one of your concept lessons at the beginning of the year.

Let me take a little detour and expound on this particular subject for just a bit. If your class is not fulfilling your imagined vision of how they should act and you've been using consequences to change that unacceptable behavior without success, ***change the consequences! They are not working!*** Retreating back to nearly every behavior management course I've ever taken, the specialist say that if you consequence three times without a change in the behavior, then your consequences are ineffective.

Of course, the TRICK is finding what consequences will work... try everything and then come up with something else – just don't give up – and don't assume you're being effective after three tries if the problem still persists. Clearly, when the same kid misses recess three out of five days, missing recess is not changing the behavior. It doesn't matter to that kid. Something matters to that kid – it's up to us to figure out what it is and use it. Get help from the parents – ask them what kinds of things are important to their child then figure out a way to use that information to help you manage the unwanted behavior(s).

Let me get back on track here, get on with our concept lesson, and give an example or two: Every day when it's time for my fifth graders to sing, I can say, "*Sit on the end of your chair, hold up your music, and sit up straight with both feet on the floor.*" OR...rather than just tell...I can <u>TEACH</u> the ins and outs of that same requirement, *one time*, and avoid having to repeat myself *every time*. It takes time the first time, but typically, it only takes one time - so in the end, it ends up worth it. Here's how I do it: "*Imagine if I were on a great baseball team <u>with you</u> and I walked up to home plate, it's my turn to bat, and I stood like this* (demonstrate a lethargic, one-handed swing while the scenario continues). *Here it comes...the pitch and we have...STEEERike one.* (She swings and misses!) *From the stretch...and the pitch...high and inside! STEEERike two!* (Still lazily swinging the bat with droopy arms and inattentive stance.) *The pitcher's ready to deliver the final pitch of the inning...he checks the runner at third, the wind-up, and the pitch. The ball miraculously meets the bat, bounces straight back to the pitcher but ricochets off his glove! The shortstop misses the back up because he's running toward second and the ball bounces off the pitchers' glove toward third. (The crowd goes wild!) The lethargic, lazy batter has a hit and an RBI. Now...the crowd falls silent, the oo's and ah's can be heard inside the hushed murmurs. The lead-off batter* *struts to the plate. He gives both shoes a solid whack with his bat, ridding his cleats of nothing. He pops his knuckles, tugs at the Velcro on both batting gloves, making fidgety, unnecessary adjustments, takes a few high-velocity practice swings – smacking his back with the bat so the pop resounds throughout the dugout, grabs the bill of his ball cap and gives it a snug little tug, and finally he steps into the batters box. He digs a groove, shoves some dust away with his toe, holds his hand up to Blue - signaling time, and finally, he grasps the bat with both hands, takes a couple more practice swings, ending with the tip of the bat pointing to left center. He is confidence incarnate! (pause) We have the wind-up...and the pitch. STEERike one! He backs out of the batters box, repeats his preparation process without omitting a single detail, returns to the plate, waits for the pitch, then STEERike two! Once more, he steps out of the box – checks for signs, repeats the progression, steps back in – and - STEERIKE THREE! YOU'RE OUT!* (The demonstration ends but discussion begins.) *So, think about it...which one of these two players would you most want on your team? The one who got the base hit and the RBI or the one who just struck out!?* Most of the kids agree they want the one who got the hit and RBI. (Then I proceed to the next skit.) *Your basketball team is playing for the league championship and the week before the big game, your coach introduces two new potential players to your team. Even though you don't want any new players, if you have to choose, which one of these two people would you pick?* (I demonstrate an uncontrolled dribble across the room, a clumsy jump stop, I bend over, spread my knees apart, and "granny-style" chuck the basketball into an imaginary basket.) *It goes in!!! Two points for your team!! Now it's time for prospective player number two...*(with great precision and skill, I dribble down the court, moving like the wind, drive the lane, go up for a lay up, switching hands in mid-air so the shot is away from the defender....and miss the shot!) *The crowd groans in disappointment. No points for your team from this guy! The question is...which player do you want on your team? The one who made the two points or the one who made zero points?* Most of the kids agree they want the one who made the points – but a few are catching on...so they vote for the one who missed the lay up. (Scene three: at the bowling alley, I am the first bowler and the commentator) *The first bowler lines up his left toe at the dots, makes a smooth, coordinated approach, slides, has a nice follow-through and good spin on the ball, hits his arrow – third from the right, the ball sails down the alley, but wait - the ball plunks into the gutter just before it reaches the pins. Bowler number two picks up* her ball, doesn't bother to put her fingers in the holes, just hugs it close, casually strolls up to the foul line, bends over, places the ball between her feet, and gives it a two-handed shove. *After what seems like an eternity...the ball ever-so-slowly bobbles it's way down the alley but eventually bumps into the head pin which starts an amazingly slow sequence of events. Like dominos in slow motion, the pins topple, one onto another and after sixteen and a half minutes, all ten of the pins are laying down. There wasn't even enough momentum by the ball to trigger the automatic pin reset but...she got a STRIKE! Which bowler do you want on your team?*

With good direction, the conversation between students should lead to the assumption that the three not-so-talented athletes just got lucky while the three who did not contribute to the team's points, have so much more potential to contribute to the whole in the long run than the "lucky" ones. Additionally, the "lousy-but-lucky" players *look* terrible, appear to be either poorly coached or not coached at all, they look "dorky" in their delivery, and they make your team look bad. They are not a good reflection of your team's potential, skills, or coaching. On the other hand, the three athletes who failed to accumulate points for the team have clearly spent hours practicing, know the game, have great mechanics, make the team look good, appear to be well-coached, and well-prepared. *Aren't THOSE the kinds of players you'd rather have representing you?*

The connection to music is this: Just like the "lucky players" who seemed successful, of *course* you can still get a sound out of your face when you're slouched in your chair, legs curled beneath you, and back bent over your music that's sitting on your lap. You can still sing and if you're a good singer, you might even sound decent...but just like the "dorky-looking" athletes, you make yourself look like you've never been coached or you have a rotten coach. You look like you don't know the right way, and should someone walk in the music room while you're singing that way – some serious conclusions are going to be drawn regarding you, your class, and especially, your teacher!

This connection to something they know and relate to seems to burn an image in their minds because, after this little skit, seldom do I have to remind them to sit up and hold up their music. They seem to understand after all that...and hopefully, the memories of those crazy skits will last a lifetime.

I don't neglect to mention the physical health, better sound production, and resonance reasons for good singing posture – but that comes well *after* the aesthetic, emotional, personal value is driven home. **Pre-teens are really into looks and image – why not capitalize on that?**

22. ***"STOP"*** is such a teacher's friend! Say it and then just wait for the "stop" to happen. You may have to repeat it, but don't clutter it with any other directions. "STOP" is clear, inarguable, and unmistakable. You *must* wait for the "stop" to happen, though, or it loses its value. If you continue talking, it dilutes your direction. It weakens your authority. It destroys your integrity. And they will learn they do not have to follow that directive. Remember, just wait or try something else, but do not continue until you have their undivided attention! Don't overuse *"STOP"* either, or it will become ineffective and ignorable (Is that a word? ☺ Let's use it, even if it isn't, OK?!).

23. ***VARIETY IS THE SPICE OF LIFE!*** *"STOP"* should work, especially if it's consistently enforced from the very beginning, but be prepared to change that command to a different word if *"STOP"* starts losing it's effectiveness. Sometimes, repetition can cause kids to tune you out and then the workability of a direction like *"STOP"* can be diluted. Some teachers use *"Freeze,"* others just have keywords. I had a student teacher who taught the kids to freeze or stop anytime he said, *"DOLPHINS."* I'm not necessarily endorsing that, even though it worked at the very beginning. I watched it eventually become totally ineffective and actually become an instigator of comments, nonsense, and disruptive behavior.

24. ***THREE STRIKES AND YOU'RE OUT!*** Strike one: stand up. Strike two: move to the door. Strike three: turn around. You can often solve "noisy" problems by asking the offender to *"please stand up."* Don't miss a beat in your instruction, don't jabber off on an explanation. Just say, *"And when you see this symbol, (Jessie please stand up), then you know that you are going to be reading treble clef rather than bass clef."* The reality of having to be different by standing is typically quite enough for her to know you're not going to allow talking while you're talking. If *"please stand up"* doesn't get the job done, the next step is *"Go stand by the door, please."* This is strike two…and works well because the student is still in the room, able to hear the lesson and participate, still within your jurisdiction, yet, is separated from their audience. If he/she continues to be disruptive, then ask the student, with a more I'm-disgusted-and-I'm-getting-really-exasperated-and-tired-of-your-nonsense tone to *"…turn around and face the door."*

That tally's to quite a sufficient number of warnings. If the disrespect still doesn't stop, it's time to resort to another consequence: I have the student write a letter to his/her parent(s). That can be accomplished on his/her own time and is covered in more detail later in this chapter under the topic: *COMMENTARY, KID-STYLE.* Or, if it becomes an issue to get anything out of him/her, notify the office that you are sending the child down for an out-of-class experience! ☺

25. **_WHAT'S YOUR NUMBER, PuhLEASE?_** When students refuse to quiet down, I call their bluff. I exaggerate my movements, search around for a pen or pencil, (even if it's right in front of me – so it buys some time and draws attention to what I am about to do,) I open my grade book, flip through a couple of pages so it looks like I have a very specific location for the information, and say, *"What is your telephone number, please?"* I write it down. Sometimes I also ask, *"Do you live with your dad? What is his name, please?"* I actually have no intentions of making a call, but the kids don't know that and they generally settle down because they're assuming I'm going to be having a little chat with mom or dad and they're busted. One time, a particularly obstinate child refused to give me his phone number. So I just jotted down a quick request for it on a Post It note, sent another student to the office for the information, and deliberately made certain he knew I have my ways…whether he cooperates or not. Help students realize you are going to get your way – one way or another – and they are not the ones in control.

26. **_YOU HAVE A CHOICE:_** I try never to press a child into a situation where this is necessary, but unfortunately, sometimes it just happens. You may have a student who absolutely refuses to do something you've asked. If you can't ignore it, you must deal with it. An example of a particular situation would be, he won't move out of the middle of the room while the other kids are skipping, or she sits down on the risers in the middle of a performance, or maybe she's throwing a temper tantrum that is disrupting the whole class. I speak in a calm voice and say, *"Jay, you have a choice. You can either get up like a big boy and do what I've asked you to do or I will call for help and we will move you. Now which do you want? You move you or I move you?"* Most of the time, Jay will do what he was asked, but if he doesn't, it is IMPERATIVE that you follow through with your proffered option. Either you remove him or her from the situation or you get help from

your Principal or another teacher. When things get this serious, it is better to have another teacher to witness what is transpiring, anyway.

27. ***TOTALLY OUT OF CONTROL!*** If a child goes completely berserk in your classroom, the best thing to do for everyone's sake, is to remove all of the other kids from the room rather than trying to move the troubled child. In so doing, you're separating the audience from the out-of-control student and securing their safety should the situation escalate. Know ahead of time where you can go with your class should this kind of episode ever happen. It's only happened to me a couple of times in my two and a half decades in the classroom, but it's best to be prepared, proactive, and have a plan.

28. ***PROXIMITY IS YOUR PAL!*** For the smaller, more insignificant, but still disrupting behaviors, let proximity be your pal. As you are teaching, just mosey toward the culprit. Your nearness often is all it takes to squelch the undesirable activity. Sometimes it takes the added "teacher look" my girls so often talk about – but between the two TRICKS, your interrupters usually settle down.

29. ***RANDOM NOISES, RANDOM RING!*** When students are working together in groups and talking is permitted, I sometimes enlist the aid of an egg timer to help all of us work toward maintaining an acceptable noise level. I simply explain that I am setting the "good egg" timer for an undisclosed, random amount of time. When the timer goes off, we stop and consider the volume in the room at the time the bell sounded. If it was acceptably quiet, we get to add a minute to recess or some other appropriate compensation for being a "good egg." If it was deemed too noisy when the timer sounded, there is no consequence but there is no prize, either. The timer is regularly reset for various duration's between rings, until the project is completed. It is fun to see how hard the kids will try to control the noise level, regardless of the reward, just in anticipation of the ring! I think it would be a fun way and effective way to manage the eternal problem of cafeteria noise, too, but that could be another whole book, couldn't it?

30. ***WHAT TO DO WHEN YOU'RE THROUGH?*** Rowdiness, noise, behavior problems, and other forms of interference often develop when students complete seat work before others finish. Teachers can be proactive and avoid the trouble as long as kids are provided something rewarding, fun, and entertaining to do once their work is *correctly*

completed. This is when art, music, reading, and game centers come in handy. If the work is incorrect, it's back to the drawing board for them.

31. *EMT, PARAMEDIC, AND TEACHER:* Just as those who are trained in human rescue must first identify and evaluate a problem, react appropriately to the particular incident and individual, then respond with the correct level of urgency; *so too, must a teacher.* There are very few careers where one must react so *instantaneously*, accurately, appropriately, and efficiently to such constantly varying circumstances as the EMT, paramedic, nurse, doctor, and TEACHER. Some situations may best require the crisis response team to provide *quiet, reassuringly gentle support and encouragement.* Other situations, however, dictate *drastic, radical, and immediate reactions* to take place. Because of these different responses, emergency medical personnel often establish a triage. It is obviously not appropriate to treat all victims with the same sense of urgency or with the same procedures. While some people need immediate, urgent personal attention, response to others can safely be delayed.

We teachers must be prepared in exactly the same way. Not unlike the paramedic confronted with a problem, we have our own teacher-arsenal of responses and procedures we carefully consider before reacting…a sort of mental triage. Some situations and students require teacher-reactions that are appropriately urgent and radical. Some can be delayed or no reaction is deemed necessary. Some just need quiet, reassuringly gentle support and encouragement. With ahead-of-time planning and a personal philosophy on how we want to react, we will make our teacher-reactions appropriate for each individual situation and not use the same caliber of urgency for every individual.

Let me explain, a child who is a first-time offender should not receive the same reaction or consequences from his teacher as a repeat offender. What is fair for one is not necessarily fair for another – what is fair is whatever *is best* for the people involved. **Please do not have blanket reactions.** *Talk with* the gentle-spirited, cowering, insecure, or frightened child and manage him differently than you manage the constantly disrespectful troublemaker. I include brief lessons for my classes explaining how reputation and "track record" can, should, and *will* have an effect on the way I will react to them if placed in a disciplinary role.

I realize this is quite a controversial topic and many may take issue with my opinion, calling it inconsistent and unfair. I know that many believe that when *any* student breaks *any* rule, it is only fair for him to receive the *exact same consequences* as any other child. There are an ample number of teachers in our schools who believe that wholeheartedly and prove it by punishing first-time offenders who made a mistake, are full of innocence and regret, with the exact same consequences assigned to one who is in trouble *every single day*, shows no remorse, and more than likely, will repeat the same behavior tomorrow. We all need to cut the poor first-time offender some slack and not be so rule-based and insensitive that we forget we are dealing with human beings, *little ones* – at that, with very real, sometimes very fragile emotions!

Understand please, that I'm not referring to serious offenses that hurt or have the potential to hurt someone else! I'm talking about offenses that only hurt themselves, their grades, their sense of responsibility, or anything that is not dangerous or destructive to others. Students who are dangerous, even first-time offenders, must be dealt with in a severe manner. In fact, if the offender is dangerous, it is no longer our job to manage the behavior – it should immediately be referred to someone of higher authority.

32. ***LIMIT LECTURES!*** (After my reponses to #31 in this chapter and #20 in Chapter Five, no doubt you're wondering how on earth I could, with good conscience, add *this* LIMIT LECTURES topic to my TRICKS!) Avoid lectures – they have a minimal effect, irritate, frustrate, and often make enemies of more than the recipient because it bothers nearly everyone. If you've got something to say, say it, ONCE, and drop it. Variations on the same theme is not appropriate in this instance! (Did I prove my point?) ☺

33. ***FORCE REMORSE!?*** Juxtaposed opinions constantly complicate this issue. Many people, particularly counselors and teachers, immediately make children apologize when they've done something wrong. I've seen some authority figures even make two fighters hug. Others do not force remorse, because they deem it insincere and therefore, valueless. Proponents say making a child apologize teaches kids how and when it's appropriate to express regret. Opponents believe it teaches kids that it is alright to lie. The fact is, if a child has recently done something wrong, more than likely, he or she has absolutely no feelings of remorse – unless, of course, it's remorse *for themselves* for getting caught or punished.

203

I have an opinion (go figure) that is a compromise and actually, has proven quite effective. I do *not* make anyone apologize after messing up. We do, however, discuss very succinctly how they've messed up, how it affects others' feelings, and how what they've done can effect their own reputation. Then, I question, guide, question some more, and prod until I get them to be able to answer the question, *"Since we've already decided that what happened probably hurt someone, what would be the right thing to do about it?"* They're usually so pre-programmed to answer, "Say I'm sorry" that they're really not thinking about what that response entails, they just want to get the issue over with. So I take it a step or two further and ask them if they even care that the other person might feel bad. If I hear the answer I want, we proceed, if not, we spend a little more time on that step. The next step is having them tell me what they could say that might make the other person feel a little better about the whole situation. Once I get them where I've lead them, I suggest they write a note, complete with a brief synopsis of what happened, their opinion of the whole thing, and their apology. I ask them to let me read it first, just so I can see that they really are apologetic and don't need a little more counsel. I don't set a deadline for the apology letter, but I keep track of them until the note is written and delivered. Sometimes it takes awhile to reach the ability to sincerely feel empathy for someone else. The longer it takes, the more talking, urging, and explaining I do, so they're just getting more input regarding the subject of apologizing.

SAYING *I'm sorry* is relatively easy...but when a lesson *and* letter take the place of the easy words, kids are far more likely to remember the rather lengthy apology process. The hypothesis is, they will more carefully select their words and actions next time so they don't do anything that merits an apology.

34. <u>*ANTICIPATE NEED AND AVOID THE PROBLEMS:*</u> There are a few proactive TRICKS you can utilize to help avoid some of the disruptive problems you may encounter:

➤ Establish clear expectations.

➤ Regularly reassure all students of your faith in their ability to succeed.

➤ Make it personal...call students by name.

➤ If they are reluctant participants, give them forewarning that you are going to call on them: *"Jen, I will be calling on you for an answer to the next question."*

➤ Give compliments – make them look and feel good in front of their peers. Image means a lot to pre-teens.

➤ If they say a wrong answer, help them save face by turning it into a correct answer: *"You know what? That will be a perfect answer when I ask _____. Remember that and I'll come back to you. OK?"* Then be sure to get to the question that matches the already-given answer.

➤ Obstinate kids are worse than reluctant kids – they usually can't be *made* to do anything! If you have one of these in class, find out just what he/she really loves doing and use that as your ally. Try: *"Hey Tori, let's make a deal. You work for ten minutes and then you can _____ for ten minutes. We'll just trade off."*

➤ Smile when you teach.

➤ Build relationships outside of your classroom with individuals. The lunchroom, library, playground, hallway, and even their regular classroom are great places to reach these kids.

➤ Offer to tutor a child with his math, reading, or spelling. The little extra time you are willing to share with someone who is struggling might just make a difference in the way he/she behaves in your music class.

35. **_STRESS FRACTURES:_** Not always, but *sometimes* some of the most inappropriate, irritating, obnoxious, patience-trying behaviors are not as much a matter of choice, but a child's way of responding to stress. Stress and worry affect all of us. It can fracture *our* ability to concentrate, to learn, to be civil, even to feel well! You may be able to de-emphasize unwanted behaviors just by being a friend and soothing their fears. If you have students whose behavior manifests itself in one of the following ways, you may be able to help *a little* by spending some extra time with them. The kids who need to be de-stressed are those who are constantly:

➢ Whining, crying, always complaining, wanting to touch you or pull on your clothes.

➢ Seem constantly confused.

➢ Needing reassurance, creating things to tell you, tattling, concerned more with other people's business than their own, and interrupting.

➢ Bossing and wanting to dictate everyone, including you.

➢ Frustrated and easily annoyed

➢ Disruptive

➢ Blaming others and bullying

➢ Shutting down, offering no response, wearing a blank expression, or sitting and staring.

So what can you do during this time you spend with them? Recognize their strengths and let them know you've noticed. **Talk to them**...and get them talking so you have a chance to listen to them. **Compliment them** – maybe they completed their work on time, perhaps they scored well on a test, maybe you caught them helping someone without being asked, maybe they didn't complain a single time during recess! Allow your **vocal inflection** to either calm or boost them – whichever they need. If they are low and flat, speak energetically, fast and with excitement – let your enthusiasm sound obvious. If they are aggressive, angry, bossy or out of control, speak in a calm, reassuring, quiet voice – don't let their intensity elevate yours. **Ask questions...**maybe it will help them think about something else and get their mind off of what's bothering them. **Use humor and play.** If you can tease them in a friendly way or make them smile, they might come out of their funk. If they are completely unreasonable and can't be persuaded out of their mood, sometimes it works to say, *"Help me understand. What could I do for you so you won't be so angry?"* or *"What would be the TRICK to getting you so you're not always interrupting class?"* or, *"What would make you feel better?"* or, *"What could I change or do differently so class is more interesting to you?"* or, *"Let's play a game. You get to be the friend and I'm* *going to tell all of your friends that they get to boss you around for a whole hour. How would you like that game?"* Sometimes, putting them in a position where they can recognize and react to the situation they are putting others in, helps them see the same picture that you see regarding their behavior. This "game" might teach them to empathize, but beware, analysis like that can backfire, so tread carefully.

36. ***IS THERE A DIFFERENCE BETWEEN TATTLING and TELLING?*** You bet there is! I take class time at the beginning of each semester and as needed between terms, to cover my own personal definition of tattling. Most dictionary definitions explain it as divulging information or incessant chatter. That definition is too broad for a teacher who has to deal with tattling five out of every five days. My definition is: "***Tattling*** is when you tell me something just to ***get someone else in trouble. Telling*** is when you tell me something just ***to get help for someone else***." We play out some tattling versus telling scenarios…enough so that I am convinced they understand there is a difference. Some educators may argue, *"But you want a child to tattle if he or she has seen someone do something destructive like graffiti-ing or stealing something."* True, very true. But, ***I* will solicit that information** when the time comes, *if* it comes. To complicate a simple definition of "tattling" and "informing" with "what-if's" isn't very age-appropriate for elementary students. If a student is hurt by another student – it is *telling* because that student needs help for someone – in this case, themselves.

Be very cautious though, not to completely ignore the "tattles." We kinda have to listen with one ear while the other ear is playing deaf to "tattling" because bullying and meanness easily disguises itself and happens more than we realize. We *have* to deal with those issues.

If you notice that kids are constantly coming to you and tattling on others, you've given them reason to know they can get results by telling. They have discovered an acceptable way to get someone else in trouble. You've taught them to tattle…by reinforcing it.

35. ***RECESS AND GRUMPY KIDS*** can be a tricky situation to handle. I *can* dictate a solution but I have found that making the ones with the grumpies sit down and figure it out, can settle the problem more efficiently than anything I might say or do. I just tell those involved to figure out what happened, how to solve it, and then to come and let me know when they can explain to me exactly what happened and their solution. As soon as they've come up with the answer and shared it

with me, they get to head back out and play. More than likely, they've missed quite a bit of their play time during their figuring out time and they will, more than likely, always remember what will happen when they tattle and avoid it next time.

36. ***COMMENTARY, KID-STYLE!*** One of the best TRICKS I've *ever* used is to have rule-breaking offenders *write their own note of explanation to their parents.* They simply list the progression of events that took place up to the point when trouble was addressed. It is not an admission of guilt – though it often portrays itself as that. When you have the student write it rather than you, it's presented in their own words, the parents find out what has transpired, and you don't have to make that phone call.

Calling, to me, is *the scariest* of teacher-to-parent interactions. It scares me for several reasons. First, intonation and body language are virtually absent in a phone conversation – so both parties stand a chance of misunderstanding the meaning and misinterpreting the motive and comments of the other. Second, facial expressions, shimmering eyes that show kindness, and smiles that ease the pain can't be seen or felt, so words without that added human touch can be hurtful. Third, telephone conversations can easily catch you off guard and have you giving answers or providing information that you are not prepared to give. It is scary to be asked for anything that is not readily at your fingertips and you can't always anticipate what you will need because you can't anticipate where the conversation will go. What's worse is for someone to request your opinion – particularly when both parties are on the defensive or someone's feelings have been hurt. Every word weighs a ton – you want to only state facts and not offer your opinion, so it's much better to be able to prepare and not have to answer on the spur of the moment. If you communicate through written expression, you have ample time to carefully word your thoughts and responses. (They also have written documentation of your every word so misquoting is avoided.) Fourth, conversations over the phone can take far too many off-tangent journeys. Not only does this cause you to have to discuss things you may not be prepared to talk about or support, it makes your conversation last *forever* and often ends up with chit-chatty yak that eats up the little bit of plan time you have.

So...when a child is naughty in your class and it's time to notify parents, this kid-commentary comes in quite conveniently! Without punishing, lecturing, giving the "teacher look" or forcing blame, I simply have the child write a "Dear Mom & Daddy letter," telling exactly what has transpired, if applicable - where they believe the fault lies, and what rules were broken. I check the note for clarity and accuracy, sometimes send it back for more information or clarification, write a quick little, *"So I know you have seen this, please sign and return by tomorrow* (add date,) *so your child will be able to play during recess,"* and whip it through the copier so I have a souvenir of the transaction. The child knows his recess is mine until the note is returned and signed by a parent. This has proven to be a very successful communication and behavior management tool.

Keep in mind...if the student refuses to write the note, give him/ her a few days to decide which option is better: to write or miss recess. If, after a few days, you *still* do not receive the letter, it is definitely time to notify your principal and, of course, the parents. At this point, the situation has escalated beyond the original misconduct. Now your student is snaking into the world of rebellion, disrespect, and defiance.

I used an analogy when I had a student adamantly refuse to serve five minutes of recess for talking. In response to that rude refusal, he was instructed to write a kid-commentary. In spite of my repeated clarification, he insisted that serving five minutes of playtime and writing the note were admissions of guilt. I asked him to imagine this scenario: *"A dad rolls up to a stop sign. He believes he stopped at the intersection but a police officer accuses him of not coming to a complete stop. It is the driver's word against the officer's word and the dad is furious about the accusation. The bottom line is, whether the driver believes he is guilty or not, if he fails to appear in court and pay the ticket, there will be a warrant out for his arrest. The court is less concerned at that point whether he was guilty or innocent of the original offense. They now must deal with the fact that the dad refused to appear when scheduled. The driver had options. He could have paid the small-by-comparison fine, he could have even constructed a not-guilty plea and eventually been finished with it. Instead, he chose to disobey the officer's instructions. At that point, his penalty, his time, his expense, and the repercussions are exponentially more costly to the driver. In the end, the officer is the ultimate authority and the dad pays some form of consequences. He may have felt as though he'd proven a point by choosing not to serve the original consequence, but ultimately, by choice, he paid a substantially higher price."* I had hopes that the story would help the little guy realize that his choices were going to cost him far more than the five minutes of recess, but unfortunately, he never figured that out.

So you're thinking, that kid refused to write – what about the little guys who *can't* write their own letter? Then…you might want to use the following as an example for the letter *you* write to mom and daddy:

Dear Mr. & Mrs. So-n-so,

Jon is such a talented little guy. When he sings, he is so good and really makes a great leader! His speaking parts for the program are so nice and loud – I know everyone will be able to hear and understand him and you will be proud when you see his performance in the show. The only problem is, and I hate to have to be contacting you about this, but he seems to forget not to talk when it's not his turn. I've reminded him but he still forgets. Today, I finally had to pull him off the risers and had him just stand and wait while we finished our rehearsal, but he still didn't really stay quiet the whole time.

He's not in trouble and I'm not cranky with him, but I think you and I both want him to remember not to interrupt, take time away from the other kids, and make some better choices.

You know him so much better than I do so I'm writing to you for some expert advice! What can we do together to help him be more successful? Think about it and please let me know if you have any suggestions that would help me help Jon. I would sure appreciate your input!
Respectfully submitted,
Debbie Gray

The basic format of any letter home, regarding a discipline problem, is first to **compliment** the child on *something*. You can mention her ability to match pitch, sit still, have lots of friends, be a strong leader, participate in discussion, nice manners, long eye lashes, straight toes, beautiful smile…anything that will help mom and daddy know you notice that their child does well at certain things and that you like him or her. The next step is to make sure they know you are **reluctant** to have to be contacting them with not-such-great news. (Remember, always write letters of compliment and support early in the year, to every child, if possible, but especially to those you predict will need some further parent-contact. This will not only help to build and strengthen your **relationship** with the child and their parents, but it helps greatly if you ever have to notify parents of a less-than-positive incident.) Finally, gently and kindly **state the offense**. Don't expound, don't elaborate, don't let your frustration and anger show, just state the facts with "soft" words. (Apply the Golden Rule to your words.) Finally, seek their **advice**. Who better to give you advice on how to manage their child than mom and dad? It empowers them, it keeps them from feeling as if they must defend their child, it puts both of you on the same team, and it helps them know you are looking out for their son's or daughter's best interest, not venting or attacking.

37. *MAY I HAVE YOUR ATTENTION, PLEASE!?* NEVER talk about *anything* they all need to hear until you have every single person's **absolute attention**. Their absolute attention means, their full body – not just their head - is *facing you*, they are quiet, and they're looking at you (not their shoelaces, their neighbor, the carpet, the fly on the wall, their hangnail, a scab, or the lint ball in their belly button!) Do not expect this to be natural for them. You MUST TEACH them what to do by telling and MODELING what "absolute attention" *looks* like. Each time someone loses his/her focus, *stop teaching* and remind him or her to look at you. Granted, this will be a major interruption for a little while…but you are a trainer…be patient and consistent…they'll get it sooner or later (sometimes later, unfortunately).

My best friend and extraordinary educator, LeAnn Dill, reminds her students before beginning a lesson, *"This is a listening time."* It is a verbal cue, as obvious as it may seem, and is helpful in directing their attention. Since hearing her use it frequently and seeing the positive results, I have adopted it and it works GREAT in the music room, as well! Me, doing it in music, also strengthens and supports what she does in physical education classes. The more you implement in your plans the very things you admire someone else in your building doing, the more concrete it becomes in the minds of your students because they experience it in classes other than just music.

Also, if you do, in fact, borrow some other teacher's idea for classroom management, be sure to drop them a note telling them that you were impressed enough with their success that you've started using it yourself. Later, let them know again how it is working for you and thank them again for the idea.

38. ***KEEP A JOURNAL FOR REPEAT OFFENDERS!*** Just as the police department keeps track of past offenses, a good teacher who constantly must deal with a student who agrees to be disagreeable, must also keep track of offenses.

My "kid confessions" make the best log of events that have taken place. I keep the copy of the letter until I receive the signed note from the parents, then shred the copy, save the original. I usually don't need any other discipline journal other than this. But if I do:

➤ I write each entry in a different color ink so repeat infractions can be seen at a glance.

➤ I do not write in pencil – it *appears* to be too easily adjusted.

➤ Place DAY and DATE on each entry.

➤ Be specific but only record facts – opinions are not only valueless, they can, in fact, reduce your journal's integrity.

➤ Keep it in a confidential location where only you know it's where-abouts.

➤ Keep all journal entries confidential.

➤ If you choose, you can include entries on the good days, too – so it's not all about disrespectful behavior, however, I do not do this. If I pull out a discipline journal – there isn't going to be *anything* positive in it - - positive things are taken care of with all of my letters, calls, and visits.

➤ If you get to enter a good report, be sure you accompany that with a note to the child letting him/her know you noticed.

➤ Allow your principal to read it periodically and ask him/her to sign at the bottom of each section read.

➤ If you prefer, you can have the student write the entry. Be sure the page made available for him/her to write does not include other entries. We don't want previous entries to be edited in any way, after the fact. This also secures the anonymity of other journaled-student entries.

➤ If you choose to write the entries, rather than the student – it doesn't hurt to let the student see what you write and know that you are keeping a running diary of his/her behaviors. Be sure though, to point out good days, too.

➤ Include actions you may have taken to alter the inappropriate behavior.

➤ Have your journal available to show when you meet with the parents...but make sure you have contacted them along the way and during the process of attempting to alter the unacceptable behaviors so the meeting doesn't come as a surprise.

I still have every discipline log I've ever written – which aren't that many because I only use this for severely behaved repeat offenders. You never know when that information might be considered valuable evidence in the event that child, as an adult, becomes a criminal. (This has happened. One of my former students kidnapped and shot a woman at point-blank range. His adult behavior came as no surprise to me having had him as a student for seven years in elementary school. Had I had a behavior log on him, a discipline journal very well would have provided unequivocal evidence that he was a long-term offender and trouble-maker. His behaviors clear back in elementary school were violent, aggressive, disrespectful, and evil-spirited.) Incidentally, the words, *"evil-spirited"* may very well be considered an opinion rather than a statement of fact.

39. ***TEACHER TALK THAT WILL TEACH YOU NOT TO TALK:***
There are a few things we just don't want to say. Here they are and here's why we probably don't want to include them in our routine speaking repertoire. <u>BIG BLUNDER BOMB NUMERO UNO</u>: *"How many times have I told you..."* <u>Response</u>: "Seventeen. No wait, maybe eighteen. I really don't know, let me ask Justin if he can remember. I'll be sure to get back with you on that one, though." (Just don't say it and you'll never have to listen to anyone give you a numerical answer to your question. If you forget and use those words – don't blame the kid for answering you. You asked.) <u>BIG BLUNDER BOMB NUMERO DOS</u>: *"I am waiting for you to get quiet...."* <u>Response</u>: "Could ya let us know what we're gonna do if we get quiet versus us just keepin' on lettin' you wait?" (Waiting for them to get quiet, and even saying those words are not your optimal choice, but OK. Saying "STOP" with authority, seems to work best. If, however, you choose to use the *"....waiting for you..."* coercion,

I'd suggest you edit the comment just a tad: *"I am waiting for you to get quiet so we can play rhythm instruments,"* etc. Just be specific about what they're going to get to do once you stop having to wait. If you have something planned that isn't terribly appealing to the masses, be honest and say, "*I am waiting for you to get quiet before we finish working on the B-section of this piece.*" If time is wasting, your statement hasn't made their noise decrease, and some kids are ignoring you, make a physical or mental list of those who *are* quiet and then say, *"Well, I've waited long enough for you. These people were quiet and so before we get back to our song, they are going to get to do the BEAN BAG BOOGIE with me."* Make sure the noisemakers just stand and watch while the others pop up for some fun. Just remember: **If you're going to say, "*I'm waiting for you to get quiet*" you better have something enticing planned so they care.** BIG BLUNDER BOMB NUMERO TRES: *"Did you like learning that song about the Barbie Doll?"* or, *"Was that fun?"* or, *"Without saying a word, go to your personal spaces. OK?"* (Each one of those *questions* can and probably will summon some kind of response. Don't ask a question at the end of a statement unless you're prepared to have all twenty-six of them respond.) BIG BLUNDER BOMB NUMERO QUATRO: *"Move over here, please."* Response: "Why? I didn't do anything?" *"Because you didn't get quiet when I asked you to."* "That's not fair. I wasn't talking!" *"Yes. Yes you were. Now move over here."* "But why do I have to? I don't wanna sit over there!" *"Because this is away from your friend, Nick, and maybe you will stop interrupting me."* "Can't I sit over there?" *"No. I told you to sit over here, please."* "But why? I won't interrupt you anymore, I promise." *"Because I asked you to, that's why."* "I can't see if I'm that far away." *"Well, then sit over there."* "I hate you. Why are you so mean to me?" *"I'm not being mean to you. I told you at least four times to stop talking and you kept visiting with your friends."* "They're not my friends." *"You were sure talking to them like they were your friends."* And so the dialogue continues. Meanwhile, twenty-six other kids are sitting there sponging up this repartee with the student versus your intentions, sincerity, and ultimately, your frustration. Bottom line...don't volley comments with kids. State what you expect and do not allow them to escort you off issue. The use of the word, *because* is a good indicator that you've taken their bait. In this example, the explicit directive was, "...*move over here*...." More than likely, they'll try to pilot you off course with a... "...*why*...." Your response **should be**, *"Move* *over here now, please."* If they try some other tactic like, *"...but I can't see if I move over there..."* You respond, *"Move now, please."* They may continue to push. If they do, sternly respond, *"This will be the last time I tell you to <u>move over here</u>. You can either move right now or I can notify the principal – it's your choice."* With broken-record responses like this, you avoid being sucked in by their get-the-teacher-off-the-issue manipulation attempts, you waste far less time, and **you** get **your** way rather than the student getting his or hers.

40. ***<u>POTENTIALLY DESTRUCTIVE DEMANDS:</u>*** Although **demanding** a little person to, *"...look at me when I'm talking to you..."* can be a powerful element of conversation under certain circumstances and definitely has appropriate moments of use, it is not *always* a real good idea. I've learned that some cultures teach that children are being disrespectful to adults, when being reprimanded, if they look directly at them. So by demanding that of them, you may be expecting them to break cultural guidelines that have been ingrained in them since birth. (Of course, it is disrespectful in every culture to be disrespectful to an adult – which is perhaps why you were demanding he/she look at you in the first place; but, I've been told I'm offending cultural tradition if I do that, so I'm sharing that tidbit with you.) Also, kids who have a history of sexual abuse may very well find it impossible to look you in the eye. Please don't force it – especially if that's a possibility. Finally, if you're dealing with a kid with behavior or emotional disorders, forcing her to look at you may become the new issue instead of your original point of discussion. You have to choose your battles and not complicate an already volatile situation with any additional demands.

41. ***<u>INTERLUDE FUN.</u>*** Having to sit still too long has a way of making fidgety kids fidgetier! (I know, it should be "more fidgety," but fidgetier is more funner to say!) I like to use interludes as personal-space swapping times. Students may spin to a new location when they hear the interlude, they may skip, crawl, or any other movement activity you can come up with – so they are less sedentary and break the lull of working in the same location at the same pace.

If it's a song where a partner is needed for the activity, there is always the possibility that someone will be partner-less. When this happens, they are told, if the numbers are even and no one should be alone, that they are to instantly shoot their hand up, look around for the other hand up, and both head toward each other as fast as possible. Not only does this little TRICK help avoid the fidgets, it can help break gender barriers, too. The more you do it, and the more fun the activity, the less they are concerned about who their partner is and more concern is placed on just finding one!

Before ever attempting any partner-swapping activity, I always spend time modeling what good sportsmanship looks like. We role play various scenarios that could potentially take place with students not wanting a certain someone to be their partner. I make it clear that our job is to include everyone...no matter what! Of course, we always stop whatever we're doing if there's a problem with not accepting someone as a partner and they find out real fast that that kind of attitude is not going to be allowed. I let them know that if someone were to ignore them or not allow them to be their partner, I would come to their aid and not let them be treated that way – so I'm not going to let them treat anyone like that, either. They understand that I am fair, but that "*picky partner pickers*" make me cranky.

If there happens to be an uneven number of students and I can't help out because I'm at the piano, they understand that they just pretend to have a partner and do the exact same motions as if someone were at the other end of their hands, facing them. It works.

42. ***EENEY, MEENEY, MINEY, MOE.*** Allowing your students **OPTIONS** can be so helpful in classroom management. For example, give "options" to a kid who is being resistant...try to be creative enough to offer more than two "options," otherwise, that child will still think you're bossing him and giving him an ultimatum rather than a choice. If you list three options, he will feel more like he's honestly being given a choice. By options, I mean, "*You may sit quietly with the others and complete your paper, you may come up here by me and complete your paper without talking, or you may sit by your best friend and complete your paper as long as you work silently.*" Don't use this TRICK if you can't come up with viable options – you *have* to be able to offer three things that *keep you in control of the situation*.

Of course, I suggest using this mostly when something seems to have the potential of escalating into a crisis. If it's just one of your normal kids acting particularly ugly for some reason, it's better not to give options at all and either make her do it, or, if you prefer, talk to her and try to figure out why she is in such a foul mood.

44. *UH OH! SOMETHING'S WRONG!* **Out of the ordinary behavior is triggered by something** – you want to be *very* careful that you don't punish or push someone into something if something awful has instigated the behavior. Don't overreact – especially if the perpetrator is not a regular problem student. Twice in my career, only *after* dealing with students who had perfect behavioral track records but their attitudes and behavior had soured, did I find out that in both cases, the kids were suicidal. The principal, counselor, classroom teacher, and nurse were aware these children had attempted to take their own lives, but none of the special staff teachers (art, music, pe, computer) were told. Because of confidentiality issues and circumstances encircling these kinds of situations, you may not ever know, so the best advice I can offer is to assume the worst, treat the changes in behavior accordingly, and approach your boss with your observations, experiences, and concerns.

45. *INTRUMENTS IN THE CLASSROOM.* Before ever actually incorporating rhythm instruments, bells, kazoos, keyboards, recorders, Boomwhackers, chimes, etc. into your lesson plans, my advice to you is to plan for the first lesson or class to be nothing more than an introduction and a time to experiment with the instruments. In order to help yourself avoid frustration, please do these things prior to allowing students to handle the equipment:

➢ Establish exactly how the instruments are to be handled, carried, played, and returned to storage.

➢ Teach them when to retrieve them and when to return them.

➢ Set your ground rules: "*You play the instrument without permission, you lose it. I am not angry with you and you are not in trouble, you just don't get to use the instrument again until next time.*" Try not to be cranky about it if they play their instrument. Just *quietly* say with a forgiving smile, "*Sorry, you need to put your sticks back in the box. Next time, you can try it again.*" **Then drop it**. (What's worse than a ranting, raving, can't-get-to-the-end-of-it lecture? If you hate those…then be sure you don't make your students endure one.) Make sure they know you're not angry at them and that they *ARE NOT IN TROUBLE*, just that THEY made a poor decision and you're following through with your promise. The little ones are probably going to give all new meaning to wailing

10

and gnashing of teeth, but you just have to ignore them – don't go soft – stay firm and don't be intimidated, persuaded, or manipulated by the tears or the wails. You just have to keep going and let them try their well-honed manipulating skills. If it persists, I've found, amazingly, that a quiet, one-sided conversation <u>in their ear,</u> stating some clear facts like: *"Don't waste your energy. You need to know that you can cry and yell 'til the cows come home and it's not going to change my mind, so you might as well stop."* Funny how it works, but it almost always does when they learn that throwing a fit is not going to get them anywhere but exhausted. It's hard work for them to work it like that, ya know?! It's hard work for you to try to teach over the drama, but you'll probably only have to do it one time for the whole class to learn that acting that way isn't going to get them what they want.

➤ Once all of your expectations are clear in their minds, they've had a chance to experiment, you will probably only have a few minutes left to actually play the instruments. But in the long run, you will spend much less time with discipline and more time with what you're wanting to do...and that's TEACH and HAVE FUN! (What an exciting and novel concept!)

46. *__THERE ARE ALWAYS EXCEPTIONS TO EVERY RULE,__* no matter how general it may be...but, if I were to share a good, useful rule with you - - I would suggest that you leave out the phrase, *"I want you to...."* Until you've established a relationship with them, many kids will prove they don't care what you want! It takes awhile of building *__RELATIONSHIPS__* with kids for what YOU want - to matter to *them.* It's better, for the time being, to make it a GENTLE but concise command. *"Please stop..."* or *"Sit down and..."* or, instead of *"I want you to have fun..."* make it, *"Don't grumble about..."* or *"Stop complaining...."* *"I want you to..."* works ok most of the time with the primary-aged kids – they WANT to please you! The older kids, however, especially if they're in sink-the-sub mode, will USE THAT AGAINST you. If they know what you WANT, they'll do the *exact opposite.* Don't give them the option – just make it a concrete, clear directive. **That is, until you've established a relaxed, respectful relationship with them.** It will be a rare occasion when someone acts badly or disrupts after you've developed that trust, friendship, and relationship with him or her. I promise.

"You don't just luck into things....
You build step by step, whether it's friendships or opportunities."
~Barbara Bush

47. <u>*GENTLE DISCIPLINE*</u>   My tolerance of classroom noise is relatively high as are my expectations for my kids, but I prefer a relaxed, more limited use of structure if the students allow. Some students just can't handle a not-so-controlled environment and need more structure, while others thrive in my music class. My free-spirited, fast-paced motivational techniques and the fun, silly and sometimes loitering-on-the-ridiculous way I teach a lesson may set the "left-hemisphere-dominates" in my classes into a spin cycle. On the other hand, I think they have so much fun and appreciate the nonsense and energy enough that it must compensate for my sometimes overwhelming personality that might otherwise irritate. Some kids would do back flips to please me. Others know that all this "fluff" is quite trivial and totally irrelevant. But, it usually provokes miles of smiles and a "didn't-even-realize-I-was-learning-anything" music class while at the same time, limiting discipline problems! I guess all I'm saying is, if you discipline gently all the time, then, when you *do* have to draw both barrels and come out with guns smoking, so to speak, the exaggerated change in your personality makes them know you mean business. If you're intense, strict, and militaristic all the time or if you're always wearing your poker face – you've already used up your ammo and have no place to go with your bluff.

48. <u>*ONE OF THOSE DAZE!*</u> It's important, as far as your tolerance for activity and noise goes, to be consistent. You'll drive your students nuts if one day they get to come in and mess around, be noisy and rowdy, then the next day, they get in trouble for acting exactly the same way. So, be as consistent as possible. If, however, you're having "one of those days," like we all have, where you know kids, noise, and activity are going to drive you nuts, then just tell the kids and let them know that *"today is going to have to be different from usual so no talking in between...."* You can add an, *"...and I mean it!"* for good measure if you're feeling particularly anxious, dazed, ill, or grumpy. ☺

49. <u>*ZOOM NO MORE!*</u> Speaking of dazed...you know how *we* can sometimes become dazed and "out of it" during a lecture, sermon,

speech, faculty meeting, or training session? I am even bad about it while driving my car. I can arrive in downtown Kansas City and realize I don't remember driving past the sports complex. I'm amazed and often even frightened by the mystery of how I got from point A to point B without even being aware of it. I guess it's the mental auto-pilot thing. You know...the drive-by-Zen thing that happens when your mind is occupied with other things or you're so exhausted that you use drive time as your brain dump time? I hope I'm not the only one who has experienced this!

Well...just as we adults "zoom off" into "never-never land," kids have an even greater capacity for zooming. They honestly don't zoom off too much during music because I seldom have any concept introduction time where they are seated for more than four or five minutes, however, once in a blue moon it is necessary for them to sit through a longer explanation than I prefer to give, but need to in order to teach it in its entirety. Anyway...I've adopted what I call the ZOOM game. It's simple, it's effective, and it can even be fun for them. Of course, your room atmosphere, your discipline style, and your personality as their teacher <u>has to be safe and fun</u> for this to be pulled off *as a game* rather than punishment or it'll go all haywire and backfire on you.

Here's how it works: After making sure they know what "zooming off" means and I've given them multiple quick examples of the times and ways I've caught *myself* zooming off, they are told that I am going to have to talk for longer than I usually do and they are going to have to stay tuned-in longer than usual in order to learn the concept . IF **they catch themselves "zooming"** before I catch them "zooming," all they have to do is stand up and sit right back down. That action *"erases the zoom"* and they're free and clear. On the other hand, IF **I catch them "zooming"** before they catch themselves "zooming," then they have to stand up until I'm finished with the lesson. It's very important to assure them they are not in trouble if I catch them, but to beware because, *"I've been doing this teaching thing for a long time and for some reason, I've just gotten really good at catching zoomers."*

The ultimate goal is to help them make a conscious effort to stay tuned-in; but when they "zoom"...the process of standing up and being able to wiggle a little helps them to refocus and tune back in to the lesson!

50. <u>*SMILE AND LAUGH*</u>...a lot!!! (Even if it means faking it!) Just like adults, kids *love* to be around happy people – or seemingly happy

people. Make a deal with yourself that you will MAKE yourself smile, giggle, and take time to laugh with your students almost constantly! Try this little experiment sometime: Without a smile, say, *"C'mon you guys...this is a singing class and you're supposed to be singing. I don't hear you. Sing louder!"* Later or at another time, with an excited smile, say, *"Holy cow you guys sound good! I can't tell who is singing so awesome and matching pitch so well! Whoever it is isn't yelling – just sounding great! Let's sing that again so I can listen more carefully!"* In both cases, your objective is to get the kids to participate better, produce more sound, and elevate their energy. See which TRICK works best for you. (Bet you can guess! I called this little TRICK, ***SMILE AND LAUGH*** not ***LOOK TOUGH AND NAG!***) ☺

51. ***RECESS REMINDERS:*** You will, no doubt, get to manage recess duty during your career. I get to for an hour every day! Lucky, lucky me! Some teachers take away recess time as a consequence then leave it to me to enforce. I don't mind – kids need to learn there are consequences for inappropriate choices. Those students are always reminded, *"Your time starts when you are quiet and starts over if you talk."* That way, their consequence is hopefully more effective and I don't have to harp at them to be quiet or feel frustrated when they're not.

52. ***WATCH WATCH:*** I have the hardest time with teacher directives that indicate one person owes five minutes, another owes ten, another 15, and someone else owes all of recess. I actually do ok with the "all-of-recess kid" because I don't have to remember to release him to play, but releasing the others at the correct interval could easily be forgotten as I'm doing the duty thing, so I have incorporated the help of an inexpensive little "recess watch." I've established a five minute row, a ten minute row, a fifteen minute row, and an all-recess row. I give my watch to one of the "five-minute owers" and put him/her in charge of *"...watching the watch,"* and when time expires, passing the watch back to a "ten-minute ower." This process takes the responsibility of remembering *off of me*, gives ownership to the student(s), prevents anyone from being forgotten and spending more time on the line than they owe, and all I have to do is move people back a row if they talk or don't meet expectations.

Over the years, I've seen other recess duty assignees have to seek out the kids who owe time in order to enforce their consequences. The kids have these tragic memory lapses and "forgot" they owed time. Granted, sometimes they really do forget; however, most of the time, I'm going to go with the fact that they want to sneak in as much playing time as possible, hope they never get caught, or hope the teacher on duty doesn't know.   I decided a long time ago I didn't want to have to do that. So, that is yet another *responsibility I place on the kids*. They know from the very beginning of the year that if I'm on duty and they owe time, they come straight to the line and begin their time. If I have to remind them, they owe their time to their teacher then the remainder of recess they owe to me. It typically doesn't take but one full recess missed for their memory to improve dramatically! (This is not about punishment, though it may appear that way, this is about teaching responsibility, honesty, and discouraging the incorrigible behavior of sneakiness.)

53. **_PLAY BALL!_** I have been blessed with a killer throwing arm. In fact, I think I still hold the softball long-distance throw at my high school, 30 years later! Anyway, I use that "gift" to help manage some of my older, "difficult" students. I get a couple of us together, invite them to bring their gloves, stay after school, and play catch for a half hour or so, on the playground. It's amazing how amazed they are that I can not only throw like a guy, but catch like my livelihood depended on it. I'm not sure if it's out of respect or just the time we spend together, but after a few after-school sessions with ball and glove, we have a relationship that no longer requires me having to discipline them in class. I'm not sure what I would do if I didn't have an arm that let's me throw a good, strong fastball, but since I do, I capitalize on that ability to make more friends.

54. **_CHALK IT UP TO EXPERIENCE!_** Have you ever had one of those little fidgets who can't stand still if their life depended on it? What to do with him or her has been an age-old dilemma. You don't really want to punish him or her for that extra dose of energy inside; but we do, sometimes, need to help control the outbursts of movement and disruption. The floor in my music room is carpeted. So, I just use a piece of chalk, draw a nice-sized circle and give the hoppity-hopper some boundaries. That's generally all it takes to subdue the motion explosions. If your floor is tile, just use a dry-erase marker. I don't like to use tape, though some people do, because it leaves a sticky film on the floor when removed, which tends to collect dirt and grime and the line becomes permanently visible.

55. ***LINING UP QUICKLY AND QUIETLY*** is always a challenge for music teachers, but it is an important concept to master early in the year so that you have as much time teaching as possible and spend less time getting the kids out of your room. There are several reasons why this is a bit more of a challenge for us than for their classroom teachers. First, they're accustomed to doing it a certain manner in their classrooms. Each teacher manages line-up time in a different way, often with different objectives and with different expectations. So for you to attempt to stay apprised of each group's routine could be quite an obnoxiously difficult job. It is virtually impossible for me to try to keep up with all classes. Some have line leaders, others don't. Some have kids line up in one line while others have a girls' line and a boys' line. Some line up alphabetically. Some line up boy-girl-boy-girl and some don't have their kids line up at all – it's just a mass exodus like in middle school or high school. Actually, there are about as many variations on the line-up theme as there are teachers in the building! There are no fast and easy rules for managing your students during transition unless you join the group and adopt your own way of doing things. That is what I have done and it seems to work pretty impressively year after year.

➢ I take the time to **define** what a good leader is.

➢ I **model** what a good leader looks and sounds like.

➢ I **explain** that I only allow good leaders to lead the class because we want everyone being lead by someone who is doing what is right.

➢ I **assign a place** for the girls to line up and a place for the boys to line up.

➢ When it is time to leave, I simply say, *"I'm watching and listening for a good leader. I wonder which line will lead the class out today? The boys or the girls? Or BOTH!"*

➢ If someone talks, I say, *"Mick, you need to step to the end of the line, please. This is a quiet line and I'm looking for leaders."*

➢ If the girls are the quietest, the boys follow them out of the room. If the boys have the most self-control and are the quietest, they get to lead the girls out. If both are equally quiet, they go through the door at the exact same time – all of them leaders! And there's usually *"cool kid spray"* for everyone who wants it!

> ➤ I avoid the whoever-gets-to-the-front-of-the-line-first-gets-to-be-the-leader syndrome by selecting the model from the line who *deserves* to be the leader. It is usually someone who earned the title by standing quietly, standing still, keeping his or her hands to self, and *walking* to line without rushing, blowing past people, pushing, shoving, or plowing through the crowd. (Remember, they know what I'm looking and listening for from our first conversation about the definition of a leader.)

> ➤ If you find that someone deliberately chatters in order to be moved to the end of the line, you have a simple solution to that, too. Just move that Mr. or Ms. Congeniality between two less talkative students. If that doesn't do the trick, you can always move him or her to the other line. I have used that hesitantly and sparingly – maybe twice in years, but sometimes the little noisy mouths can't figure out where the POWER OFF button is. The best way to get them to clam up is to put them out of their element and away from their same-gender audience.

56. ***HAVE SOME FUN YOURSELF!*** Don't be afraid to get silly, use your imagination, and **join in** on the fun in your room! Don't TELL your students to move and then stand back and watch! Do whatever you expect them to do! Tell them to crawl – YOU CRAWL! Tell them to hop – YOU HOP! Tell them to spin – YOU SPIN! Seeing an adult doing the same activity they are doing is not only fun for them, it reassures them that it's OK and it makes them feel secure. The more the kids see YOU entertaining and enjoying yourself with music, the more THEY will do the same. Don't be afraid to let the kids get silly, use their imagination, and have some crazy fun, too. Sometimes we worry too much about what it might look like from the hallway peering into our classrooms, what your principal or other teachers may think of you. Try not to base your activity, your discipline style, or how much you discipline on what others might think. As long as your students are acting appropriately and aren't so loud that they are disturbing someone in the next county, let them go. Put on a pair of earmuffs, take some Prozac, and let the fun begin.

"Teachers who inspire will do some crazy things and make some mistakes, but they do them and make them with enthusiasm!"

~ Debbie Gray

We can be good, loving role-models, we can do our utmost to lead them through the channels toward a well-balanced education, and it is our job to create opportunities for success for every single person who walks through our doors. But then…after awhile, when it comes to those special ones who intentionally buck the system or "just can't help it, anymore," we need to re-evaluate and decide when we've finally extinguished our heroic attempts and have reached the point of diminishing returns. Then our job is to *take off and soar with the ones who want to go!*

59. *JUST SAY OK!* *"Cassie, just put that down…"* "I didn't do it!" *"Caley, don't be so rough…"* "I didn't do anything!" *"Destin, give it back…"* "I didn't take it." *"Ronnie, don't let go…"* "I didn't let go…" *"Markey, don't forget…"* "I didn't forget." These are the responses I call the "**I didn't's.**" If appropriate responses aren't taught, these kinds of inappropriate responses spread like a nasty strain of flu or a good crop of head lice. We can always give them one of our highly revered teacherly responses and use it as one of those priceless "teaching moments." After all, it is our moral obligation as educators to let them know they actually *did* do it. (awwww…) Or, we can insist, "*Just say OK.*" If that doesn't work the first time, <u>add emphasis with a name</u> tag, "*Just say OK, Carlton.*"

More often than not, they'll try to argue and add a few more self-defense statements in an attempt to purify their reputation, cleanse your accusation, and develop their ego, but all they need to hear from you is, "*Just say OK.*" Stick with it until they say it, then leave it at that. ("Teaching moments" can escalate the situation into a challenge or argument. If you want to, you should, but I suggest waiting a bit later so emotions have had time to ease.) You see, offering appropriate words to say provides them with an appropriate, non-condemning, face-saving, inarguable response. The student is relieved. The teacher is relieved. The tension is relieved. How do you spell relief? "*Just say OK.*"

Debbie Gray

Chapter 9

SERIOUS STUFF
Or...

WARNING...DANGER, DANGER (Will Robinson)

1. ***ALWAYS, ALWAYS, ALWAYS WRITE YOUR SAFETY RULES AND EMERGENCY GUIDELINES INTO YOUR LESSON PLANS AND THEN PRACTICE THEM!*** Do it at the very beginning of school, do it again at grade card time, and do it anytime in between if procedures change. Don't just *explain* to the kids where to go in the event of a fire, tornado, earthquake, or lockdown, *walk them through it.* And, walk them through it more than once, reviewing the importance of being silent and moving quickly. If an accident or emergency would ever occur while students are in your classroom, you will want them to be safe. You will also need to show that safety rules and emergency procedures were taught and practiced with every single one of your students. Document, document, and then, document some more. When we have a school-wide drill once a month, it's easy to forget that only one class is getting "walk-through" practice, so it's very important to actually plan a lesson around each drill. You don't need to spend a long time - - and I would only do one particular kind of drill per day, but drills can be one of your "concept areas" you teach at the beginning of each quarter to every grade level.

2. ***DON'T EVER LEAVE STUDENTS UNSUPERVISED.*** If you're in the hallway, every single child needs to be with you. Never, *ever* leave ANYONE alone...not under any circumstances, not even for "just a minute!" They must be within your visual range if you do have to slip out. Just grab someone from the hall, call the office for help, send a student after someone, call for your neighbor, or take the kids with you. Just don't leave them in the classroom, playground, or hall unattended. This also applies to students dismissed from after-school activities. You must accompany them to the door and wait with them until their rides have arrived for them.

3. *CONCENTRATE AND REMEMBER WHO YOU GIVE PERMISSION TO LEAVE YOUR CLASSROOM.* Whether you're on recess, hall, lunchroom, bus duty, or in class, it is so easy to just nod permission to a request to go to the bathroom, the office, library, etc. It is far too easy to get preoccupied with the remaining students, your instructions, or the activity, and forget all about who has left the room! It would not be as difficult if you use seating charts and chairs, but I don't. First, I advise you to always have the student tell you when they return. Second, I would suggest you always send a buddy with a student, no matter where he/she has to go. Make sure the buddy is dependable and bright so you don't have to worry about them plotting a skip day together! Plus, you're more likely to miss two kids than one if you get busy and forget. (Hey...it happens! Especially in huge choir classes with 60 or more kids!) (Hey...if they disappear – it's your responsibility!) (Hey...that's an enormous responsibility!) Third, you could have a spot on the chalkboard dedicated to "CHECK OUT" and have the kids write their name on it when they leave, erase it when they return. Some people use a hall pass – so at least they know someone's gone. Or, the easiest thing is to just make a conscious effort to pay close attention to who you dismiss.

4. *DON'T ASSUME THAT TAKING PICTURES OF STUDENTS IS OK.* I can't explain it but I suppose some parents have valid reasons for objecting. But if you plan to photograph *any* student individually, for *any* reason, whether it be for a bulletin board, program, college assignment, National Board Certification, the newspaper, the school paper, *anything at all*...it's a good idea to contact the parents to make sure it's OK. If you're dealing with a parent who has a particularly litigious track record, get a signed release from them. Although I have been lucky enough not to have faced trouble because of photographing students, others in my school have – so just be aware and take care!

5. *DON'T ASK TO SEE IT.* If a child tells you her tummy itches or she has a rash, it's just better to pass that baton directly to the school nurse. Do not pass Go, do not collect $200. As a mommy or daddy and as nurturers, it's almost second-nature to say, *"Let me see...."* Resist that urge. Probably nothing would ever happen, but we just don't ever want to know for sure.

6. *DON'T EVER SUGGEST TO A PARENT THAT A STUDENT NEEDS TO BE TESTED,* treated, seen by a doctor, medicated, be

checked for ADD, ADHD, etc. or anything similar. I've been told over and over that districts can be held financially responsible for expenses incurred when a teacher has "prescribed" professional help. That's one place none of us want to go…so don't take the risk. I am not even close to a legal advisor, so I can't be exact, but I make sure I don't say anything that even resembles a suggestion. I suggest you discuss with your principal exactly what can and can't be said during parent conferences. From what I understand, it doesn't even pertain only to official parent/teacher conferences, which means, if you run into a parent or guardian at the grocery store and make the suggestion that they might want to take their kid to the doctor, that their student needs professional diagnosis, meds, or a professional evaluation – you can be in trouble.

7. ***STICK TO THE FACTS…JUST THE FACTS!*** When conferencing with administrators, specialists, police, and parents, or writing a formal report on a student, it is very important to speak or write *only of facts*. Save your opinions unless specifically asked and even then, tread carefully. In an already uncomfortable situation, offering your opinion seldom benefits anyone - not to mention the fact that the experts don't generally care what you *think* – all they want is observable evidence. So, it's a good bet to avoid saying things like, *"He's just a big ol' mean bully to all the poor, little, helpless kids who are smaller than him!"* Instead, say something like, *"Yesterday, while on his way to line up, he shoved one little guy out of his way and made him fall down,"* or *"She stomped on the smaller girls' toes and made her cry."* These are opinion-free, emotion-free statements of factual observation.

8. ***WATCH YOUR WORDS!*** Never say *anything* to a student or parent that you wouldn't say if your Superintendent of schools were standing right there with you.

9. ***THINGS YOU SHOULD* NEVER , EVER SAY *TO A PARENT*** …during a conference, in an informal conversation, when writing a letter to a parent, or when making comments on a report card!

   1) Your child has delusions of adequacy.

   2) Your son is depriving a village somewhere of an idiot.

3) Your son sets low personal standards and then consistently fails to achieve them.

4) The student has a "full six-pack" but lacks the plastic thing to hold it all together.

5) This child has been working with glue too much.

6) I would not allow this student to breed.

7) When your daughter's IQ reaches 50, she should sell.

8) The gates are down, the lights are flashing, but the train isn't coming.

9) It's impossible to believe the sperm that created this child beat out 1,000,000 others.

10) The wheel is turning but the hamster is definitely dead.

I received that *silly* email a long time ago and just tucked it away under my NEED A CHUCKLE file. I think it was titled: ***Don't you dare ever say it!*** The author is unknown-to-me, but I thought the comments would be fun to include. They definitely make a strong point about what ***not to say*** to mommies and daddies!

OK...all nonsense aside. On a more serious side of this "don't-ever-say-it" issue are a few things that seem obvious, but I will include them, nevertheless, just to instigate some thinking and careful scrutiny about what might easily slip in to an "encouragement lecture." Imagine receiving a telephone call from a parent that goes something like this: *"I have a bone to pick with you, Ms. Know-it-all teacher! My two little girls are crying and driving me crazy now because they said you said, '...pay attention, ask questions, study and work hard so you don't end up living in a trailer or being a trash collector. Well, I'm here to tell ya, Ma'am, we live in a fine double-wide and I make a good living driving a trash truck! Now tell me...did you really say that to my girls?'"* There are many jobs or places to live that one might fill in on either one of those blanks – but even if it's something from a familiar movie like "living in a van down by the river," that might just fit too close to or *be* home for some of your students. We have no way of knowing what kind of circumstances our kids might be living with, have lived with, or are facing. So just be aware of those kinds of things and choose your words carefully.

10. ***DON'T EVER INSINUATE THAT MOMMY OR DADDY IS WRONG***. It's just not a bridge you want to cross. Except in such cases as Hannah's. ☺ Wait…I mean…Emily! (In case you're totally confused now or the Hannah-Emily comment is an enigma and bugs you, you can check back in chapter four, number three.)

11. ***CONFIDENTIAL***! Remember that all information kept on a student should be confidential. I know I'm repeating myself, but I must because this isn't your basic read-from-front-to-back kind of book and this is one issue that is very reasonable to reiterate.

12. ***NO CORPORAL PUNISHMENT.*** Don't ever discipline a student with anything other than words and acceptable consequences, regardless what your district policy may be or what parents might suggest. In other words, protect yourself by adding this 11th commandment: **CORPORAL PUNISHMENT** (hitting) **IS NOT TO BE ADMINISTERED TO ANY CHILD FOR ANY REASON.** Sit on your hands if you have to – but do not touch a child when you are angry!

13. ***SEND STUDENTS TO THE CLINIC*** if you have even a morsel of doubt about his/her welfare. I want to share two stand-out-in-my-mind experiences that I will never forget! Luckily, I was never blamed for either situation. But in retrospect, I know how easily I could have been! Picture this: I am doing recess duty on a beautiful spring day. A third grader comes up to me and tells me he has fallen and hurt his hand. I give him some motherly attention and the option to go to the nurse or continue playing. Without shedding a tear, he went back to the kickball game and played hard until the whistle blew. I found out the next day that he had spent his entire evening in the emergency room finding out that he had not just a broken arm but had a *fracture* severe enough that it required surgery! He came back to school several days later sporting a cast with four bruised and chubby fingers protruding from it. I felt horrible that I didn't make him go straight to the clinic. On the other hand, he seemed fine. It was a judgement call – and I clearly judged wrong.

The second time I got fooled was when a student came to me during my lunch duty shift and told me his back itched. I did kind of scratch his left shoulder area for him but I must admit, I was more interested in getting him to sit back down in his seat and remember that getting out of his seat during lunch was against the principal's rules. The next thing I knew, the nurse was in the cafeteria administering an Epi Pen injection because he was having a severe allergic reaction. I had no idea!

My point is, I have just learned that it is really imperative for me to send complaining students to the clinic for a more thorough evaluation and a written record that they were seen by the school nurse. I opt to err on the safe side. Just think about it…if a student bumps his head ever so slightly and you tell him he is OK but then some complication arises, you stand a much higher chance of being held responsible than if you just go ahead and send him to the clinic. Let the health *professional* check him out, and send him back to you. Then you've cleared yourself of that decision-making and liability. I know it can be a hassle. I know it can be habit forming for some children. I know it can put you in a less-than-favorable position with the school nurse – but, when I consider the possible alternatives, I do it anyway – in spite of the possible ramifications.

14. ***RESTROOM REQUESTS*** can be a *great* barometer of the effectiveness and the interest evolving from our lessons. If you have a trail of I-need-to-go-potty kids, you should probably re-evaluate your lesson…because it's boring and they're wanting to bail. Don't let it hurt your feelings, just make some small adjustments. When class is fun, I seldom have anyone ask to "go potty." When I do, it's typically an isolated case. But let the lesson lose momentum, and here they come…in hoards! If that happens, and it typically does when they're seated and expected to be quiet and listening, I dismiss the *one* who first asked, then I *quickly* change the activity to something where they're up and moving, even if it's just a couple of minutes long. Usually, the can-I-go-potty line disappears because they don't want to miss out on the fun. Most of the time, I can go back to the lesson that induced restroom requests. But I try to save it until the very end of class to finish up. Potty time can happen on their way back to regular class, when it is already ordinarily scheduled.

15. ***LET 'EM GO IF THEY ASK TO GO:*** If a child asks to go to the bathroom, I *just let them go!* You can ask, *"Can you wait for a few minutes?"* and then if they return asking again, you KNOW they really need to go. I suggest you just send them when they ask. We surely

don't want one of them to wet their pants because we thought what we were teaching was more important than their need to "go potty." With older kids, you might think, *"...they should be old enough by the time they're twelve, to hold it."* You know, *you're right.* But what if they're not? What if it doesn't have anything to do with their age? What if they are having a diarrhea attack? Maybe it's a girl who will only ask you to go once a month? We can't possibly anticipate that, so it really probably shouldn't be up to us to decide if a child "needs" to go to the bathroom – we can't possibly know what they are experiencing at that moment. (The Golden Rule comes to mind here, again.)

Some kids have medical problems that may require them to use the restroom frequently. We are usually, *hopefully*, made aware of those circumstances. But, since I can't remember all the special circumstances of all 500 of my students, I don't trust my memory – they ask…they go. Then there are those who may have a urinary, kidney or bladder infection. Maybe *they* don't even know about it yet. All they know is something doesn't feel right and they *want* to go to the bathroom. We can't know. They ask…they go.

Granted, there are those lil' boogers who just want to go to ditch class. If you suspect that, send one of your *"primo"* students along to accompany them. That has an amazing way of expediting their business and taking the fun out of skipping. You're not risking the volatile repercussions that can *and will* crash in on you if something exasperating and embarrassing *does* happen. Choose your battles… **this is not one of them, trust me.**

16. ***ABC A***ssistance needed in the **B**athroom, better **C**heck! If a student lingers too long in the bathroom, it is wise to notify the nurse, aide, or another teacher to follow-up and make sure everything is OK. Sometimes they are ill, sometimes they've soiled their clothes and are helplessly wondering what to do, and sometimes they're just messing around, killing time, and need to be busted!

17. ***TEASING TROUBLES:*** Teasing is such a hurtful thing and what may seem insignificant and petty to us can be traumatic to a little person. Put a stop to any and all teasing. But equally important, if you are aware that someone is picking on another, share that insight with everyone on staff who may come in contact with the picker and the pickee! It takes the whole school community to stifle that kind of ugliness, so spread the news. This issue does not fall under the confidential guidelines.

18. ***CHARLES IN CHARGE*** is not such a good idea! Teachers often appoint a class "monitor" or "helper" who is in charge of reporting misbehavior or "taking names." Sometimes, like assigning a line leader, it's an honorary position that's passed around the class from day to day or week to week. Please DO NOT ever place any child responsible for the behaviors or reporting of the behaviors of other students! There are several reasons I believe Charles *shouldn't* be in charge: First, consider the confusion in their minds when they are accused of tattling when they tell on someone and you haven't solicited the information from them, but the same exact thing is considered "reporting" or "monitoring," *not* tattling, if you've assigned them to tattle. Secondly, I know from first-hand experience that it can be an awful task. My daughter was repeatedly placed in the *"take names while I'm gone"* role. Can you imagine how many enemies she had the potential of creating had she actually accepted that assignment?! Asking kids to tell on their peers divides classmates, builds animosity between kids, encourages tattling, and has no positive value other than perhaps to cover what is the teacher's job. Finally, it is the teacher's responsibility to be *proactive* in managing the kids in class. Responding to reported misbehavior is *reactive*. It is being provided a list so you know who should be punished. Let's change it to CHARLES, *NOT* IN CHARGE!

19. ***DO NOT HAVE STUDENTS PLUG OR UNPLUG ELECTRICAL EQUIPMENT*** including stereos, lamps, computers, electric pianos, fans, projectors, ANYTHING! It only takes one harmless spark, one short circuit, one small shock and you have some serious explaining to do!

20. ***OUTLETS?*** When kids are sitting on the floor, they are eye-level and much closer to electrical outlets than you realize. Outlets and kids mix like oil and vinegar…"lettuce" keep our eyes open.

21. ***DO NOT ALLOW STUDENTS TO MOVE EQUIPMENT!*** It's always nice to have a hand when moving the piano, when the overhead projector needs to be taken back to the library, the TV/VCR needs to be rolled to another room, or the risers need to be set up or torn down…but resist the desire to deploy students for those tasks!! One pinched finger, one smashed toe, one dropped television, and you are going to have some more serious explaining to do. It is just another one of those bridges you just don't want to cross! Plus, document in

your lesson plans that you have reviewed this rule at regular intervals to all classes.

22. ***NEVER SEND STUDENTS TO YOUR VEHICLE TO RETRIEVE SOMETHING YOU'VE LEFT IN THERE!*** This seems so silly, I guess, but I've seen it cost a fellow tenured teacher her job. She sent a student to her SUV for a couple of jump ropes in the front seat. Evidently, her military-issue firearm was somewhere in the front seat area. The student never touched it but must have mentioned it to someone. The teacher no longer has her teaching job. Most of us will never have a gun in our car, but what about the bottles, the magazines, the paperbacks, medicine, cigarettes, or videos you may forget are sitting on the floor or seat? What may seem thoroughly benign and innocent by our standards may very well pose as ammo against us for an anxiety-stricken, protective, over-reactive parent. They *are* out there, ya know…so my advice is…just don't take any chances.

23. ***NEVER SEND MEDICINE VIA A STUDENT TO ANYONE.*** Students should not even deliver cough drops for you. If you think of the possibilities, choking, allergic reactions, or a lozenge stuck up the nose, they are just not problems you will ever want to endure.

24. ***NEVER GIVE MEDICATION TO A STUDENT*** (unless it is an Epi-pen or some other form of treatment for a life-threatening emergency and only then if there is no one else to administer it).

25. ***COLLECT HOME, CELL, AND EMERGENCY NUMBERS*** of all students you may be keeping after school hours when the clinic and/or office are inaccessible. This list is also important to have with you on a field trip, at a party, skating rink, hayride, concert, or any other activity where you are the person in charge. All it will take is one emergency and you with no way to reach a parent and you will totally understand the importance of this advice.

26. ***BE AWARE OF RESTRICTIONS*** There are some people who may not pick up some kids. Make sure you know who these people are and are able to enforce that security.

27. ***DO NOT KEEP YOUR SCHOOL KEYS, SECURITY CODE, AND I.D. BADGE TOGETHER.*** Every day I see teachers with their building keys connected to their security badge! I wear mine, too,

but I do not keep them together at the end of the day...especially not in my car. I've seen them hanging from rear view mirrors. If they ever misplace them or their vehicle is vandalized and they're stolen, whoever finds them will have building access. At least if the keys are separate, there is no way to connect the keys to the building they unlock. I'm not sure I would want my picture attached to a set of lost keys to my school, anyway, ya know? It is pretty incriminating!

28. ***SOME WORDS ARE NO NO'S!*** There are a few **words** that we, especially as elementary teachers, need to think about before we use them in class. I suspect that when teaching high school, student explicatives don't need to be quite so guarded. But it is truly amazing how innocent little words can get you into deep CA CA at the elementary level! Tell students to sit on their pockets instead of their buns or bottoms... and definitely don't say "*butt*"or anything else resembling that word. Have them "fold" their legs rather than "sit Indian style." Don't let your daily-use words slip into your speech – even if they seem non-offensive. Be careful what you say and how you say it to other staff members or parents. There are probably little ears (or big ears) somewhere in the vicinity.

29. ***NEVER ALLOW A STUDENT TO LEAVE*** SCHOOL WITHOUT RECEIVING DIRECT PERMISSION FROM THE OFFICE. (This includes even going outside for recess, or on a field trip, etc.)

30. ***CARRY YOUR KEYS FOR SECURITY.*** Our building is locked down 100% of the time. Every door is locked. The only access into the building is through the front door, by the office. A door bell and security camera is by the front entrance. The lock must be released from inside the office before the door will open. Most faculty members have a master building key and keep them on their I..D. lanyard so building access is never limited to the front door. I learned that lesson the hard way when I took a class *outside* for a fire drill and discovered that my keys were *inside* with my purse. I was locked out, by myself, with 25 little people depending on me to keep them safe and get them back inside the building.

The best way I've found to manage my keys and badge, since I'm so scattered and need easy methods of organizing, is to keep my school and car keys in the same pouch in my purse. When I lock my car, I exchange my car keys for the building keys. At the end of the day, when I reach for my car keys, it reminds me to replace them with my building keys. My I.D. badge, lanyard, and whistle hang on tack in my room.

31. ***I TAKE MY CELL WITH ME ANYTIME I GO OUTSIDE THE BUILDING*** whether it be for an emergency drill, an out-of-doors activity, or recess duty. We have walkie-talkies we carry when outside, but I keep my cellular, too. As a rule, I don't make or accept personal calls, but I *do* have it in the event of an emergency.

32. ***WHISTLE WHILE YOU WORK.*** I like to keep my whistle on my lanyard with my identification tag. That way I never leave it "in the other coat" or "in my other purse" or "in my pants pocket." Having a whistle with you at all times is a safety issue, too. If there were ever an emergency or a situation where confusion and noise broke out, your voice would be negligible over a crowd of frightened students. Having a whistle on your person at all times gives you a better chance at controlling a situation should one ever arise.

33. ***WHISTLE ONCE – FREEZE; WHISTLE TWICE – LINE UP… FAST! PRACTICE!*** I enforce this rule about as rigidly as any rule I have. I make the students practice it, react to them, and line up fast every single day. It only took one tragedy to teach me a lesson I will never forget. It was probably my tenth year of teaching. I was outside, in charge of recess duty. It was a typical, warm, autumn day and approximately one hundred fifth graders were playing on the west playground. Technology at the time wasn't nearly as advanced as it is now. Walkie Talkies and cell phones were unavailable. Someone ran out of the building to inform me that the service station a few blocks south and west of school had been robbed, the cashier had been shot in the head, the gunman was still armed, and on foot – last seen heading north east. Our west playground, crawling with eleven year olds and one teacher, was directly in his path! We had just gotten outside to play so when I blew the whistle to get them to line up – they just looked at me like deer in the headlights, trying to figure out why I was making them line up already. Some argued, some did actually line up, but most just stood and balked. I yelled at them to hurry and line up *fast* – but they were so torqued about having to go in so soon, they drug their feet, barely moved, and I could *not* get them to hurry! This situation rushed the adrenaline with such force through my system, it actually made me feel faint.

I eventually did get everyone inside without mishap, the robber was apprehended long before getting close to school, and everyone was safe in the end (except the cashier who died on his way to the hospital,) but oh how differently that afternoon could have ended! From that day on, my kids know – I mean, KNOW that when that whistle blows once, they are to freeze and listen. If it blows a second time, they know they better run as fast as their little legs will carry them and line up! There are some serious consequences for those who fail to follow those directives. **Safety is not a negotiable, friendly, I-*hope*-you-do-what-I-say issue.**

If a situation develops where the kids don't run to line after the second whistle, you might want to add a third whistle. The third whistle will be blown as soon as you believe there's been ample time for everyone to run and get in line. The deal will be, *"If you're not in line by the time I blow the whistle again, you will owe that time tomorrow out of your recess since you made us wait on you."* It's amazing how fast they can line up if they're not interested in missing play time!

34. ***KEEP YOUR COOL!*** I stuck this little ditty in the WARNING! DANGER! DANGER! section because it has the potential of really ruffling feathers! Of all the outside stressors I deal with as a music teacher, these two kinds of situations are probably *the* most difficult for me to face! Parents, often with best of intentions, will use withdrawal from my choir rehearsal or performances as punishment for their kids. Today's parents are constantly forced to find effective consequences for unwanted behavior. So, in order to have some leverage, they seek to find something the child likes a great deal to take away from them. Far too often, it's choir. The bottom line for all of us to remember is, in the end, parents will do whatever *they* choose to do. But you might try to head this off at the pass by adding something in a newsletter. Students' participation in choir is not only a personal avenue for fun and musical development, but also a very important part of the success of the whole. Let parents know that everyone is counting on every single child. One missing link in the chain weakens the entire production. Use your own words and write with sincerity and passion. Hopefully you will be able to sidestep this unfortunate issue. If you discover a great way to avoid this problem, please write to me and let me know – I can use some more ideas! So far, I think it has happened to me, at least once, every single year I've taught.

Another issue you may face that has the potential of really forcing self-control is that dreadful letter that comes a few weeks, or worse…a few days…before a huge performance, notifying you that a son or daughter will be doing something else (more important to them) the night of your program, rather than coming to perform in the show. As torqued as I may feel, I try, usually unsuccessfully, to find the silver lining – like: *"At least they've told me ahead of time so I have plenty of time to be miserable, worry, and stew over what I'm going to do now that one of my main kids will be missing."* I receive one of these kinds of letters about once per performance, I am still not used to it, and it still upsets me; nevertheless, I have to accept it so it doesn't make me crazy! Here is how I typically try to handle it –

> Dear Mrs. Yadidittomeagain Didn'tya,
>
> Let me start out by just telling you how much I enjoy Owen! He is such a talented kid, is *very* smart, and so much fun to have in class and choir. Thank you for sharing him with me! Also, thank you very much for giving me the advanced notice of him being gone on the night of our concert! Knowing this far ahead of time, I should still have time to reassign his speaking parts, give that new person a chance to memorize the lines, practice them, and it also affords me time to change the script for the announcer so she can relearn and practice saying the long list of narrators names with the new speaker's name inserted. The choir will also have a couple of chances before the show to practice facing the new speaker instead of Owen during the introductions. (I know it sounds simple but it can be tricky with 65 kids and 20+ different introductions, as you can well imagine!) Though I'm sad Owen will miss the evening show, I don't blame him for wanting to go to the big concert that's in town that night. I'm glad he can still be here for the afternoon assembly – which will begin right at 2:30. I really appreciate your heads up! Thanks!

Now mom and daddy know several things: **1.** His priorities are forcing a huge domino reaction within the choir…with a considerable number of changes having to be made. **2.** His choice to be gone has affected the entire choir. **3.** He is sacrificing his part – totally, not just for that evening performance. **4.** I'm not a grouch but she can bet her bottom dollar, not on her life will I entrust any more special parts to Owen in the future! There are too many kids who would do *anything* for a part all their own. For me to give it to someone who doesn't appreciate it enough to make some sacrifices to keep it, would be so unfair to the die-hards who wouldn't miss the opportunity for *anything*! I wish I could include in my letter, (but of course I can't) *"What if everyone decided to go to the concert? Then where would we be?"* And I'd also like to be able to say, *"For every performance you miss, you have to sit out a performance."* That can be a real effective consequence or deterrent when the next performance means getting out of school a half day and having lunch at McDonalds after the concert! But I've chosen to avoid that consequence because it only breeds more trouble for myself in the long run, it causes hard feelings, and damages relationships.

Oh well…there are some people we'll never understand because their priorities aren't with loyalty, commitment, or responsibility to the whole but to ol' number one. I've seen it for 25 years, I seriously doubt it will ever change. Let's fact it, we can't change the fact that they choose to do something other than participate in the concert - except to make the performance so irresistible that nothing else tempts them away, but to think who and what we're competing with makes that a rose-colored-glasses expectation.

A decade ago, I was allowed to grade down on effort when a student didn't show up for a concert, but that is not the case any longer. In elementary school, I guess most of us have no leverage to *make* kids come to perform. Once they're in upper grades, the music teachers actually do lower grades for not attending a performance that they've worked all semester to prepare. With all that said, let me add another perspective to the whole mix.

Experience has helped me understand and soothed some of my stress about performances. I am incredibly proud of my family, but that's not why I included their information back in the Debbie's Dossier section. I think it's cool to realize that because of the varied interests, skills, and activities of Mike and the girls, I am able to write from a vast variety of experiences and perspectives. These seem to help my vision and understanding of the *whole* growing up process. I understand what it's like to assure that my kids studied hard and often in order to earn great grades! I know what it's like to juggle years and years of ball games, practices, coaches' requirements, inflexibility, and the dedication it takes to play sports at those higher levels. I value having a life outside of work and the world of music! The racing community has opened an unbelievable new window of insight and understanding. I understand how a hobby can dictate time, energy, and schedules. I realize how the involvement of one family member can affect other family members beyond their control. I know what it's like to have daddy away and have to manage the family alone. I understand dreams and goals and what it takes to reach them. So, I also understand, *particularly at the elementary level*, that my students and their parents are faced with exactly the same obstacles, detours, and decisions that we faced.

As busy as lives are, there will always be conflicting schedules. I've come to learn that *it's unwise to make kids choose between music and whatever*. It is not healthy for you. It causes stress, crabbiness, and builds animosity. Plus, the sad truth is, many are going to choose their *whatever* over music anyway, if forced into making a choice between the two. Honestly, my first ten years of teaching, I got totally bent out of shape and cranky from fretting over the competition with outside activities that drew my singers away from participation in music activities. Then I had kids of my own – kids who happened to enjoy *sports* more than *music*. Now I try to avoid making kids make that choice. My spring concert, which was always in May always conflicted with baseball and softball games! So, rather than lose kids to the game, I moved my spring concert up to April so my performers wouldn't have to miss a **game** – maybe only a practice. I've learned to look for ways to accommodate others as much as possible. I look for ways to prove my respect for their interests, too. I request ball game, recital, gymnastic event, bowling, and motocross schedules, then show up and watch. It doesn't take a lengthy stay to show parents and kids that what they do is interesting and important to me. It has become obvious that

I can connect better with honey than vinegar.

After all these years, I know if someone "has to pitch a ballgame" the same night as our concert, the show will go on. Life as we know it will not cease to exist. When he or she is 20 and I'm 50ish ☺ it's not going to matter. I know it's a tough pill to swallow, particularly after being inundated with the demands of a music school, but I hope this helps destressify you by peering at it from several different perspectives. Now…enough of that little detour…to Debbie's Dossier! Let's get back on track….

35. *__MAKE SURE YOU ARE TRAINED IN HANDLING BIO-HAZARDOUS SITUATIONS.__* I am so far from being an authority on this topic, I can't even express it, but I do know that *any* body fluid,

be it saliva, urine, feces, and especially blood, must be handled with care and in a very specific way – for your own safety and the safety of others! It hasn't been that long ago that if someone got a nosebleed and dripped on the floor, I'd just swipe it up with a paper towel, wad it up, give it a toss, wash my hands, and go on with class. Yeah… not like that any longer! Just be sure you find out exactly what your district's policy is and what it takes to keep you and your kids safe and healthy.

36. ***KNOW ALL PROCEDURES IN THE EVENT OF A CRISIS.*** If your school has no crisis management plan, now is as good a time as any to help establish one. Most of us have basic fire, tornado (at least in the Midwest), earthquake, and "lock down" drills. But there are some rather obscure processes beyond where to put the kids to keep them safe that need to be carefully considered. You sure don't want to have an armed intruder, a storm hit, a hot water heater explode, a hostage situation, an earthquake, a flood, or any other horrific, life-threatening or casualty-strewn episode happen without being *totally* prepared and knowing exactly what *your role* will be. The process may include calming the masses, managing the ensuing chaos, and dealing with injuries, frightened students, parents, emergency crews, emergency vehicles, and the media. Just to give you some starter ideas, I am including *some* of the procedures that LeAnn Dill and Jo Watson, leaders of our Building Crisis Team, devised for our school. You will, of course, have to make adjustments to suit your circumstances. Here are some things you might consider when designing your Crisis Management Plan:

➤ **Establish a chain of command.** (This should include non-office staff members as well as staff members in various areas of the building.) Establish the order of the command chain. Make your list at least ten people deep so someone is in charge and understands his/her duties in the event that the normal Principal, Vice-Principal, Counselor, chain of command is impossible.

➤ Assign the following duties and have informed back-up personnel for each. Assign someone to:

1. Confirm information regarding emergency/crisis.

2. Make definitive decisions regarding crisis conditions.

3. Assess the need for assistance. Request assistance.

4. Notify emergency services. (911)

5. Notify Central Administration Offices.

6. Activate Crisis Team

7. Vacate building or notify everyone to follow emergency procedures.

8. Monitor student needs and exits.

9. Act as "runner."

10. Aid classroom teachers, if needed.

11. Issue information between those in command.

12. Turn off utilities: main gas line, electrical and gas appliances. (Though typically the custodian, other staff members *should know* where and how to do this.)

13. Lock doors to limit access to building

14. Direct cars/buses until local emergency teams arrive.

15. Secure necessary documentation in event of building evacuation. (Health & Enrollment cards.)

16. Attend to injured students and staff until EMT arrives.

17. Have a walkie-talkie and be in assigned locations.

18. Monitor special needs students.

> **Establish:**

1. Locations where everyone should meet, also plan an alternate location or plan B.

2. List of cell phone numbers of all staff members.

3. Methods to signal each type of emergency. (You may need a discreet signal to notify staff of an intruder and alternate ways to notify of storm and fire in the event the electricity is off.)

4. Relocation options for staff and students in the event of an extended evacuation.

5. Location for parents to meet with their children. (This is for staff to establish *ahead of time* but not necessary for parents to know this information.)

6. Teachers should have a blanket and protective gloves in their room.

Chapter 10

LESSON PLAN LESSONS

TEACHING TIPS AND TRICKS OF THE TRADE

"Leave as little to chance as possible.
Preparation is the key to success."
~ Paul Brown

Between great textbooks, hours and hours of college classes, tremendous professors, your own creativity and talent, your experiences in music and your knowledge of little kids, I have no doubt you already know how to prepare, teach, and extend the learning of every concept we need to help our kids understand. This book, and particularly this section, was designed to give you some additional ideas to expand your lessons and just be able to do it differently once in awhile. I've only addressed the very basic concepts, but you will find that some of these TRICKS can be altered a little and used for guided practice, introductions, or reinforcement activities for other concepts, as well.

One of the "biggie" steps I've taken to make *me* a better teacher is to have taken as many teaching and discipline courses as I can find. I've studied Jim Fay's - *Love and Logic*, Lee Canter's -*Assertive Discipline*, James Dobson's - *Dare to Discipline*, James Thompson's – *New Solutions to New Problems*, Hank Benjamin's – *Teaching in a Hyperactive Society*, Carl Jung's *Psychological Types*, Isabel Meyers & Kathryn Brigg's – *Type Indicator*, David Keirsey's – *Please Understand Me - The Keirsey Temperament Sorter*, Kathy Nunley's – *Layered Curriculum & Brain Based Research*, and most recently, Judith and Joseph Pauley's book: *Here's How To Reach Me: Matching Instruction To Personality Types In Your Classroom*. There have been others, but these are the HOT TOPIC names with the HOT TOPIC program theories that have dictated management processes in the past decades. (I urge you to stay abreast of the newest research and theories pertaining to education but also to take the time to study the "oldies but goodies," as well.)

There are a number of impressions I came away with from all of these courses. The first is that I have every type of learner in every single class that comes to me for music. Therefore, I must vary my teaching to ensure

245

my instruction methods correspond to various learning styles so students will succeed! It is overwhelming! There are visual, auditory, kinesthetic, and just plain reluctant learners. There are the Reactors, the Rebels, the Persistors and Promoters, the Workaholics, the Passive Aggressive, the ISTJ's, ENFP's, and the ESTP's with all variations on that theme, the ESL, ED, BD, LD, ADD, ADHD, EMH, and everything in between! We have the students with articulation problems and various other speech hurdles. The other thing I came to realize is that if I am to be the facilitator for the success of all, I have to take this ubiquitous aggregation of people and teach them what the state and I believe to be important. We are all faced with the same challenge and we are all "spinning plates" with inclusion, diversity, learning styles, and multiple intelligence's complicating our task! It is definitely an overwhelmingly monumental assignment!

There are still those among us who resist the notion that we need to teach in different ways and that *"it worked when I was in school – it can work now!"* In response to that, one of the best analogies I can think of that helped me sort through my thinking about these different types of kids we see and the need for teaching them within their own framework of understanding – refers to mans' best friend:

THE CASE OF HARLEY AND CASEY

My sister, Pam, has a beautiful Golden Retriever named Casey. Although Casey is fleet-footed and active, she would not make a good watchdog! Granted, her size and barking might discourage an intruder. But she, like all typical Golden Retrievers, is adaptable, friendly to everyone, gentle in temperament, and committed to carrying things around in her mouth... including the intruder's crowbar!

Although being a watchdog isn't her forte, Casey does have remarkable ability when it comes to retrieving! She would *love* to swim through icy-cold waters to retrieve a dumb duck decoy....even if it wasn't supposed to be retrieved. One of her most favorite things in the world is to be wet, play in mud, and, almost like a little Kindergarten boy, pounce in puddles...but ponds and lakes are even better as far as Casey is concerned.

Retrievers were bred in England and Scotland back in the late 19th century, with the sole purpose of retrieving birds. Although Casey-girl is very willing and trainable, her ability to retrieve is an inborn trait, an ability she can't help, an innate characteristic of hers. No one had to teach her how to do it. Retrieving comes easy for her and is a natural activity she enjoys.

Casey's temperament shows up when Pam makes Casey do something Casey doesn't want to do. She just sits, becomes passive, and ignores Pam by looking the other way. She waits. She balks. She sulks. She does not want to move. *However*, Pam has learned that with some quiet coercing, gentle urging, maybe a treat or a bit of kind-hearted prodding, Casey will stand up, tuck her tail, lower her head, and do exactly what she's been told to do. If Pam would be gruff, stern, and yell at her, Casey would shut down – collapse into a bundle of cowering unwillingness.

Then there is Harley! Whoa…is Harley ever another story! Last year for Christmas, we gave Pam a solid black Great Dane puppy named Harley. Just a year later, her "cute little puppy" is over a 140 pounds of pure bred muscle and still growing! When she stands up on her back legs, that "cute little puppy" towers considerably over six feet! Her shoulders are already three feet high and her head and neck account for nearly another foot of dog! Unfortunately for Pam, Harley doesn't seem to realize she's monstrous in size. In spite of a couple of brief obedience classes, she still *acts* like a puppy and believes with all her heart that she is still a lap dog!

Harley is a gentle giant. But although her elegance, magnificent size, muscular body, speed, and endurance make her strikingly noble and splendidly majestic, her courage, loyalty, protective nature, and aggressiveness when provoked, is *extremely intimidating*, to say the least! Let me just say, I would probably not terribly mind being a dumb duck decoy in Harley's presence, but I would never, in a million years, want to be an unannounced guest in her home - - I appreciate all my appendages far too much! I've heard, this giant breed of Dane can be traced as far back as the year, 407 when they were <u>bred</u> solely as fiercely-loyal *protectors* and accompanied soldiers into battle.

Just like Casey, Harley's temperament shows up when Pam makes Harley do something Harley does not want to do. She backs up. She lowers to a crouch. She bares her wicked teeth. She growls. (My mom says, "She looks *evil and possessed* when she has to do something she doesn't want.") Harley is strong, strong-willed, and *obstinate*. No amount of bribery, coaxing, begging, or soft talk will inspire Harley. It takes a commanding voice, some *serious* coercion, some muscle forcing the issue, and a considerable amount of towing by her collar. Then, Harley lunges, throws her head around convulsively in an attempt to escape, and quite intentionally, puts Pam's wrist *in her mouth, wanting more than just about anything to clamp down and induce pain,* before eventually conceding and doing what she's been told to do. Because of the ensuing, inevitable battle, Pam is always reluctant to make Harley ever do anything. Yet she knows, if she doesn't control her behavior, Harley will be an unmanageable, unliked, disrespectful adult dog.

Are you catching my point? Both dogs have similarities in their general nature and gentle temperament, but both have natural, inborn instincts that dictate their behaviors, temperament, reactions, and abilities. When forced, Casey reluctantly succumbs – Harley definitely fights back and resists. To expect Harley to retrieve and Casey to protect is somewhat farfetched, though feasible and possible. Successfully teaching that would clearly take an inordinate amount of patience, time, and highly specialized training.

This "inordinate amount of patience, time, and highly specialized training" is our aspiration when educating the Casey's and Harley's in our classes. Just as these two pets have very distinctive behavior, heritage, environment, and pasts that dictate the way they act and the abilities they demonstrate, our students are very much the same way!

In case you're still somewhat skeptical and believe that all students will learn – regardless how we teach, as long as they listen, take notes, study, and try… I have to share another story to help you understand about these different types of kids we see, and grasp the importance of teaching to different learning styles. This happened to me just last Friday when having lunch with a fellow special-class teacher:

MY FRIEND MARY

My good friend, Mary, met me with such enthusiasm and energy about something she'd learned in an in-service that morning, that she could hardly contain herself! *"This is such great information!"* she assured me. Together, we started mulling through handouts she'd collected from the workshop on POWER WRITING. She couldn't wait to get back to school and teach the 1-2-2-2-1 formula for writing a paper. As she proceeded through her explanation of this process, I could feel my anxiety rise like the mercury in a thermometer during mid summer, in Missouri. The more she talked about these numbers and this "formula," the more agitated I grew. Not at *her*, of course, but at the concept! By the time she concluded with, *"Isn't that just the coolest thing, ever!?"* I was so distressed I was grappling for the right words to express myself – and nothing would come out of my face! I, Debbie Gray, was making red-flag history being *speechless*.

Eventually, I assembled some semblance of order in my thinking and uttered out something that probably came off very offensive, *"**I don't like that, at all!** My palms are all sweaty and my heart has been palpitating* *since you first said '1-2-2-2-1!'"* Clearly, poor Mary was confused and the look of astonishment on her face sent me reeling back to reality with my insensitive verbal response to her excitement, echoing through my head. I stammered, clamored, and cajoled, trying desperately, without success, to make up for my coarse and caustic comeback. We had already stood up to leave, were putting on our coats, and I guess my words froze her in mid-reach through her coat sleeve. She just stood there, dumbfounded at my reaction.

In *my* non-analytical, creative, non-data-based, right-hemisphere-dominant world, numbers would only get in the way of creativity. Numbers would stifle my ability to think! ***Numbers scare me!*** Numbers, to me, represent failure, disappointment, and anxiety. Numbers are my baggage! To attach numbers and formulas to something I love, like creative writing, is like…attaching something I abhor to it in an attempt to make it better! To me, connecting numbers with writing is like putting anchovies on pizza, English Walnuts in brownies, mixing cherries with chocolate, or serving turnips with filet mignon! *You just can't do that to me!*

Mary, who thinks more balanced, is more logical, organized, and systematic, wishes she had known this formula before anguishing through her National Board Certification responses because, *"…It would have made all that writing so much easier!"*

To you, I say…THIS is prime and very close-to-home proof that we need multiple ways of teaching the exact same thing! To the Mary's out there, 1-2-2-2-1 will make that proverbial light bulb finally come on in their heads. To the Debbie's out there, just say, *"In your first paragraph, write your statement of fact or thesis, then write three paragraphs to support that fact, then restate your first paragraph in different words. Title your paper, put your name on it, and bam! Turn it in."*

Having this clearly imbedded in my brain, I challenge myself to come up with a variety of ways for kids to learn every concept I teach! The Casey's, the Harley's, the Mary's, and the Debbie's need to learn. In this chapter, you will find some general as well as very specific teaching devices and lessons that will help you help everyone in your room, be successful.

1. ***HANDS ON:*** As often as possible, give your kids things to touch, feel, manipulate, and do. This will be your treat to the kinesthetic, tactile learner in your midst.

2. ***ARTISTIC OPPORTUNITIES:*** Give students chances to produce answers, study guides, etc. in art form. Allow your visual learners

to use videos, technology, and their artistic talents in any medium to express themselves. For example, they could make posters, program covers, illustrate songs, draw a cartoon that goes with the lyrics to a song, design a sculpture that the others can write a song about, or create a music video. Just make sure your visual learners have an outlet for their talent – they will be so excited and you will be pleasantly surprised how much they know when they can show it to you instead of tell it to you!

3. *__TALK IT UP:__* Every class has auditory learners – that means they prefer just hearing or can learn just as easily by hearing the information. Unfortunately, many teachers, particularly college professors, only meet the needs of the auditory learner because they lecture. TELLING is fine, CONVERSATION is great, DEBATE can be fun – but remember, this is only one inlet for information that leads to success in only one group of learners.

4. *__RICH TEXT:__* Some students prefer the more traditional path of learning and that is via the textbook. So…just keep in mind that the text is not ousted because we're expected to do some creative teaching, but don't use it exclusively - it is just *one avenue of many* to reach our kids. Keep it in your arsenal of TRICKS!

5. *__TECHNOLOGY:__* I incorporate as much technology as I possibly can into my lessons! We use the TV for current events – like the Grammy's. I incorporate video segments into nearly every class - on a daily basis. I use music computer programs like *MUSIC ACE* and *FINALE.* The Internet is available for information collecting and homework assignments. I run PowerPoint shows for instruction as well as review and reminders. And I am learning about sequencing and MIDI so I can eventually share that information with my students. We live in the age of technology; there's no denying, so I do what I can to make sure my kids know that music is keeping up rather well!

6. *__WRITING IS GOOD:__* Writing not only means essay answers or written reports, it can include writing **poetry** – that carries the potential of being added to a melody to make a song; **stories** – perhaps with sound effects or dynamic markings; **plays** – impersonating composers or explaining music careers; **lyrics** – whether they be "piggy-back" lyrics or lyrics to an original melody; **lesson plans** – give each student a topic to teach to their class; **compare and contrast** – write impressions of different

pieces of music or an art piece with a musical piece that includes similarities and differences; **evaluate** – have students write reflective comments about a performance, an assignment, or a listening example; **opinion poll** –find out what popular groups, songs, and musical styles the kids listen to at home. You can ask them to write about what they like most about music class and what they wish they could change about it. This can be very insightful as long as you're not prone to hurt feelings and can use it as constructive criticism to help make your program even better than it already is! Writing opportunities are endless however, I can't use it as much as I think beneficial, particularly in the older grades because of time constraints. (On this note, let me give you a synopsis of my fifth grade year so you understand what I mean. My fifth graders do a full-blown, costume, scenery, props, solos, the whole shebang performance in December. Since I only see them once a week for 45 minutes and retention from one week to the next is nearly nil, I have to start my Winter Musical preparations the beginning of October! As soon as the December performance is over, I immediately begin teaching the entire fifth grade Singfest music. Singfest is an all-district activity made of select fifth graders from every elementary school that culminates in an after-school workshop followed by an ALL-STAR concert that evening. Teaching at least six pieces, all with at least two parts, descants, and in multiple languages, requires that I start in January in order to have them prepared to sing in late March. The day after that concert is over, I begin preparing for D.A.R.E. graduation – which usually entails *at least* three songs. If I'm lucky, one of the Singfest pieces is appropriate for D.A.R.E., but more times than not, that isn't the case. Finally, the fifth graders sing for their big graduation from elementary school. This ceremony has grown to become quite a spectacular event, complete with cake, punch, parents, decorations, awards, fancy clothes, flowers, photos, and great music. My performances are backed up like jets waiting to land at Heathrow or O'Hare…there is just not much time for *teaching curriculum*, anymore…except what I can sneak in within the context of the performance prep!)

7. **_ASSESSMENT FOR ALL:_** When assessing comprehension and mastery, try stepping out of the traditional test box and offer this: *"You have learned a whole bunch these past four weeks! Rather than taking a test so I know how much you know, use your favorite method of choice – art, music, plays, poetry, story, research, anything, anyway*

*you want, to **tell** or **show** me EVERYTHING YOU'VE LEARNED!!!*
Be sure not to leave anything out!"

8. <u>**WRITE YOUR PLANS IN PENCIL:**</u> ☺ (Give God the eraser.)

9. <u>**SOUVENIR OF ELEMENTARY MUSIC:**</u> Every once in awhile, come December, just for fun, a surprise, and good memories, I slip in a non-educational activity in lieu of a regular class format. Every Christmas, I teach the song JINGLE BELL ROCK. I collect as many versions of it as I can scavenge, (vocal, instrumental, men singing, women singing, children singing, solos, duets, full choirs, and various musical styles) and burn them onto one CD *if I can*, so they're back-to-back and I don't have to fumble through lots of different records, tapes, and compact disks in order to keep the background music continuous. While the variations are playing, we create a simple souvenir or gift: *a jingle bell rock.* All of us bundle up, go outside, everyone finds their "perfect" rock, we wash them, then dry them with hair dryers (provided by me), and simply hot glue a jingle bell that I've purchased in mass quantities from Hobby Lobby, Wal-Mart, or craft store, to the top of the rock. It makes a fun paperweight or conversation piece for the coffee table.

Another fun project we do is to make our very own ROCK CONCERT! This is typically a fall or spring project because it takes more outside time to search for rocks so we want warmer weather. You will need: One two-inch flat rock per child, 10-12 small rocks per child, permanent markers, one Popsicle stick per student, a hot glue gun, and copious amounts of hot glue. I usually provide the flat, "base rock" by purchasing a bag of river rock from the lawn and garden section, but you don't have to do that – the kids can bring in their own or just use the ones they can find laying around the school playground or just use the ones they can find laying around the school playground or parking lot. (My school happens to neighbor a city park, so we have an ample supply of gravel from which to choose.) Anyway, the project requires the larger rock for the base of the "concert stage" and a bunch of smaller rocks for the "singers." We wash and dry them; then, with permanent markers or paint, (I have used both but prefer the markers because there's little-to-no clean-up), we draw tiny round circles for the mouths and eyes of the "singers." The next step is to hot-glue the small rocks to the base rock, making them as up-and-down-looking as possible so they resemble a bunch of singers standing side-by-side on riser rows. To complete the project, the project needs a sign. The kids snap a Popsicle stick in half, rub it on concrete to smooth off or shape the edges and make both sides match, then neatly write the words *ROCK CONCERT* with magic marker on one-half of the Popsicle stick. The other half of the stick is the vertical T-portion of the ROCK CONCERT sign and is glued to the "base" rock before the horizontal part of the stick with the words on it, is glued across the top of the vertical stick.

These projects are fun and inexpensive. Former student's come back after being out of school for years and tell me they still have their jingle bell rock or their ROCK CONCERT paperweight! One girl told me she'd made ornaments out of jingle bell rocks and that's all she had on her dorm room Christmas tree! You just never know how far-reaching your influence may extend.

10. ___ALL DOTS ARE NOT CREATED EQUAL:___ Do you realize that staccato dots *above or below* a note can be confused with the dots *after* a note like a dotted quarter note? Don't forget there are dots on either side of a double bar line that we call a repeat sign, too. We who have spent years in private lessons often see those things as entities unto themselves while kids who've never seen them before, see them *as dots.* If you tell them that a dot means *staccato,* they're going to assume that every dot on the page means *staccato.* Now that you know these are confusing to kids, just be sure to point them out and make sure they understand the difference and that dot-location is integral to it's meaning.

11. ___CRESCENDO:___ Point out that the abbreviation, cresc means the exact same thing as the symbol for crescendo. Your kids often struggle with verbalizing their confusion. Save them the trouble and verbalize it for them while pointing it out to them. While you're at it, help them figure out why a page will have the abbreviated word and then three measures later use the symbol.

12. ___IT LOOKS LIKE AN EGG IS IN THE END!___ I use *silly* but fun reminders to help kids learn, understand, and remember. After drawing a mental picture with a story and showing a photo of a black snake swallowing a hen egg, I connect that visual to *"It looks like there's an egg in the end of an English horn"* **Egg** – **End** – **English horn** – all begin with the letter **E** so it's **E**asier to remember! (Crazy you say! I know! But it works.)

13. ***THREE T'S AND A CURLY FRY, PLEASE!*** Another silly anecdote is one I use to help students remember the instruments of the brass section: Tuba, Trombone, Trumpet = the 3 T's. I keep an order of French fries and curly fries (from Arby's) in my cabinet, ready to pull out and inquire what kind of fries we have. I ask them to identify how they look different. Then, I pull out my picture of the French Horn and ask them to tell me which kind of FRENCH FRY the FRENCH horn resembles. The FRENCH fry…wait! I mean, the FRENCH *horn*… looks like a curly fry! It's craziness – I know – but they remember craziness so well!

14. ***STRINGY FAMILY:*** We always allude to families when talking about the instruments in the orchestra. Why not give the instrument families *family* titles, as well? For example, the bass viol is THE DAD, the cello is THE MOM, the viola is the BIG SIS (or big bro – your choice), and the violin is the BABY. Kids relate to sizes and family units – this can sometimes help them relate to the instruments and can be used in nearly every section of the orchestra.

15. ***YOU SIT DOWN TO EAT JELL-O, YOU SIT DOWN TO PLAY THE CELLO:*** Using sentences like this that reflect familiar daily experiences to not-so-familiar information help draw both together, making memorizing a little easier. It doesn't hurt that Jell-O and cello rhyme and are spelled nearly the same. Granted, repetition of these sentence-cues helps more than anything.

16. ***READ ABOUT REEDS:*** Write a story or, better yet, have the kids write a story with characters who are double reeds and single reeds. It will be easy to illustrate, too! Offer both reeds so the kids can hold, pass around, and analyze them and discover why they are called single and double reeds. You can provide some red thread, give them three Popsicle sticks, take them outside to the sidewalk, show them how to rub them down on the rough surface of the concrete to thin out the edge, and have them use two to "make" a double reed model and one stick to make a single reed model. If you want to add some yummy fun to your lesson, offer ice cream and give double and single dip cones to your class. To reach still more kids, remember, the word double and single can also be associated with baseball or softball when talking about a "double play" or a "double" when a ball is hit far enough that the batter gets to second base. Show the kids how to look at their finger as it touches their nose – identify that as double

vision. You could always share a stick of Doublemint gum or have a Double Bubble bubble-blowing contest! Helping kids associate the familiar with the non-familiar builds confidence and helps them chain new information with already mastered information.

17. ***OBOE VS CLARINET:*** To us, the differences are obvious and it's easy to identify these two very similar instruments, but for little kids, they look so much alike, in spite of the concentration on double and single reeds, they still seem to get them confused. Try everything you can come up with to help clarify this information in their little heads – but one successful TRICK I've tried was to bring in a large plastic straw. I smoosh it together so they see a flat opening instead of a round opening, but I point out that there's still a top and a bottom to the straw. Then, I demonstrate how I have to shape my mouth into an O-shape to suck on a straw. With this background, I introduce the Oboe...exaggerating my O-shaped mouth, repeating the O-sound as often as I can without annoying the heck outa them! ☺ Next, I offer an example of both instruments and ask which instrument looks most like it has a straw you could suck out of when playing it? Of course, they nearly always answer the oboe because of the double reeds' shape resembling a straw. (It doesn't hurt if you've already mentioned before that the double reed resembles a straw.) The next step is obvious; we connect the O-shaped mouth to the O-shape needed to suck on a straw, to the "straw-looking reed," to the O in the word oboe. It all fits together nicely, but it takes lots of showmanship and concentration to be able to keep their attention, pull it all together, and make sense in their little brains.

18. ***MY CONTRA 'TIS OF THEE...*** Contrabassoon, for some reason, seems to be such a foreign word for little ones. They don't usually have too much trouble remembering the word, *bassoon*, but helping them remember the first two syllables of contrabassoon is often a real challenge. There's not a good rhyming word for *contra*, no familiar synonyms, nor have I been able to come up with a familiar "connector" word, so...when introducing the *"new weird word,"* I sing the phrase, "MY CONTRA TIS OF THEE, sweet land of liberty, of thee I sing." During questioning and review, if they need a cue to help them remember, I just hum the tune and they get it every time! (You don't have to say it...I *know!*)

19. **_THE LAST STRAW:_** Use a big ol' fatty malt straw as an ultra basic process of how a slide trombone or slide whistle works! Hold a thick straw parallel to your body, pinch it hard at the bottom, blow in the top like you blow across the top of a bottle, then, using the fingers of your other hand, as you blow, pinch the straw and slowly slide them upwards toward your lips. The pitch will glissando higher with the lessened area for air to circulate.

20. **_STEM DIRECTION:_** When writing notes on the staff, kids seem to struggle with stem direction. For some reason, they think that has something to do with pitch or duration. I've used a few different ways to help students learn which direction the stem goes. Of course, this is assuming we want the kids to understand why some notes are, in their words, "upside down." This little rule of thumb doesn't, of course, apply to music written with harmonies all written on one staff. 1. I have discovered it helps to incorporate an analogy to football with the middle, "B" line on the G clef, as the "50 yard line." The notes on one side are trying to cross the 50 yard line, heading up, while the notes (above) the 50 yard line have the goal of going (down) to score." 2. The other analogy that has proven helpful is to draw waves on the B line of the G clef staff and tell the story of the notes underwater needing to reach to the surface – and those above, in the air, are also trying to reach the surface. (I found out the hard way that you can really confuse them if you call it "SEA LEVEL" because they're thinking "C" level!) 3. A way you could show *why* notes have to have varied stem direction is to make a diorama. Use a large shoe or better yet, a boot box and lay it on it's side so it resembles, from the student's perspective, a TV of sorts. Using markers, make a horizontal line exactly in the middle of the bottom of the box, reaching from the far left to the far right side of the box. That will "B" your "B" line, assuming you're using the G clef. Now make a stem out of a small stick or dowel. Trim the stick so that when the end of it touches the "B" line, it either reaches to the top or the bottom of the box. Next, connect a note head to the stick. This can be made of cardboard, foam, or anything round or oval – just try to make sure it's diameter fills in the spaces between lines. Finally, add the two lines above and below your "B" line to create a staff. Now you have an ideal visual to explain why the stems have to go down and sometimes they go up. As soon as you try to move the "note" above the "B" line, it won't fit because the stem bumps in to the top of the box. You add, *"The way music people fix that problem, is just to turn the note over so the*

stem goes downward; then you can move that note anywhere above the "B" line without the box interfering with the stick." The same can be modeled by turning the stem going down on the "B" line, then attempting to move the stemmed-note lower. It can't happen because the stem bonks the bottom of the diorama. The solution is then to turn the note over so the stem goes up, then the note can move lower on the staff.

21. ***BREATH SUPPORT:*** I love to use juggling scarves to teach long, deep breaths and diaphragmatic breathing – with the goal of trying to make the scarf hit the ceiling. I use the music *Freeze* from Greg And Steve - *Kids In Motion Songs for Creative Movement,* (Youngheart Music, P.O. Box 6017, Cypress, CA 90630) – so the kids get the "freeze" time to let the scarf drop to the floor, time to not blow, and recuperate. It's great for referring to each time I'm talking about breath support – especially for *pianissimo* parts that still need intensity and a controlled, full breath supporting it. The kids love it, too! There's a secondary benefit, as well. It wakes them up…gets them breathing nice and deep, gets their blood circulating, and gets them up on their feet after sitting at a desk most of the day.

22. ***INSTRUMENTS OF THE ORCHESTRA LESSON:*** Lesson objectives: Students will be able to identify, by name, timbre, and family, all instruments of the symphony orchestra. The lesson is divided into segments - lasting over the course of *at least* five class periods.

  ➢ The music room is visibly & audibly focused on musical instruments. Actual instruments are hanging from the ceiling, on the bulletin boards, and will be removed for the kids to hold and examine more closely throughout the lesson segment. Photos of other instruments are on the walls, a video of an orchestral performance could be playing, a PowerPoint show could be displaying families, categories, and instrument names, and a jigsaw puzzle of instruments could be available. Orchestral music could be playing as frequently as possible upon entering, exiting, and during class. *The goal is to saturate students with orchestral sights, sounds, and experiences!*

  ➢ Each day of the five will begin with one family introduction from our MEET THE INSTRUMENTS filmstrip. A video segment introducing one of the four families of the symphony orchestra

257

(Strings, Woodwinds, Brass, & Percussion) can be used as well, but in addition to the film strip, not instead of.

➢ A guest performer will be invited to play and demonstrate the instruments for the class. There will be a sign up schedule for any student with an instrument or access to an instrument and/or performer, to show, demonstrate, and/or play at any time during the lesson segment - during class time. You can use your school paper to recruit instrumentalists from outside your building, too! It's amazing how many kids are surprised to learn that a parent knows how to play an instrument, that someone had one stashed in the basement or attic, or that a grandpa knows how to play! It is fun and very enlightening for all involved!

➢ Students, in small or class-sized groups, will play a slap, slap, clap, clap, snap, snap game of Categories, naming the instruments from each family, and then switching families in order to include more instrument names.

➢ Instrument baseball will be played to reinforce the learning of the instruments. Students are divided into two teams with the teacher as the "pitcher." Before being shown a picture of an instrument, the student "at bat" determines the "pitch." First bases = identify only the family; Second base = identify family & instrument; Third base = identify family, instrument name, & another instrument in the same family. Home run = family, instrument, another instrument in the same family, and some additional fact about the instrument pictured.

➢ Students may play INSTRUMENT BINGO. (IF you choose to do this and want to play the game with audio segment examples, remember, you must TEACH them the timbre of the instruments before expecting them to know them or the game is not educational – it's a guessing game based on luck rather than knowledge. If you choose audio excerpts, they need to hear AT LEAST three different solo examples and one example within the context of a piece for it to be enough to identify and learn the sound. Even this is a marginal amount for identification – but too many of us assume that one, maybe two examples are enough. Three examples are the absolute minimum! If that is not possible, BINGO can also be played with just the physical identification of the instrument

- which, at primary level, is, in my opinion, quite age-appropriate. Learning to recognize timbre is an added bonus and appropriate for intermediate-age students; but I've found it typically takes much more experience with orchestral sounds than we can provide in one unit of study.)

➢ **Culminating Activity to assess mastery**: Students may choose to do at least one of the following projects. Please allow students to set their own date for presenting their project, let them see you write it down, have them sign beside the date that it will be ready, and they are then accountable for the project's completion at a certain time rather than you enforcing a due date.

A. **FAVORITES.** Write a three-page paper that includes:
  1. The instrument you would most like to play.
  2. Explain why you would like to play that particular instrument.
  3. Provide at least one photo of the instrument.
  4. Your own drawing of the instrument.

B. **PRICES.** Check on prices from at least three music studios/stores in an investigation to find out:
  1. The cost of private lessons.
  2. The cost of instrument rental & purchase of the instrument(s) you would most like to learn to play.
  3. The three instruments that are the cheapest to rent. The three instruments that are the cheapest to purchase. Include prices.
  4. Write a report with your findings.
  5. Plan a time with your teacher to present your project to the class.

C. **RESEARCH PAPER.** Write a paper with research of the history and/or development of one of the following:
  1. Any orchestral instrument.
  2. The orchestra
  3. One of the *families* of instruments in the orchestra.

D. **MOVIE TIME.** Watch the PG-rated movie, MR. HOLLAND'S OPUS and write a two-page newspaper review of the show that includes:
  1. What the story was about so your opinion either encourages others to watch it or discourages others from watching the movie.
  2. The scenes in the movie that were believable and why they were believable.

3. The scenes in the movie that were not very believable and why they were hard to believe.
4. Your favorite part about the movie.

E. **ATTEND** a live orchestra performance and write a "critique" that includes:
1. All instruments that performed in the concert.
2. The number of instruments in the orchestra and how many performers there were in each section or family. (Not always the same. Most percussionists play every instrument.)
3. The tunes or songs that were performed during the concert.
4. Which instruments performed a solo.
5. The Conductor's name.
6. The name of the Concert Master/Mistress.

F. **GAMES GALORE.** Create/make a game that reviews the instruments of the symphony orchestra that we can all play in class. The game may be a board game with all necessary pieces to play or a game show format with contestants and necessary parts to play.
1. The game should include pictures of the instruments and at least some recordings of timbre (the sounds they make).
2. Practice explaining how the game is played or, if it's a game show, practice being the host.
3. Schedule a time with your teacher for the class to play your game.

G. **ART.** Make a mural poster that includes pictures and labels of all of the instruments of the orchestra. Pictures may be:
1. Photos
2. Drawn or colored
3. Magazine pictures
4. Any design, any size you prefer.
5. Schedule a time to present your project to your class.

H. **COMPUTER.** Design, save to a disk or CD, and present to class a PowerPoint project introducing the instruments of the orchestra.
1. Include all four families and all of the instruments we have studied.
2. Include photos with instrument names labeled.
3. Include sounds, if possible, and identify the instrument making the sound.

4. Time how long your presentation takes, then schedule a time with your teacher to present your project.

I. BE THE TEACHER. Design a written test.
1. Provide a picture of each instrument.
2. Provide a listening example for each instrument.
3. Schedule a time with your teacher to administer the test.
4. Provide a copy of the test for each student in your class.
5. Prepare to GIVE the test.
6. Grade all tests.
7. Return all tests to students with corrections made on their papers.

If students have access to the Internet at school for research, computers for word processing, recordings for audio needs, and art supplies, old catalogs for photos, these projects could be done during class. Most have access to those items at home and *could* be expected to complete their projects as a homework assignment rather than using class time.

I just always have to remember, any assignment like this could be OVERWHELMING if they do not KNOW the material they are expected to use in the project. We don't want to create frustration - we want them to enjoy music, their project, and showing it off to their classmates.

23. <u>*NOTING NOTATION*</u>: I use flashcards for starters, to teach <u>*rhythmic notation*</u>. After *I* read the pattern, they echo me until they can read them without my prompts. Next, we apply that knowledge to a rhythm instrument. This appeals to everyone, but especially to the kinesthetic learner. For the competitive spirits, we like rhythmic dictation using lap board or chalkboard relays. The most difficult is dictation by *listening* to the example played on *melodic* instruments.

The next concept is that music moves in three different ways: <u>*leap, step, and repeat*</u>. I show them on the board what each pattern looks like when written on the staff. To reinforce this concept kinesthetically, we imagine we're standing on "the world's largest keyboard." I teach which way is up on the keyboard (right) and which is down or lower (left). First, I dictate *verbally* (like Simon Says) directions for them to "step up; leap up; repeat; leap down; and step down," gradually increasing the tempo in which I call the directions for them to move.

Once they understand the concept of movement in music, they <u>*read*</u> examples, first from the board and later from actual written songs.

By this time, we are thoroughly engaged in transferring verbal skills into musical skills.

I introduce the <u>names of the notes</u> the "old fashioned way." The spaces spell the word F A C E and the lines are an acronym for E-every G-good B-boy D-does F-fine. Working in groups or with a partner, they create their own acronyms. At the chalkboard, I say a word that can be spelled with the letters in the musical alphabet and then they use notes on the staff to write the word. Another way I teach note placement is by using my five fingers as a "staff." You can buy an inexpensive ring, where the stone would normally be, hot glue a flat black magnet with a stick for a stem. Slide the ring note over your finger for "on the line notes" and for "on the space notes," clamp together your "staff" fingers, holding the "note" securely between them. This visual helps little people remember that the line (your finger) goes right through a line note and that the space note must touch both lines above and below the note. It's great for a high-speed review.

Have the kids use their own five fingers as their staff, then have them point where the notes go on the "lines" and "spaces." You can even have a class project where they can make their own "finger notes" that can be tossed in a coffee can and used over and over, again. It's a fun method for checking mastery and allowing your kinesthetic and visual learners to make associations by touch and see.

Each student has a <u>plastic keyboard</u>. From a single reference note, we "play" the three ways music can move, first by verbal dictation and then by reading it from a staff. Finally, we connect their first lessons of *rhythmic* notation with the *melodic* notation. Most students are then able to apply these concepts to their voices and instruments!

Our favorite "test" is "<u>Just Play It</u>" baseball!

➤ The "batter" gets to choose his or her "pitch."

➤ A first base "hit" involves reading only <u>rhythmic notation,</u>

➤ Second base requires the "batter" to read <u>note names.</u>

➤ Third base requires reading the <u>note names *in rhythm*</u>.

➤ A "home run" means the "batter" has to <u>play</u> the example on diatonic bells or keyboard.

➤ Incorrect attempts are outs. Like baseball, three outs, and the other team is up to bat.

24. ***VOCABULARY VISION:*** I believe I have a learning disability. You've heard of attention deficit disorder? Well...I have **RETENTION** deficit disorder! (That is, of course, not an original concept, but it is close enough to home for me not to have possibly instigated the thought – of course, that would have to assume I retained enough memory to come up with it.) At first, I considered it a real detriment to my success but as the years have progressed, I have come to realize that what I originally identified as an obstacle has instead, become an opportunity. In order for **me** to learn, I have to break a concept into it's most fragmented and fundamental elements. By learning how to do that for myself, I now share those same techniques with my students. There are some ideas in the Bulletin Board chapter, to help people recall names of composers. Now I will offer some fun TRICKS to help remember musical terms:

Many music vocabulary words seem to cause students to struggle with not only remembering definitions but also which word goes with which concept. For example, many kids get INTRODUCTION confused with INTERLUDE; and HARMONY is often reversed with UNISON. I have a rather unorthodox way of helping them keep words like these clear in their heads:

➤ It seems so obvious, but then...the old saying, "You can't see the forest for the trees" applies here. When teaching INTRODUCTION - I ask them if any of them are ever like me and have trouble keeping the two words INTRODUCTION and INTERLUDE straight! I tell them that I've figured out a way that helps me. I teach them the proper or correct way to introduce one person to another. Then, we do a little Name That Tune game by playing only the introductions to familiar songs and having them identify the song from the short opening music. Next, I draw a verbal correlation between introducing someone and introducing a song...,one is with words and one with music. Then, I write the word INTRODUCE on the board...in a deliberate, over exaggerated motion – I delete the E and add the suffix, TION. I can't tell you how many times the kids go, "Oooohhhhh I get it now!"

263

➢ For HARMONY & UNISON confusion, I help in one obvious way, by discussing UNI as in unicycle and more familiar to them, UNIcorn. The best way to help them remember is by slipping and saying "uniSAME oops, I meant unison." They can remember that the notes are the SAME so I try to use "SAME" every time I can. I use music that has different staves for each vocal part in order to show ONE line for ONE part and ONE line for ONE other part. I find this is easier than showing one and two parts written together on the same staff.

➢ With HARMONY – I write the word on the board – show them how it looks when TWO staves are used for TWO different parts – and then I draw a line on the "O" of HARMONY – changing it to an "a" so it looks like: harm**a**ny. I emphasize that if there are MANY parts, it is *harder,* then I slip a letter "d" between the "r" and the "m" so it's har**d**many. I certainly go on to tell them not to call it "hardmany," but "harmony," and "if it helps you remember, USE IT!"

➢ Internet help: There's an AWESOME website I use for examples of HARMONY. It's funny and the different parts are "clickable." http://svt.se/hogafflahage/hogafflaHage_site/Kor/hestekor.swf

➢ Same thing with the vocabulary word, "DICTION." When you use the word, write it on the board, too – and add an "ary" in smaller letters to the end of it – so DICTION becomes DICTIONary. It will help them remember and connect DICTION to the way they pronounce words.

➢ The words TEMPO and STEADY BEAT seem to be used interchangeably in little kids' minds so I made a SPEED LIMIT 45 sign that looks *exactly* like those on the highway. The only difference is, MY sign says TEMPO LIMIT 45.

25. **_SOUND WAVES, CREST AND TROUGH:_** These are terms that have been on the science portion of our states' standardized tests. I like to use jump ropes, photos, and rubber band demonstrations to help students learn the parts of the sound wave (crest and trough) and how the distance between the two reflects the pitch of the sound wave. Another science test offered an illustration of glasses filled with different amounts of liquid. The test asks which beaker would have

the lowest sound if hit by a mallet. This can be very confusing to teachers and students because when we blow into a bottle with different levels of water, the pitch is exactly opposite that of those struck with a mallet. This is a lesson you can teach in the music room and still not be venturing far from your music curriculum. A fun and memorable way to demonstrate sound waves, vibration, and the eardrum as a receptor is to tightly stretch some plastic wrap over the open end of a plastic cup, then secure it with a rubber band or hair tie. Next, put a few grains of sand, sugar, salt, or best because of size, uncooked rice on top of the plastic "drum." Have a student stand near the rigged cup, hit a drum, metal lid, snare, or anything that makes a significant sound, and watch what the granules or rice do. Explain how this is the exact same way their eardrum collects vibrations and sends the information to the brain, translated as sound. If you're so inclined, you can add to that lesson how important it is to protect the eardrum from extremely loud sounds so the sound transmitters aren't permanently damaged.

You might check with your classroom teachers to find out if there are any other concepts on their grade level tests that are music-related and could be taught or reviewed in your class.

26. ***DYNAMICS PRACTICE:*** Have a *FORTE* DAY! Have a symbol indicator some specific place in the room where a dynamic marking lets students know, as they enter, that everything they do that day must match the volume symbol. *FORTE* DAY means everything that is done, whether it is stomping instead of walking, yelling instead of talking, playing the bells forte, lining up forte, stacking chairs forte, etc. is done throughout the entire class. (Plan ahead for this one and make sure you're in the mood for it or you won't be once it starts.) Be sure, if you feel it is necessary, set some limits *before* you turn them loose or you may be so sorry. You can have *PIANISSIMO* DAY or change your *FORTE* DAY into a *PIANO* DAY, if it gets to you before the end of class. These *PIANO* days are great to have when you're not feeling your best! It's fun, it makes memories, and it helps your kids associate *everything* they do with a dynamic marking. Without even realizing it, they are learning, having fun, and thinking about the term of the day. Enjoy!

27. ***COMPARE, CONTRAST, SIMILARITIES & DIFFERENCES, COLUMNS, etc.:*** A great deal of emphasis is being placed on particular word usage in standardized tests. The more we can use the same vocabulary in the music room that is being used in the classroom

and on the state tests, the more we help to reinforce the usage and understanding of test terminology, the more we are helping our fellow classroom teachers teach, and our students to succeed.

Get a list of key terms used in your states' test at all grade levels, then adopt that vocabulary into your lessons as often as possible. We're all in this together – and music people have a great opportunity to prove that music fits into lives rather than being a little extra piece of life they just happen to experience once in awhile.

Chapter 11

QUESTION AND ANSWER TIME

1. QUESTION: What does your ideal classroom environment look like?

Environment tends to mean the surrounding area, but to me it is the entirety of all the surrounding *conditions!* So…I will begin with the students…for they have the most fluctuating control of classroom conditions.

Students in my active classroom must first be *respectful* of others' attention, space, and abilities. Second, they must be attentive – I teach them to be *active listeners*. I show them what it looks like, when it's appropriate, and why it is important to adopt active listening skills into their skills for life. I teach that being an *active listener* means:

- Facing the speaker (with their body, not just their face)

- Being absolutely quiet

- Looking at the speaker and doing nothing else

- Following the speaker's movements and making adjustments to face the speaker; and…

- Nodding the head gently but ever so seldom to acknowledge attention and understanding.

Physical environment is equally important to the ideal classroom. My room now has or has had plants, a forest & waterfall mural, a water fountain, a lava lamp, lamps, a comfy overstuffed chair, carpet, end tables, pictures on the walls, family photos, and pillows. I like to include pictures of my house, my pets, my car – anything that helps them to realize I am a person who lives just like they do. It is my goal to make it feel safe, *homey,* and different from a traditional school setting. It's more comfortable for me, I know it is for them. (I've had students who were living in a van – I make sure they have a place that feels like a home.)

267

2. QUESTION: Regarding student behavior, what is appropriate in your ideal classroom?

- Students treat others the way they would like to be treated.

- Students are active and involved.

- Students are attentive and *looking at the speaker*.

- Students are respectful of other's space, comments, and property.

3. QUESTION: What behaviors are most disruptive to you?

Students with hyperactive tendencies, behavioral issues, and emotional disorders often interrupt learning; not only for themselves but also for the other students in class. Every child within our large district, who has been identified ED/BD, meaning they have emotional or behavioral concerns, attends our school. Some of these students are very severe cases with aggressive, explosive personalities, abusive behaviors, and defiant mannerisms. Many act as if they are void of morals or conscience. Some of these kids are probationary main-streamed so I have them with their regular classes. Sometimes, I also see them as self-contained, all together, at one time, so the extremes in behavior we *see* may be disproportionately more than the typical elementary school music class. I don't know that for sure, though. I am thankful for our team of experts in handling these special-needs students.

Constant motion and impulsive behaviors of the hyperactive child can and do disrupt class. But not paying attention always seems to be the most difficult for *me* to help. Constant motion is a familiar element for every student in my energy-laden, action-packed music classes. Consequently, a perpetually moving, hyperactive child would, more than likely, never even be identified as "hyperactive" in an observation. The impulsive behaviors also do not pose too much of a challenge or disruption. The 45 minutes each student spends in my class is divided between activities, concepts, introduction of new materials, and movements that change about every four to seven minutes, *depending on the response of the class*. The students may be sitting on the floor, standing, laying down, standing and balancing on a chair, or striking some other unusual pose during an introduction element. Then, within seven minutes or so, they are back to an activity that gets them moving from their "home" or "personal space." The alternation of *quiet-and-still* to *noisy-and-busy* usually is a natural way of avoiding impulsive actions and benefiting the hyper student. They are busy and they are happy.

I believe the most disruptive for *me* – not necessarily the other students in the class, is the student who finds it virtually impossible to focus on anything except his or her, what I call, "particular thing of significance du jour." It may be a miniscule piece of fuzz, a dripping faucet, a shoelace, a window shade, something that has happened or is going to happen, or the "faces" in the grains of wood in the door. No matter the level of activity, the sounds or lack of sounds, the authority in proximity, or the creativity applied to make a useful, fun lesson, *that* perseverating personality finds it difficult to pay attention. I catch myself perseverating over how to prevent the perserverator from permanently perseverating! ☺

After I get the other students on track and springboard them into the lesson or activity, I am sometimes able to use a little one-to-one time and pull the in-his-own-world friend who could not pay attention in a quiet, non-disturbing way, back to the lesson. These students are the ones who were *not* singing when the class was singing. But when it became listening time, they decided to provide us with their best rendition of the tune we, as a class, had just finished! These are the students who do not want to play the instruments while the others play. They want to bang on something and make their own music when everyone else has stopped and moved to something else. The lag time is uncanny.

The one child I am thinking of in particular, I do not believe does this for attention or even purposely for that matter. At least, that is not his primary intent. He is just not able (or *maybe*: willing) to concentrate on the activity at hand. He seems to have a delayed response mechanism that kicks in after observing others doing it. As you can well imagine and have, no doubt, experienced yourself, this is a very disruptive, frustrating, and noisy situation.

Students who do not pay attention, for whatever reason, are the ones who are clueless when it comes time to actually begin the assignment, turn in the project, get into groups, or whatever action has been clearly defined. This student blurts out questions when the others have already begun. This student *"doesn't wanna do it"* because he or she does *"not know what to do"* because of *zooming* during the information or springboard time. Students who haven't been in tune with class are often bothering other students, handling things no students are allowed to touch, or finding some kind of mischief that will either entertain them or get them some needed attention – whether it is positive or negative – it's still attention.

When they are not paying attention and I have to take time to "bring them back" to the rest of us or restate the obvious in order to get them to join in, it takes time away from those who have listened and *deserve* one-to-one attention. I must admit I do not like it nor is it fair when my attentive kids receive less of my personal time and attention than the naughty ones. If the disruption persists after a fair warning, the disrupter – regardless of his or her diagnosis, excuses, reasoning, whining, fit-throwing, or threats - is removed from my class so the other students are not shortchanged. I have several options, listed in order of preference: 1. Send him/her to another (predetermined and preplanned) unfamiliar-to-the-student-and-different-age-level teacher/classroom. 2. If it is a special education student, I send him/her to the Recovery Room or back to class – whichever the ED teacher prefers. 3. Send the student to the Principal. (Incidentally, I choose not to send students who need discipline to our Counselor. I believe he/she is there to soothe and counsel students through difficult times, not be the "heavy" and carry out disciplinary procedures.)

4. QUESTION: What TRICKS have you incorporated in your teaching to help hyperactive students change these behaviors?

My primary goal is to form a **relationship** with these kids. (Hmmm…have I mentioned that already?) It takes a while, but in the end, they will usually do practically anything to please me - only because *they like me*. They like me because they like how I treat them. Until we get to that point, however, I use some traditional strategies to help me help them stay focused.

Proximity has been my good friend. I can usually tell ☺ who these boys and girls are so I make sure I am close to them during discussions and whenever I am covering directions. I draw them into the conversation by using their names, smiling, asking them questions, providing them the opportunity to add to the conversation, asking for their help, and getting them to contribute in some way so I can encourage and compliment their input – regardless of how menial it may seem. And sometimes, depending on the student, I might gently touch him/her or their chair prior to the question being asked – helping him/her to focus *ahead of time*. ***Compliments*** about *anything* help make kids want to do better and try harder.

With one of my more severely hyperactive students, I found that she could be more successful when outside stimuli was reduced. Several times, I have pre-recorded directions that are spoken a bit slower and more in depth than usual, placed her with a study carrel, and plugged her into headphones. By listening *only to me* through headphones, in one space where movement is limited by the length of the cord, the bordered study area, and my repeated use of her name, she has gradually learned how to pay closer attention and to key in on important directives like, FIRST, LISTEN THEN WRITE, and WHEN YOU ARE FINISHED. With that added personal touch, she knows exactly what to do, how to do it, when to do it, and where to do it! The cassette tape recorder experiment has proven quite beneficial.

I extended that same TRICK to record tests for those who struggle with reading and I have incorporated videos in my lessons for those who are decidedly more visual or kinesthetic learners. As soon as these kids have even the hint of success, we talk about how they feel and how good it feels to do well. I write them notes letting them know I've noticed and am proud of their accomplishments!

I have learned that *if it's possible* to eliminate the element that frustrates the learner and *if I can* avoid the things that cause the learner to shut down, then I have helped to eliminate the shut down!

Most of the time, the elements that frustrate the most are a lack of self-confidence, poorly-behaved peers, or a significantly short attention span. Some students simply cannot concentrate long enough to absorb the necessary information. We all need to remember that **teacher talk** is a dead end for most hyperactive students. Remember the Charles Schultz classroom scene in the Peanuts cartoon where the only thing heard from the teacher was, "*Wah wah wah wah wah wah wah wah?*" I'm convinced that *that* is all many kids hear.

Have you ever shown a musical in class or observed during a performance? What happens when the spoken dialogue ends and you come to a song? Nine times out of ten you'll have to address talking or some other inappropriate behavior. Why? To kids, the music dialogue is insignificant. Unfortunately for teachers, as soon as activity ends and someone begins to speak, the little boogers usually begin to fidget, tune out, and shut down.

271

So…to help combat that inability to "stay tuned in" while I am talking, I fluctuate my speech. I change volume frequently. I alter my tempo. I talk with silly sounds or with a foreign-sounding accent. I slowly but constantly move around the room. I add pictures or props whenever possible. I add pauses for emphasis. I lean close and scoot further away. I use lots of facial expressions and smile. I use student' names constantly throughout my talk. I remind them to, *"…face me… look up here."* I squat to their eye level or teach while kneeling or sitting. I touch a shoulder, pat a back, or stand nearby. I realize that I am competing with TV, video games, and computers! I guess I would say that although I am sincere, I am a professional actress *all day long.* (And yes…it's exhausting!)

Sometimes these tactics prove effective. Sometimes nothing I have tried helps. I keep devising and trying new TRICKS though. Unfortunately, more strategies bomb than produce good results. Nevertheless, I know there is *some* way to keep every student interested and focused on what we are doing and ***it is my job to figure out what it takes***. (Remember those rose-colored glasses? Yeah…they're on.)

I believe my first priority is to win them over. If I can "bait" them, "catch" them and "reel" them in, they will *like* to come to my class and then the biggest hurdle is over. I am a risk-taker and believe me; I have learned from *lots of mistakes.*

5. **QUESTION: Are there any *other* TRICKS you would like to share regarding the hyperactive child?**

Often times, hyperactive students have a natural resistance to authority. I have also figured out that most of them have an intense interest in a few select things. I combine those assumptions to create a strategy for helping them to get work completed.

I have two compelling assumptions: First, perhaps if I do not assume an authoritarian mentality, I will not be *"resisted."* Second, one of the most curious interests these students have is in one another. These kids are magnets! It takes exactly one half of a day for a new, hyperactive student entering our school to team up and become best friends with one of our resident hyperactive kids. They are simply drawn to each other – usually *before lunch.*

Ironically, I learned that one particular group of boys perform better when I encourage them to work together. In most of their other classes, they are separated – either physically or emotionally. They are not allowed to work together in the same groups, they are not allowed to sit at the same tables, and in some places, they are not even allowed to talk to each other. Granted, together they *can* (and sometimes do) feed off of each other's inappropriate behaviors and create a wouldn't-be-so-bad-to-retire-early-after-all feeling for their music teacher. Yet, I have discovered that if given clear expectations and an understanding of the _privilege_ they have of being _trusted_ to work together, sometimes they have produced remarkable work!

An added bonus is that they *respect* me simply because I respected them, trusted them, and gave them a chance. It is amazing what wonderful things emanate from mutual respect! If working together doesn't work this time, I assure them that when we do another group activity they can have another try at working together. The TRICK is to make sure they know I have high expectations for them, that I'm counting on them, and that I know they can do it!

Another strategy I use comes from knowing that all kids, but especially these kids, need *instant success*. In light of that understanding, every single day I teach a new song by ROTE. I don't make them search through written music that is complicated with notes, verses, choruses, musical symbols, foreign language, and words that whip by too fast for the average reader. I teach them by call and response. They can't help but feel successful because they are "spoon fed," so to speak, every step of the way! Each song has actions or some kind of choreography designed especially to help their memory process and to get them moving. More often than not, they have been sitting in class, taking notes, working with paper and pencil, or doing something that has kept them relatively sedentary. When they get to music class, they know they get to get their sillies out, expend some of their pent-up energy, and leave class having learned something brand new, silly, and fun! Rote learning gives every student, hyperactive or not, immediate success. Before they leave, they know a new song they can sing to someone when they get home that evening. That, in turn, produces additional reinforcement, which brings them back to my class a day or so later, *anxious for more*! I like to think of it as job security - based on student success.

After having written all of this, in retrospect, I think the bulk of my success lies in the fact that the kids like me because they know I care about each one of them. I know special things about each one of them. I believe in them and I am going to compliment them again and again.

6. QUESTION: If you could choose the one belief that you feel is most integral to your teaching approach, what would it be?

I believe we all have to believe that every child wants and needs special time, love, understanding, patience, kindness, and appreciates the security that stems from a strong **relationship**. I have seen new-from-other-schools boys and girls enter my music room for the first time who are completely defeated and deflated. These boys and girls come in with a chip on their shoulder the size of Milwaukee and a cranky attitude that could put Zig Ziglar in a foul mood! Repeatedly, I have seen those same students blossom into participating, cooperative, happier children. The trick? No trick. Just the relationship built by spending time with them, caring about them, understanding their confusion and frustrations, patience with their special needs, and kindness no matter what they do wrong. That's not to say they get away with doing wrong, it just means that my reactions need to be based in compassion rather than frustration.

7. QUESTION: You keep talking about relationships. How do you go about bringing you and a hard-to-reach kid closer together?

Unfortunately, there is not a catch-all answer to this question, but I can share an example of how I worked toward developing a relationship. Remember Devin? Luckily, his class was my last class before my lunch break. One afternoon, I asked him to stick around after class for about five minutes. My first unanticipated job was to convince him that he wasn't in trouble just because he was asked to stay late. That actually worked in my favor because he was so pleasantly surprised to find out it was a good thing in my class to get to stay after, rather than a bad experience!

Once he was confident, he was free from that worry. We <u>sat down on the floor together</u> and I told him how much I enjoyed having him in class and that I really liked him a lot. I told him that I respected him and that I thought he was one of the most perceptive kids I'd ever met. His response to that was heartbreaking. He looked down to the floor, rolled a piece of carpet fuzz between his fat fingers, paused for what seemed like an eternity, and in an almost angry voice said, "*Why would you say that!? Nobody likes BD kids around!*" I responded, "*First of all, you're brilliant! I've never had a student with such an incredible vocabulary and understanding of really complex things! I really mean it, you are one of the smartest fifth graders I've ever known!*" I also told him, "*I said that I like having you in class because I meant it. And, the biggest reason why is because you always, not sometimes, but always come into my class respectful toward me."* I said, *"Devin, you have never, ever been rude, mean or disrespectful to me – and you could have been just as easily as the others, but you never have. It's easy to respect you right back! You'll probably never, ever know how much that means to me that you've chosen to be nice to me all the time."*

He finally looked up, eye to eye, and said, *"Thank you Mrs. Gray. Nobody's ever said that to me before. Can I go now?"* and then allowed me to hug him. He responded the way he did because I truly believe him...nobody ever *had* said that to him and it touched a feeling, an emotion...I could tell. I also know that he asked, *"Can I go now?"* because our visit was drifting into *his* lunchtime!

I just knew, after the conversation that my objective from then on was to build a relationship with Devin that would help him over the hurdles of loneliness and anger that he lived with day in and day out. A few weeks later, our after-class conversation meandered into another discussion about him being Jehovah's Witness and how he *"knows it's right"* but he *"hates being left out of birthday parties and holiday celebrations."* He explained to me that that's part of the reason he gets so angry about things. Even though I had no answers or advice about that particular subject, it indicated to me that he felt safe with me and that he felt like he could talk to me about deep, hurting things that were bothering him.

9. **QUESTION: What do you do about transfer students moving into your school who are reluctant participants?**

Most of our transfer students are regular-ed students, but many transfer in because of our BD/ED specialty. I don't push any of them into joining in but I do adjust the lessons so that talk time is nearly nil and fun time dominates. With the help of other students who have already learned that music is fun and full of new information, those new kids *gradually* move into the action. They like to fit in and choose to conform to the behaviors and movements and participation level of the other students. It reminds me of how some people step into cold water – one toe at a time, so they can get used to it...gradually. Eventually, they're completely immersed. Some people, however, jump in, either head first or with both feet, *all at once!* While some take *forever* and others never give it a second thought, the end result is the same. I think most kids want to be a part of the action. They want to be respected. They want to be liked. They want to be accepted.

And they want to feel safe. They just take different amounts of time to reach the point of feeling comfortable giving it a try. Echo songs are one of my favorite tools for welcoming these newbies! I sing, they echo – they're not forced into anything uncomfortable and it's obvious they don't have to have any prerequisite learning.

I learned long ago, that no matter how determined a general-ed student is not to participate, when left alone to observe and unforced to join in, he or she becomes an active participant within three class periods! Giving them their space and their own time frame gives *them* the control! It doesn't hurt that I try to design the class activities to be *irresistible*.

Granted, some kids just never dive in. I consider each situation independently. If a long time elapses without their reluctance switching toward participation, I seek advice from their teacher, their parent, my principal, and our counselor. They are all better prepared to deal with severe individual situations like that.

10. QUESTION: What do you do if a student just doesn't like to come to music and prefers art or physical education over your class?

It's fine! I don't worry about it *in the least* and I certainly don't take offense. God gave all of us choices, abilities, and preferences and He gave our kids in my building EXTRAORDINARY art and PE teachers! It is no wonder they love going to those classes!

The majority of the kids like to come to music class, even if it's not their "most" favorite special class. The ones who don't like it, often come around. But I always let them know it is ok if music isn't their favorite. When given permission to go ahead and favor something else, it seems like it makes what they don't choose feel safer. They become much more accepting because they know *I know* it's not their favorite special class but that it is also OK to prefer something else.

11. QUESTION: Do you believe there is a positive correlation between a good education and classroom relationships?

I am absolutely passionate in believing that relationships affect student attitudes, academic achievement, relationships with peers, and basic performance! I believe this because I am witness to it on a daily basis. Our intermediate ED/BD program, at one time, had a population of seven boys and our primary program had thirteen boys. The younger boys were manageable and were, for the most part, making great strides in personal relationships and social skills. The fourth and fifth grade group was another story. Every single one of those boys was a spoon – always stirring up trouble, always provoking, always interrupting, always volatile, always shifting the blame.

I worked hard to build a **relationship** with those boys by learning details about what *they* loved and what interested them. I knew Devin loved to play the drums. I used that little insight to focus on building a relationship with him *first* because he had the most profound problems. He was also somewhat of the "Alpha male," so winning him over meant winning over the majority of the class.

For starters, I bought a STOMP OUT LOUD video and showed small segments so the boys experienced how music could be made with non-traditional musical instruments. They were absolutely mesmerized! During our next time together, we created rhythmic instruments out of *everything!* We banged on the soles of our shoes. We pounded on coats with different materials to see if they sounded different. We tapped glasses with water in them. We even played plastic cups that I collected after a KU basketball game! I gradually extended that lesson, first with hand-held rhythm instruments, then later; I brought out five snare drums. All along, these boys who were determined not to learn anything, were learning rhythm by reading, by imitation, by discovery, by rote, and by echo! They were having fun, too!

My next step was having them "accompany" music on the radio. Now, camouflaged with fun and interest of playing an instrument, they were learning *musical styles* - because I station surfed. They listened to the different styles of music, various tempos and dynamics, and "played" their percussive accompaniment accordingly.

By mid-year, I honestly believe Devin would have taken a bullet for me and he, who was the single most difficult student in the building, gave *me* very little trouble, NO attitude, and, in his words, *"LOVED coming to music class!"* The **relationship** was my goal; the learning was my objective.

Once I had Devin as an ally and knew what it took to keep him that way, I methodically aimed at Tim. Tim loved cars, so I started bringing him photos of my husband's racecar. I took him to the parking lot and gave him a personal tour of my Corvette. Tim came in every day expecting to hear about or to see something new. This was a child who would rather do anything rather than come to school. I set it up so, as soon as he arrived in the morning, he checked in with his classroom teacher, then came to see me. For quite a long time I made sure I had something car-related to show him. Eventually, I weaned him off of tangible things like posters, pictures, models, etc. and we just talked. Tim's attitude toward me was pretty positive and by the end of the year, he had finally started participating in music activities where before, he just slammed stuff around because he did *not* want to be there.

And finally, my most heart-wrenching story is about Phillip. Phillip was our feral child. He had lived alone – on the streets for *three years* before someone found him and took him in. He had a raggedy, too-small, lightweight Royals windbreaker that he wore to school every day. Phillip never ever took his jacket off, hot or cold, inside or out. As Missouri winter rolled in, that lightweight, threadbare jacket was all Phillip had to wear. As I'd stood out there on the playground in my -60 F rated coat and hood, there was Phillip in his tattered nylon Royals coat. The first time I saw it, I asked him if he was cold. He, of course, said, "Nope." I told him I had a cool, aqua, purple, and black HORNETS Starter jacket at home that Jess had outgrown. If he would ask his "uncle" if I could give it to him, and it was OK, he could have it. The next day, Phillip told me it was OK. Having anticipated that answer, I'd brought the coat and gave it to him. I never saw the Royals jacket again. Because of a little extra time and a too-small coat, I had another friend who came to see me every day at recess. We talked, he followed me around awhile, and then we both went about our business for the day. Before the end of that year, Phillip was mainstreamed, coming to my music class with his regular class and was no longer having to go to his BD/ED self-contained classroom on a regular basis. Once again, these three boys serve as **proof that positive relationships are directly related to positive success in school.**

12. QUESTION: How do you help students who choose destructive or self-destructive behavior?

Happiness is a primary deterrent for destructive behaviors. Happiness, at least partially, is being able to find enjoyment in **relationships** with people. Destructive and self-destructive behaviors tend to occur when someone believes others have given up on helping them find happiness. Granted, it's far more complex and enigmatic than this. But foundationally stated, if I don't give them someone to trust and help them know I care what happens to them, they're going to lose faith in *happiness through people* and resort to seeking it elsewhere.

Working to develop a closer relationship with students, being a good listener, proving to them that I care, and giving them unconditional friendship are *starters* for helping them avoid the downward spiral of unhappiness with it's potentially destructive reactions. I want to escort kids out of that defeated feeling by making sure they know that I'm not going to give up on them and that I believe in them.

Another component of helping kids feel loved and appreciated is by establishing some boundaries for them. I decided this was important after one of Micah's friends told me that he had been allowed to do anything he wanted for as long as he could remember. He mentioned that everyone thought he was lucky and envied him, while in reality, he felt like his parents didn't care about him. Sadly, he admitted, "...*if they cared about me...they would have made some rules.*" Another guy who is now twenty-one told me, "*It's obvious you love your girls. You don't let them do stuff that can hurt them. It's so cool that you want them to call before they leave! I could have a wreck and lay in a ditch all night and my dad probably wouldn't even miss me.*" It is obvious that kids need to know we care about them and we can demonstrate that care by setting some guidelines and holding them accountable.

The TRICK is in the way you *establish* the rules. If you state them as "RULES that *better not be broken,*" you're setting yourself up to have to deal with rules that have been broken. If you state them as "RULES because *I want you to be safe and I care about you,*" then your chances of them accepting them are far better.

13. **QUESTION: What do you believe is the most consequential component when giving students effective ethical and moral counseling?**

Regardless of the *words* a teacher speaks or the lessons he or she introduces, unless students *feel* respected and safe in that teacher's classroom, lessons of moral counseling fall on deaf ears. Modeling is one of the best teachers but is only effective when the model is held in high esteem. That comes from a trusting adult-student **relationship**, consistent encouragement, patience, and two-way **respect**.

Music is a perfect medium for blending friendships, *feelings*, and character building with morals. It is not only good for the individual but for our communities to teach an old "Golden Rule" concept in new ways. We live in such a socially toxic world that it is good to help young people recognize and *feel* the results of good basic human

279

qualities. Qualities, morals, and values that should transcend time and culture without being controversial. I create opportunities through discussion, songs, lessons, stories, and activities so they can *feel* what it is like to experience prudence, justice, fortitude, temperance, patience, honesty, generosity, and then we learn to envelop everything we do with *empathy*.

Teaching music is so much more than teaching music.

Music is our opportunity to touch the hearts of others.

14. **QUESTION: Can you offer an example of moral counseling that you've done with your students?**

Watch at a baseball game, during an assembly, or at the circus. Typically, adolescents are disrespectful during the National Anthem and Pledge of Allegiance. This disrespect is visually and audibly evident through body language, chatter, and lack of participation. We discuss ways we can show respect to our country during the National Anthem and Pledge of Allegiance. 1. Remove hats. 2. *Stand still* and face the flag. 3. Do not talk. 4. Participate.

I videotaped my fourth graders as they were singing the Star Spangled Banner during a rehearsal. During playback, I asked the students to watch only themselves and judge if they were 1. Attentive and standing still 2. Singing, but moving around, or 3. Not participating and active.

Then, I **told a story** of seeing a soldier at the Tomb of the Unknown in Washington, D.C. where a bee buzzed around his face for the longest time before it landed right on the tip of his nose. I explained how we stood watching that soldier allow that bee to crawl up *inside* his nose without even so much as a flinch. His job was to honor that symbolic burial place for all those who have died for our freedom. The selflessness of his actions that hot, humid afternoon epitomized his respect and self-discipline.

After some discussion, I shared some personal experiences while visiting several communist countries. I specifically addressed particular incidents, behaviors, and sights that reeked of government control and lack of freedom. I expressed my pity, without using that word, for those people so unbelievably affected by the harshness and inflexibility of their militaristic government. The students listened in amazement. They were shocked to realize how much they take freedom for granted.

The closing statement of my stories went something like this, "*I admit, I used to do the pledge every morning in school out of habit. I never really considered what it meant or even what I was saying. Have you gotten to that point? Ever since I got to see how people live who have no freedom like we have, I no longer take it for granted. In fact, I am offended at ball games when the cheerleaders, fans, and players do not show respect. They primp and giggle, stand slouched, and/or act silly during the anthem. I don't really blame them – only because they just don't know. But I know...and now YOU know just how precious our freedom is, and how thankful and respectful we should be. Next time you are a part of some tribute to our freedom and our nation, do two things. First, be a good role model for others who don't know what you know about people who have no freedom of choice. And, second, notice who stands quietly and respectfully and who are among those who take their freedom for granted.*"

15. QUESTION: What were your objectives for that lesson?

Students will stand quietly, at attention, and remove hats during the pledge and anthem. Some Americans choose not to participate in the saying of the pledge or the singing of the anthem. They have that right to choose! Nevertheless, if they live in America or are visiting America and enjoy the freedom America provides, they also must be respectful of the rights of others who wish to pledge their allegiance!

16. QUESTION: Did you have an assessment strategy for the lesson?

Yes, however, please understand that not all assessment requires written or formal evaluation. In this particular moral lesson, after the stories and discussion, students performed the anthem again and a second video taping was done. The students *discussed the contrasts and similarities* of the first video before the story, with the second video after hearing an explanation of why we should not take our freedom for granted.

17. QUESTION: How did the students react to the lesson?

The kids giggled, pointed, and thought it was funny as they watched their rambunctious behavior during the first, *pre-lesson* taping. I gave them the freedom to make comments, laugh, and yes, even make fun of the actions of some in class. After the story lesson, I replayed the first video and this time, there was no nonsense during the viewing and the kids quietly assessed their behavior. The stories of the soldier and the experiences in the communist countries clearly effected the way they performed, reacted, and interpreted the video. When I showed them the second video – to see how they acted after I spoke with them, they agreed that their behavior was much more solemn, respectful, and was "more appropriate."

Some classes, for some reason, were more callused than others – my stories for them were adjusted to carry a bit more impact than with those classes that were more intra- and inter-personally dominant and more naturally empathetic. I inserted more detail, opinion, and *emotion* to the story. I incorporated more imagery and I asked the students to *imagine* how it would feel to live in a place where....

18. QUESTION: Does your general approach to discipline promote your students' ethical development?

I believe it does. My goal is for their moral development to be intrinsic and that is a growth process that is better evident in the long term. Each class is included in discussions at least three times each semester about what we want our music class to feel like regarding kids and their behavior. Then, we talk about why their mental pictures are important and how we can set goals to maintain the kind of class they imagine. Incidentally, I call them *"goals"* rather than *"rules"* and that seems to give offenders less reason to break a rule. It is weird to "break a goal" and often daring to "break a rule." It is a matter of semantics, but I have discovered that it is an effective word choice. We do not even discuss consequences unless circumstances force that issue. But we do talk of *"soft reminders"* that I can give to help those who are having trouble, to get back on goal. When discipline does become a problem, I can generally make eye contact, smile, and shake my head as a gentle reminder to stop. At least, that is what I find to be true with the majority of the students I have had in my classes year after year.

Students who are either unaccustomed to my teaching styles or refuse to work toward the same classroom goals, receive the same in-class reminders but then, after class, I catch them on their way out and visit with them. I begin with the good things they do, first. I let them know that I've noticed and appreciate the positive contributions they have made to our class...in kid-talk, of course. Then, before I talk about their inappropriate behavior, I say something like, *"Don't let me forget. I need you to deliver a message to ___ after we're finished visiting today…I know I can trust you to get the job handled responsibly.*" (Now they know I trust them and I value their presence). At this point, I tell them how their behavior has interrupted class and shows a little disrespect. I explain how I wish they would not do that anymore. I make sure they know that I realize sometimes they might forget, so I'll give them this little signal of smiling, shaking my head and winking – then they know it's my *kind* way of saying, *"Please stop doing what you're doing."*

I think this method of discipline builds moral development because he or she is choosing to have *self* control rather than *dictated*, external control. They then have a choice in the matter, and they are reinforced for making wise, respectful decisions. We are both winners.

19. **QUESTION: Do you have any teacher-set consequences for misbehavior that you believe promote moral discipline in your classroom?**

Sure. Misbehavior needs to be met with appropriate consequences. We have all learned how the severity of the consequence should match the severity of the inappropriate behavior, how we need to be consistent, and to hold students accountable. But, I believe that promoting and developing a caring, moral community of kids is not a singular lesson, consequence, or strategy but rather, a multi-faceted, ongoing learning experience.

Kids seem to like to listen to stories about my experiences, my family, my thoughts, and my dreams. So, I share the story of how my husband and I sometimes hire students to help us for special occasions. I explain that when I used to look for someone to baby-sit our daughters, I was careful to choose someone who was responsible and trustworthy. I was looking for someone who I knew would act the exact same way whether I was in the house or gone. I asked them, *"You know how kids sometimes act perfectly responsible as long as the teacher is in the classroom but as soon as she steps out the door for something or a guest enters the room, that same perfectly behaved child, causes trouble? Why would that kind of person be a bad choice to baby-sit for me?"*

I extended the lesson about working hard and staying on task. I told them, *"Mike races cars, you know, and he is always looking for someone he could pay by the hour to help him work on his racecar. He doesn't necessarily need someone who knows about motors or transmissions as much as he needs someone who would be willing to wash and wax it, sort equipment, and do other little tasks that take Mike's time away from actually working on the motor."* Then I asked, *"Why do you suppose he would want someone willing to work hard and stay on task?"* The answer soon became clear that if he was willing to pay someone *by the hour*, he didn't want someone who took four hours to do a one-hour job.

I combine both of these real-life stories and asked the students to work with a partner and decide: 1. What is the moral of these stories? 2. What are the natural consequences? 3. How do these stories, the moral, and the consequences apply to our music room? 4. How do these stories have anything to do with someone's reputation?

20. QUESTION: What were your objectives for the lesson?

- Students will realize that the way they behave in school reflects how they will behave outside of school.

- Students will realize they are leaving lasting impressions upon others by the choices, the actions, and the work ethic they choose to adopt now.

- Students will learn that they will be assessed or judged by others according to the way they choose to act in school and the reputation they have now may very well follow them throughout their lives.

21. QUESTION: What was your assessment plan for this lesson?

Students were asked to reflect on the kind of impression they have left and the kind of reputation they have established with each one of their teachers. Then, they were to fill in the following form, pretending that *they are me, discussing them* - placing their own name on the application line:

I, (student name) am applying for a job. My elementary music teacher, Mrs. Gray, has been asked to fill out this referral and make comments about the kind of student I was in her class throughout elementary school. Her comments: _____

_____

_____

_____

❑   I would hire this applicant **because**: _____

_____

_____

_____

❑   I would NOT hire this applicant **because:** _____

_____

_____

_____

Upon completion of the form and while I read their responses, I ask the students who realized that they had not done their best in creating a good, moral reputation for themselves, to write some goals they might use to help change their reputation between now and the time they graduate from fifth grade. For the students who rated themselves high but who are clearly out of touch or in denial of the reputation that accompanies them, I have them re-evaluate their answers. If they still fail to recognize the kind of impression they're leaving with others, I contact the counselor, reveal their form, and have the counselor take over with his/her expertise. For those students who have a wonderful reputation – and thankfully, that's the majority of our kids, I ask them to take another sheet and fill in the form with ME as the applicant and they, the employer. This is very insightful for me to learn from a student perspective!

22. QUESTION: What influenced you to become a teacher?

Good memories last a lifetime!

Rather than my answer being *what* influenced me to become a teacher, it is *who* influenced me to become a teacher! It has always been the *who* more than the *what* that has inspired me!

I remember resting on my little plastic, blue and yellow, fold-up mat watching Mrs. Reagan, my Kindergarten teacher, waddle around the room during nap time, and knowing that some day I was going to be a teacher, *just like **her!*** She met us every day at the door and gave us a big, grandma, flabby-armed hug. She smelled just like a grandma too, and she treated me so special - as if I was her only grandchild. Then Mrs. Schmidt, my "very best first grade teacher," was pretty, and nice, and smiled a lot too, so then I changed my mind and wanted to grow up to be *just like **her!***

For some reason, my memory has blanked out most of second grade except for remembering wonderful, gentle-spirited Mrs. Riggens walking into class on Monday mornings with a basket brimming with homemade jelly she'd made just for us over the weekend. During that year, we got to sample just about every flavor of jelly imaginable - thanks to her generosity and talent! Sometimes, she even brought yeast rolls and let us smear as much jelly on them as we wanted!

I also remember watching the sky roil and turn pitch black one second grade morning. I was *always* afraid of storms when I was little, but I was especially scared when I wasn't at home. We were reading together when there was a blinding flash of lightening followed by an enormous crash of thunder, then the lights flashed a couple of times, stuttered, and the room filled with an inky darkness. I remember the hush – I remember how everyone sat stunned – holding our breath and wondering what was going to happen next. Dear Mrs. Riggens smiled, glanced around the room at her obviously horror-stricken eight-year-olds, gently closed her book, told us to push our desks against the wall and to meet her in the middle of the room. She pulled out a huge, soft quilt from her closet, fluffed it to the floor and gathered us all in to sit down. She talked so quietly that morning – *smiling the whole time.* Lights out, she opened the windows and pulled the blinds clear to the ceiling – making a gigantic wall of windows. It was quite the opposite reaction I would have expected! Instead of closing out the storm, she invited it in! She whispered. She smiled and winked. Together, we were listening to the rain and counting the seconds between lightening and thunder. We tallied the number of times we heard thunder and saw lightening to see if they were the same and I got so engrossed in her "experiments" that I completely forgot about being afraid. She promised us that when we heard fifteen rumbles of thunder, she would bring out a surprise! 13....14...15....she lifted her chubby little body off of the quilt, shuffled to the closet and presented us with a huge bucket of fresh strawberries! Since they weren't washed, she insisted that we reach outside the windows, hold them – one at a time - in the rain, and get them all clean to eat! Every single second grader in my class and Mrs. Riggens had damp arms, red lips, and berry stains all over our fingers! What began as a scary, even sickening mid-morning, ended in a warm, fun-filled, story-making memory. (It does reflect, however, how images and feelings are seared into our memories without a teacher ever realizing the lasting impact of his or her actions.) Mrs. Riggens was awesome!

In third grade, I remember like it was yesterday, Miss Viebrock read a chapter or two of the entire collection of Laura Ingalls Wilder's Little House books *every* day after lunch recess! It was truly the highlight of my elementary career. It may have been a coincidence, although I doubt it, but she read about the scorching hot sun in Little House on the Prairie while we were sweating and our hearts pounding after a miserably hot, late summer recess. On the days we would come in with fingers and toes numb from an icy wind, we heard about the House in the Big Woods and the effects the freezing winter had on the Ingall's family. When it was spring for us, it was amazingly spring for the Ingall's family, as well. Miss Viebrock taught me how to write in cursive, and how to multiply numbers. Right before we headed home every day, we got to sit on our desks (unheard of!) and sing songs until our bus number was called! She taught us a new song nearly every week! To this day, I honor that wonderful person by teaching my third grade music students every single song she taught me thirty-five years ago! I still loved Mrs. Reagan, Mrs. Schmidt, and Mrs. Riggens, but wow! Miss Viebrock…oh my, I wanted to be *just like her!*

As elementary school floated by, having had tremendous teachers, my goal of becoming a teacher was reinforced year after year. I remember making mental notes to be *just like Mrs. Dunn*, my fourth grade teacher, when somebody did not follow directions in my class. She always solved the problem so quietly and privately, carefully selecting just the right time so the offender lost no dignity. Mrs. Dunn's husband died in the middle of the year when a tree limb fell on him during a storm as he was walking out to the mailbox. I never got to see her again after that.

Mrs. Erdman, my fifth grade teacher, was so ahead of her time as an educator. She always let us work in small groups, and even *neater*, she *always* had some huge, all-class project going on throughout the year. It's funny what you remember. Martha Smith was one of my best friends and her dad was the manager of a grocery store. He made what I remember to be a *huge* box with wooden sides about five inches high. It covered the whole top of two reading tables in the back of the room! Mrs. Erdman let us build our own city, complete with houses, courthouse, post office, corner café, library, and bridges – everything was made by us out of Popsicle sticks! Our town had streets of *real* gravel we collected outside on the playground, trees from *real* tree branches, ground made of *real* dirt, a beach with *real* sand, and even a *real* volcano that later erupted with the addition of baking soda and vinegar! That project lasted almost all year and we got to work on

287

it any time we completed our assignments and scored well on them. What a great motivator, eh? What fun memories!

One of her other projects was a bulletin board sized mosaic! Anytime we had free time at the end of an assignment; we could go to the mosaic and glue small shapes of construction paper to the wall to add our contribution to the total picture. That picture was much like a color-by-number print only we filled in the areas with geometric shapes no larger than one inch square. It took the biggest part of the year for the mural to take shape – but my what an awesome accomplishment and sense of being partly responsible for making that picture come together. Yep, I *knew* I wanted to teach a cool class like Mrs. Erdman's and to be *just like her!*

Then there was **Mr. Paul Sanders** – the <u>character</u> who stood before us as a sixth grade teacher and spoke in accents, taught class in some foreign language – just so we "could hear what it sounded like," and played the accordion or harmonica at the close of the day around a construction paper bon fire – "just like the settlers did years ago." Mr. Sanders was such a mood-setter as well as a *master storyteller!* We were always much too busy being entertained to think about doing anything but paying attention to him. By the time I had completed sixth grade, I had decided I wanted to be *just like him!* (Well, I suppose not the *him* part ☺, but I did want to *teach* just like *him*.)

It's obvious that there's a little bit of each one of those teachers in me now – *even the flabby arms!*

CHAPTER 12

Thoughtful Thoughts To Think Through

and...

Exceptional Educational Email

"One of the symptoms of an approaching nervous breakdown is the belief that one's work is terribly important."
- Bertrand Russell

SOME WORDS OF WISDOM
FROM THE OLD GRAY MARE

Our work *is* terribly important. In order to stay mentally healthy, physically well, and *not burn out or breakdown*, we *must* keep *everything* we do for school in perspective and realize there are actually other things even *more* important! It is far too easy to let our teaching responsibilities infiltrate every aspect of our lives, taking away from the important things. Being a master teacher has the ample ability to suck time out of us like a vortex because the commitment and responsibilities are enormous! That's just the way it is. Teaching has an uncanny way of completely consuming a person's life, particularly if the teacher has the Super-Teacher syndrome.

I have watched as *remarkable* teachers transferred, resigned, or retired from our building and I remember being so melancholy and thinking how they could *never* be replaced. As humbling as it is, though, I must admit - I was wrong. I've been forced into the realization that *none of us* is irreplaceable! I can tell you because I've watched it happen over and over. It honestly only takes a couple of weeks, at the most, for people to adjust to the absence of a dear friend. The world that once so lovingly embraced us, soon returns to the busy-ness of life, is forced back into overwhelming responsibilities, gets caught up in day-to-day activities, buries their noses back in their massive TO DO lists, and no longer feels the vacancy. I don't say this to discourage anyone or be pessimistic, but the truth is – there is always someone waiting in the wings, eager to fill in wherever we leave off! I tell you this because it is imperative to realize and I tell you this to help you keep your job and the hours you devote to it, *in perspective!*

If we are completely cognizant of this easy-to-be-overworked-easy-to-be-taken-for-granted-and-easy-to-be-replaced phenomenon, it will help us keep our schoolwork in perspective. We won't stay after school until eight or nine o'clock every night preparing for the next day. We won't think we *have* to be at school before the sun rises every morning. We won't take home crates of papers to grade every single night that take away from our personal time! We won't put our family second to our job, we won't deem it necessary to come to school sick rather than stay home and take care of ourselves, and we *will* realize that though we may want to and think we can, we are not going to save the planet with our selfless teaching job!

We do *what* we can, the *best* that we can; but,

we <u>must</u> *prioritize* our personal lives and relationships

over our work or it is difficult to enjoy both!

On a daily basis, we're inundated by the media, friends, and educators with phrases like, "…work to keep your life in *balance!*" or, "*Balance* your career and your personal life…." But the fact is, you can only BALANCE those things when BALANCE is appropriate. I submit to you that *true* balance is probably inappropriate during most stages in your life. You will probably find your "balance" will be dramatically tipped in favor of your new career when you first begin teaching, particularly if you are single and childless. However, when that wedding comes around or that first baby joins your life, there's no way your *balance* will be equal. Instead, the natural turn of events will tip the balance in favor of time spent with your new spouse, baby, and family! *And well it should!* This is a time in your life you will never get back once it's past so don't ever feel guilty for prioritizing it above all else. You may be thinking, *"Hey, Gray…Don't state the obvious stuff with me!"* I know…*I know.* But, I'm telling you – there's an overemphasis on BALANCE these days and when you aren't able or don't *want* to equally balance work and home, it tends to make you feel guilty and stressed.

I don't think you should ever feel guilty for not *balancing* career and home as the experts suggest. I agree that there is a season for every purpose and the *different stages* in your life will tip the balance in *different directions* toward *different priorities*. This is how it should be, so don't be discouraged or feel depressed about it. Do your best at school…do your best at home, and if work is keeping you from doing your best at home, then it's time to rethink your priorities and look again at the second paragraph of this section.

I was waiting on an order at a local fast-food restaurant and reading the *wallpaper,* of all things! The words I saw were so simple, yet so profound:

"All you can do is all you can do, and all you can do *is enough*."

Take some time right now, to read my HOUR GLASS called "TAKE TIME." There is much to be considered and much to be remembered within the text...please enjoy.

"TAKE TIME"

Take time to **smile**; it is contagious
Take time to **forgive**; it helps you heal.
Take time to **think**; it is a source of strength.
Take time to **rest**; it's your chance to recharge.
Take time to **read**; it is the foundation of wisdom.
Take time to **play**; it is the connection to feeling young.
Take time to **be quiet**; it is the opportunity to experience God.
Take time to **be observant**; it's the opportunity to help others.
Take time to **anticipate need**; it is a gift seldom forgotten.
Take time to **love** and **be loved**; it is God's greatest gift.
Take time to **laugh**; it will brighten your soul.
Take time to **dream**; it is your future.
Take time to **pray**; it is God's power on earth.
Take time to **listen**; it is the best way to show you care.
Take time to **worship**; it is the best way to honor your Father.
Take time to be **thankful**; it is the best way to experience God's goodness.
Take time to be **compassionate**; it is the best way to touch the hearts of the hurting.
Take time for **children**; it is the most positive way to touch the future.
Take time to **appreciate;** you may be the only one who does.
Take time to be **friendly**; it is your path to happiness.
Take time for **others;** they need your support.
Take time for **God**; He is our eternity.
Take time to **write** – often.

"Teachers plant trees under whose shade we will never sit."
~ Anonymous

"School is a building that has four walls – with tomorrow inside."
~ Lon Watters

I received the following email some time ago and stashed it away thinking I would refer to it again, maybe tomorrow. There are lessons to be learned from proverbs, folklore, traditions, and stories. Tomorrow finally came. I share this tale with you, just as I have with my kids, and in so doing, honor the anonymous author who fashioned the words.

"Build Bridges"

Once upon a time, two brothers who lived on adjoining farms fell into conflict. It was the first serious rift in 40 years of farming side by side, sharing machinery, trading labor and goods as needed, without a hitch. Then the long collaboration fell apart. It began with a small misunderstanding and it grew into a major difference. Finally, it exploded into an exchange of bitter words followed by weeks of silence.

One morning there was a knock on John's door. He opened it to find a man with a carpenter's toolbox. "I'm looking for some work," he said. "Perhaps you would have a few small jobs here and there. Could I help you?" "Yes," said the older brother. "I do have a job for you. Look across the creek at that farm. That's my neighbor. In fact, it's my younger brother. Last week there was a meadow between us, he took his bulldozer to the river levee, and now there is a creek between us. Well, he may have done this to spite me, but I'll go him one better. See that pile of lumber curing by the barn? I want you to build me a fence -- an 8-foot fence -- so I won't need to see his place anymore. Cool him down, anyhow." The carpenter said, "I think I understand the situation. Show me the nails and the post-hole digger and I'll be able to do a job that pleases you."

The older brother had to go to town for supplies so he helped the carpenter get the materials ready and then he was off for the day. The carpenter worked hard all that day measuring, sawing, and nailing.

About sunset, when the farmer returned, the carpenter had just finished his job. The farmer's eyes opened wide, his jaw dropped. There was no fence there at all. It was a *bridge* -- a bridge stretching from one side of the creek to the other! A fine piece of work -- handrails and all -- and the neighbor, his younger brother, was coming across, his hand outstretched. "You are quite a fellow to build this bridge after all I've said and done." The two brothers stood at each end of the bridge and then they met in the middle, taking each other's hand. They turned to see the carpenter hoist his toolbox on his shoulder. "No, wait! Stay a few days. I've a lot of other projects for you," said the older brother. "I'd love to stay on," the carpenter said, "but, I have many more bridges to build."

Good teachers build good bridges – and lots of them!

~ Debbie Gray

Keep your relationships with your spouse, children, parents, siblings, friends, and even acquaintances positive and strong. We are told again and again, that circumstances outside our classroom shouldn't affect our performance. In a perfect world, that is very true, but the fact of the matter is, our worlds are not even close to perfect. We all face problems that, no matter how hard we may try, are out of our control.

When my daddy was in Cardiac Intensive Care from March 7th clear until he died the end of May, I can honestly tell you that no matter how much I didn't want to bring those emotions to school with me, they managed to hop a ride. I *tried* to act happy and my silly, perky self, but it was such a façade. I did not *feel* happy, silly, or perky a single minute of those three months…but my job didn't make any adjustments for my feelings. I still had to plan lessons, still had to manage discipline, still had to keep students interested in learning, I still had to ACT like my life was normal, and all I wanted to do was go sit beside my daddy in the hospital or curl up in a corner and cry. My mom and wife-roles didn't stop, either, just because I didn't *feel* like playing mom or wife like always. Although daddy's illness had nothing specifically to do with *relationships*, and what was happening to all of us was totally out of my control, my point is… my long-established, positive, close **relationships** with my **mom, sister, husband, daughters**, *and friends*, are what sustained me through that horrific time in my life – it wasn't my *job* that gave me courage, it wasn't the *what*…it was the *who*. Had I not had that *people support,* I am afraid I would have crashed. I am so thankful for friends.

It's a two-way street, ya see? To have friends, you need to ***be a friend!*** This often means going out of your way to attend a shower or wedding that maybe you don't even want to go to or have the money to spend on a gift. It means, attending visitations and funerals when a cohort loses someone special, even if it's inconvenient, time-consuming, or not at all close. It means sending Get Well cards and visiting when someone on staff is sick at home or in the hospital and it means providing food, babysitting, or transportation for families who have been through trauma and are in need of a helping hand. It means keeping up on the concerns of others, "…*how's Cari doing in Iraq?*" "…*how's the new house coming?*" "…*is your mom out of the hospital yet?*" "…*what did you find out from the doctor?*" "…*when does your husband get home, again?*" "…*is it a boy or a girl?*" "…*when is the graduation party?*" Just be interested.

Being a friend is more than smiling and saying hello as you pass in the hall. WORK at building friendships! Making the effort to <u>be there for</u>

<u>them</u> during special occasions or under difficult circumstances proves that you really do care! You *will* reap what you sow!

"When a friend is in trouble,
don't annoy him by asking if there is anything you can do.
Think up something appropriate <u>*and do it*</u>."
~ Edgar Watson Howe

So, what does this little sermonette have to do with teaching school?! First, it reinforces the importance of **building relationships,** not just with our students, but with the people we work with on a daily basis. More than likely, if you're like me, most of those people will be sharing the same hallways, lunchroom, lounge, and parking lot with you for several decades – you might as well take time and build some bridges to them. It will make everyone happier and create a much more satisfying work environment. Secondly, suffering though experiences with my own downtrodden emotions made me know, first hand, just how difficult it is to think, to react appropriately to various situations, and to concentrate on something that seemed so totally insignificant in my personal scheme of things. *There is an inordinate number of our students who struggle to do well in school for the exact same reasons.* Far too many of our kids have a home life that is an absolute mess! Some are dealing with abuse, some addictions, some fear, some pain, illness, or some loneliness. Some have faced or are facing death, many have incarcerated parents, some carry baggage with them from clear back when they were toddlers. We have no idea what hops a ride to school with our students. *So if we always assume the worst has happened to them* when they aren't in the frame of mind we expect, it is far easier to treat them in a way that is loving, compassionate, kind, and understanding. **Try to remember how hard it is for you to concentrate or be interested in *anything* when something has happened that has made you miserable, frightened, or worried.**

BILL GATES' SPEECH
TO MT. WHITNEY HIGH SCHOOL
in Visalia, CA

Rule 1: Life is not fair - get used to it!

Rule 2: The world won't care about your self-esteem. The world will expect you to accomplish something BEFORE you feel good about yourself.

Rule 3: You will NOT make $60,000 a year right out of high school. You won't be a vice-president with a car phone until you earn both.

Rule 4: If you think your teacher is tough, wait until you get a boss.

Rule 5: Flipping burgers is not beneath your dignity. Your grandparents had a different word for burger flipping - they called it opportunity.

Rule 6: If you mess up, it's not your parents' fault, so don't whine about your mistakes, learn from them.

Rule 7: Before you were born, your parents weren't as boring as they are now. They got that way from paying your bills, cleaning your clothes and listening to you talk about how cool you thought you were. So before you save the rain forest from the parasites of your parent's generation, try delousing the closet in your own room.

Rule 8: Your school may have done away with winners and losers, but life HAS NOT. In some schools, they have abolished failing grades and they'll give you as MANY TIMES as you want to get the right answer. This doesn't bear the slightest resemblance to ANYTHING in real life.

Rule 9: Life is not divided into semesters. You don't get summers off and very few employers are interested in helping you FIND YOURSELF. Do that on your own time.

Rule 10: Television is NOT real life. In real life people actually have to leave the coffee shop and go to jobs.

Rule 11: Be nice to nerds. Chances are you'll end up working for one.

I'm not really sure why I stuck this Bill Gates speech in my book about TRICKS FOR KIDS. It might have something to do with the realization that there are many educators out there making well under $30,000 a year, teaching kids who will graduate and start out with a base pay that is more than double the salary of the ones who taught them how to do what they're doing to earn that kind of pay! There's something wrong with this picture, (and the way I tried to express it!). But, it's kinda fun and satisfying to know that someone is helping keep a pinch of reality in the minds of high school graduates. They've yet to sweat out the long hours of college requirements, the poverty-level living one must endure while going to school, and the all-nighters required to bust out a huge research project – but, for some reason - expect to start out financially where their parents have taken a lifetime to achieve! Thank you, Mr. Gates!

"MAKE A DIFFERENCE"

A man was walking down a deserted beach at sunset. As he walked along, he began to see another man in the distance. As he grew nearer, he noticed that the local native kept leaning down, picking something up, and throwing it out into the water. Time and again, he kept hurling things out into the ocean. As our friend approached even closer, he noticed that the man was picking up starfish that had washed up onto the beach, and one at a time, he was throwing them back into the ocean.

The first man was puzzled. He approached the man and said, "Good evening friend, I was wondering…what are you doing?" And he replied, "I'm throwing these starfish back into the ocean. You see, it's low tide right now and all these starfish have been washed up onto the shore. If I don't throw them back into the sea, they will die from the lack of oxygen." "I understand," my friend replied, "but there must be thousands of starfish on this beach and you couldn't possibly get to all of them. There are simply too many and don't you realize that this is happening on hundreds of beaches up and down this coast . . . can't you see that that you can't possibly make a difference?" The local native smiled, bent down . . . picked up yet another starfish . . . and as he threw it back out into the sea, he replied, **"It made a difference to that one!"**

You may feel like you cannot make a difference in the world today, but you CAN -- one life at a time.

~ Author Unknown

TAKE CARE OF YOURSELF

DEB GRAY'S TOP TEN TRICKS TOWARD TAKING CARE OF YOURSELF

1. Pray and play plenty.

2. Surround yourself with good friends.

3. Go to worship to stay spiritually renewed.

4. Get enough sleep, eat healthy, and exercise.

5. Get up early enough so you're not rushed before work.

6. Be organized to avoid grumpies, confusion, loss, and wasting time.

7. Hide a *spare* somewhere: car key, house key, and a twenty-dollar bill.

8. Listen to motivational tapes and Christian radio while you are in your car.

9. Collect stories, quotes, and scriptures so you have a place to retreat for inspiration.

10. Don't hesitate to refuse offers that could put you on overload. Don't feel guilty for saying no.

COOKIE POEM

The woman arrived at an airport one night
with several long hours before her flight.
She hunted for a book in the airport shop,
bought a bag of cookies and found a place to drop.
She was engrossed in her book but happened to see,

that the man sitting beside her, as bold as could be,
Grabbed a cookie or two from the bag in between,
which she tried to ignore to avoid a scene.
So she munched the cookies and watched the clock,
as the gutsy cookie thief diminished her stock.
She was getting more irritated as the minutes ticked by,
thinking, "If I wasn't so nice, I would blacken his eye."
With each cookie she took, he took one too,
when only one was left, she wondered what he would do.
With a smile on his face, and a nervous laugh,
he took the last cookie and broke it in half.
He offered her half, as he ate the other,
she snatched it from him and thought... oh, brother!
This guy has some nerve and he's also rude,
why he didn't even show any gratitude!
She had never known when she had been so galled,
and sighed with relief when her flight was called.
She gathered her belongings and headed to the gate,
refusing to look back at the thieving ingrate.
She boarded the plane, and sank in her seat,
then she sought her book, which was almost complete.
As she reached in her baggage, she gasped with surprise,
There was her bag of cookies, in front of her eyes.
If mine are here, she moaned in despair,
the others were his, and he tried to share.
Too late to apologize, she realized with grief,
that she was the rude one, the ingrate, the thief!

A semi-sweet morsel from this little poem:
*How many times have we absolutely known
that something was a certain way,
only to discover later that what we believed to be true . . . was not?*
Keep an open mind and an open heart, because . . . you just never know ...
you might be eating someone else's cookies.

DO I HAVE ALL THIS RIGHT?

After being interviewed by the school administration, the eager teaching prospect said: "Let me see if I've got this right. You want me to go into that room with all those kids and fill their every waking moment with a love for learning. And I'm supposed to instill a sense of pride in their ethnicity, modify their disruptive behavior, observe them for signs of abuse and even censor their T-shirt messages and dress habits. You want me to wage a war on drugs and sexually transmitted diseases, check their backpacks for weapons of mass destruction, and raise their self-esteem. You want me to teach them patriotism, good citizenship, sportsmanship, fair play, how to register to vote, how to balance a checkbook, and how to apply for a job. I am to check their heads for lice, maintain a safe environment, recognize signs of anti-social behavior, offer advice, write letters of recommendation for student employment and scholarships, encourage respect for the cultural diversity of others, and oh, make sure that I give the girls in my class fifty percent of my attention.

My contract requires me to work on my own time after school, evenings, and weekends grading papers and recording scores. In addition, I must spend my summer vacation at my own expense working toward advance certification and a Masters degree. And on my own time, you want me to attend committee and faculty meetings, PTA meetings, attend sports events, skating parties, carnivals, fund-raisers, and participate in staff development training.

I am to be a paragon of virtue, larger than life, such that my very presence will awe my students into being obedient and respectful of authority. And I am to pledge allegiance to family values and this current administration. You want me to incorporate technology into the learning experience, monitor web sites, and relate personally with each student. That includes deciding who might be potentially dangerous and/or liable to commit a crime in school. I am to make sure all students pass the mandatory state exams, even those who don't come to school regularly or complete any of their assignments. Plus, I am to make sure that all of the students with handicaps get an equal education regardless of the extent of their mental or physical handicap. I am also to communicate regularly with the parents by letter, telephone, newsletter, and report card. All of this I am to do with just a piece of chalk, a computer, a few books, a bulletin board, a big smile AND on a starting salary that qualifies my family for food stamps! You want me to do all of this and yet you expect me **"NOT TO PRAY?"**

I Thessalonians 5:17 we find these words: **"Pray without ceasing."**

It will help you <u>thrive</u>, not just survive!

ACKNOWLEDGMENTS

or...

THANKS!

✓ I want to thank my awesome husband for putting up with me during the writing of this book. Actually, I'd like to thank him for putting up with me since we met! Mike, you are *the best*! I love you!

✓ I'd like to thank our two daughters, Micah and Jess, who have shared their love, lives, experiences, and hearts with me, giving me perspective and inspiration from the students' point of view. Girls – you are amazing and *always* make me proud!

✓ Thank you to my mom and dad, Alice and Thurman. These two people, *the finest parents ever*, made so many sacrifices so that I might be able to take music lessons, travel with my performing groups, and go to college in pursuit of my lifelong dream of being a teacher. There was never a financially right or good time for them to afford me these opportunities, yet, they somehow always made a way.

✓ Thank you to my sister, Pam, for always putting up with me and my off-beat ways. Thanks for taking care of important family business while I had my nose in the computer writing TRICKS. You're a great friend!

✓ Noel Fulkerson and Molly Jessup – you were the first to inspire me to take this career path and I thank you!

✓ A very special thank you to Mrs. Linda Johnson, my former Principal, who made me stretch my professional self. Your wisdom continues to inspire me and your love for kids is unprecedented. What a great role model you are!

✓ Thank you to LeAnn Dill, my awesome teaching buddy, my cohort, my right arm, my left *BRAIN*, and my *best* teacher-friend! Thank you for caring about me so unconditionally. Thank you for always anticipating need. Thank you for your wisdom and advice. I have been blessed by your life.

301

✓ Thank you Taylor Hill, for helping me find the authors of all those quotes!

✓ Thank you to all the proofreaders who helped me complete this project: Randy & Sheralyn Peterson, Mary Franco, and our resident Grammar Goddesses: Melanie Caywood and Katie Britt.

✓ And finally, last but not least, thanks to Patti, Jayme, Rachel, Dan, & Jeremy, my incredibly talented student teachers, for inspiring me to write. It was you who really made me think about what I actually do in class, put it into words, explain the reasoning behind it, and write it down. Your talent and character have been very humbling for me... and I thank you so very much for your influence, encouragement, and motivation to stick with this project to the end.

Printed in the United States
30251LVS00004B/148-165